THIS GREAT JOURNEY

Photo: Bassano & Vandyk Studios.

JENNIE LEE

This Great Journey

A Volume of Autobiography
1904-45

With a Foreword by
BENN LEVY

LONDON
MACGIBBON & KEE
MCMLXIII

FIRST PUBLISHED 1963 BY MACGIBBON AND KEE LTD.
COPYRIGHT © JENNIE LEE 1963
PRINTED IN GREAT BRITAIN BY
CHARLES BIRCHALL AND SONS LTD.
LONDON AND LIVERPOOL

CONTENTS

FOREWORD

HAVING been an affectionate and occasionally exasperated friend of the author's since her girlhood, it has not been possible for me to read her autobiography except through the prism of a personal relationship. Come to that, most readers will to a lesser degree be similarly placed since every public figure, living or dead, evokes some kind of judgment from us if only in the most general terms of sympathy or antipathy. We can only be objective about an object, and not always about that.

Still harder is it to be objective in self-portraiture. There is no overwhelming impulse to put in our own warts, even if we have noticed them. So autobiographers range from the ungrudging hero-worship of a Churchill to the much rarer, headlong, incontinent candour of a Pepys or Boswell.

That it is a difficult form I know well, for I once attempted it in vain myself. After nearly ten thousand words I had not succeeded in bringing myself on to the already crowded stage at all. The inhibition owed nothing to modesty; indeed, more probably it was due to a subconscious fear that I might fail to do the central figure justice. Partly it was that, while to write of others has the excitement of exploration, to write of oneself is mere regurgitation.

But the main problem is the choice and presentation of a persona, the problem, in short, of 'characterization'. For whether you write about Emma Bovary or yourself, every line is affective: so you cannot abdicate control. You cannot throw the reins upon the horse's neck or he will come to a halt, as mine did. You may resolve that truthfulness alone shall be your arbiter but alas, truth too is impudently subjective. If it were not, honest men could agree. 'That is my truth', as Aneurin Bevan once said, 'now tell me yours'. Whether he stopped to hear it I cannot recall.

This basic problem of the autobiographer—how not to falsify himself discernibly or otherwise, how not to alienate the reader and infringe his own self-respect with an excess of claims or of mock-modesty, how, in short, to find the approximate truth about himself and brace himself for the fearful telling and yet avoid the dubious joys of exhibitionism—this problem, so seldom solved, has been solved in Jennie Lee's book by a simple expedient; it has been by-passed. For the book is not so much an autobiography, though it claims to be, as a political and social chronicle of her times told in the first person. Self-portraiture is a by-product, not a purpose. Even the earlier glimpses of family life are designed to illustrate a stratum of living conditions rather than a personal history.

And this of course is precisely what might have been anticipated. Personal privacy was not less sacred to the Bevans than chastity to our great-grandmothers. Journalists' invasions of it left them as shamed and outraged and angry as a Victorian spinster whose skirt had been hoisted ankle-high by some drunken thug in the street. That men should actually be paid for such activities instead of gaoled remained incomprehensible to them and gave rise to their long guerilla warfare with the Press. That the public life and acts of politicians should be fully on show was politically salutary but to supplement the public image with personal disclosures was a vulgarity akin to the wearing of an evening uniform traditional to a social class which was not one's own. They came from people to whom pride was a living necessity.

It was improbable therefore that the sensibility and habit of a lifetime would be abrogated in the writing of a so-called autobiography; and it was predictable that the precedence which politics had always held over personalia in Jennie Lee's life would be reflected in her book.

For she had been most powerfully brainwashed by experience, by precept and by environment from birth. So to a greater or less degree have we all. Only a minority *choose* their politics; still fewer choose their religion. For the most part circumstances choose a creed for us and all others are persistently washed from the brain. It is a humbling, even humiliating reflection. We must be nearer to Pavlov's dogs than we assume. For if we habitually exercised our powers of independent reason, however faultily, it would be an inconceivable coincidence, for instance, that virtually all Americans reject the theory of communism and all Russians dismiss the theory of capitalism. The division would be within communities, not between them. 'Upbringing' is a more effectual brain-laundry than has yet been devised either by the Kremlin or Madison Avenue.

There might be some comfort in the thought that the British community, at least, is sufficiently free-thinking to divide itself about equally between socialists and anti-socialists, were it not for the fact that we happen to be, as Disraeli mentioned, two communities. The thinking (or should one say reflexes?) of each is depressingly homogeneous. It provides the starting points for such differential social and economic theory as divides the political parties but overt renegades are few, if often notable. Just as Salisbury was born and bred into Conservatism, so equally do men like Herbert Morrison find themselves in the Labour Party through the accident of birth. Born in Hatfield, he would still have made his political mark as a man of talent, with of course the same eventual apotheosis into the peerage, but most improbably as a Labour leader. And who could doubt that Ernest Bevin, given more affluent beginnings, would have become a boardroom boss, hectoring and ruthless, rather than a Trade Union boss? Socialists by birth and socialists by conviction are perceptively distinguishable— and, as might be expected, often at odds with each other. Much of the recurrent factionalism inside the Labour Party can be traced here.

Yet some there are, a few, who refuse to have their politics chosen for them by the mere hazard of circumstances—or their religion or even their country; an obstinate minority who treasure freewill to the point where their brains remain virtually unwashable, a minority precious to those of us who, resistant to the determinism of Freud and Marx, still wanly hope for an eventual age of reason.

And by the same token there are socialists by birth who are also socialists by conviction. It would be hard to envisage the gentle Lansbury as a boardroom boss whatever his upbringing or to picture Maxton as a strike-breaker or Aneurin Bevan doing his painful imperial duty as master to lesser breeds without the law or Bob Smillie urging the economic wisdom of paring the wages of the poor.

To such as these Jennie, I think, belongs. It is true she was swept into socialism long before the age of consent, that every youthful experience conditioned her into enlistment, that nearly every adult man and woman in and about her home, in those grim days of childhood, was brave and battered and militant and invincible and fully deserving of the love and respect they earned from her with its consequence of emulation. It is true too that she was not and is not a highly rational being. Her fuel was emotion rather than doctrine. "My difficulty," she writes, "was that I had no gift for thinking in abstract categories. My mind reduced everything to the personal, immediate and concrete."

And it is true that the cognoscenti of Madison Avenue never forget that they too must reduce everything to the personal, immediate and concrete. They have analysed their clientele.

Yet I find it hard to imagine Jennie, even after a different conditioning, on the other side of the fence. And this, strangely enough, is more because she is her non-political mother's daughter than her highly political father's. "Ma Lee", whom I shall love and remember always, was everything she didn't know she was; in particular, a mighty influence. She, who claimed nothing, who saw herself (if indeed she ever stopped to look at herself at all) as a kind of dutiful nanny ministering to a clutch of boisterous, combative, argumentative giants, all outsize knights in shining armour who no doubt knew what they were about and could count on her support, if not her attention, loomed over and dimmed the lot of them; not only her own gay assertive family but the most eminent of their friends. Somehow one's eye was forever drawn to the background which Ma Lee contentedly supposed she inhabited, drawn there and fascinated and touched by that rarest form of greatness, a being without ego.

Because she exuded sanity in a dotty world, she was truly the mother-figure: we could not be frightened when she was there. There was no dark, no nightmares. She concentrated on the trivia which are the daily stuff of living and on the loving-kindness which so rarely blesses it. Within the orbit of that dear Scotch dumpling, chuckling, resilient, selfless, alert, uniquely uncompetitive and unacquisitive, her broad Fifeshire accent often barely intelligible, lay indestructibly warmth and security and reassurance. By contrast the clamant turbulence of the highly masculine world

about her, where I was so much at home, seemed somehow pitiful
and immature, though not of course to her; cabinet ministers
seemed prancing idiot-children. What she was no man could be.
Hers was superlatively the feminine contribution, hers was the
power and unclaimed glory, the feminism that feminists had
turned their backs upon.

Jennie was not her mother's replica. She had many of her
father's qualities; his evangelism, his interest in reading, his
staunchness in a fight. But, as with her mother, the mainspring of
her mechanism was in her heart rather than in her head. And
because she hated cruelty and because poverty is cruelty and
because its existence could not have been hidden even from a
rich man's daughter in those lavish years I doubt if upper or
middle-class indoctrination would have held her from crossing
the line. Like Cripps or Beatrice Webb or Trevelyan, she would
have found socialism. But she would have been led by sympathy
rather than by doctrine. For, on balance, she is her mother's
daughter.

BENN W. LEVY

INTRODUCTION

I BEGAN writing this book in the summer of 1939 in the hope that it would help me to see my way more clearly through the tangle of the years. The concluding chapters were written three years later in the midst of the second world war.

Both parts reflect the emotions of the times when they were written and so far as they have value it lies in that fact.

The wartime memories may help to explain why Aneurin Bevan was so sure there would be a Labour victory in 1945. His job in these years was immeasurably harder than mine.

There was no glory for him, no easy applause, none of the blessed relief from tensions enjoyed by those who move with the herd and are in no danger of being trampled under by its frenzied feet. He was always in danger. Someone had to man the most exposed posts. We could not all be members of a Tory dominated Coalition. We could not all find a cosy corner tucked under the protective wing of a powerful overlord fighting the war, but a different war, or at least fighting for irreconcilably different ends.

Much that was instinctively understood by fine men and women carrying on in their own unpublicised, unglamorised worlds, will one day be recorded, fact by fact, blow by blow.

But that is too big an undertaking for an introductory chapter to a new edition of fragments of autobiography written more than two decades ago. This is, at most, a preliminary documentary, a contribution to the raw material without which it is not even remotely possible to recapture the true meaning of past events.

It is a labourer's job to reassemble known facts. But only an historian of unusual sensitivity can do a worthwhile excavation job beneath the debris left by prejudice and deliberate falsification.

One day will the whole story be told? I can hear Ni's mocking, astringent, deeply tender tones. 'Of course not. All history is gossip.' Or again, a favourite quotation, 'This is my truth, now tell me yours.'

> ' O, many
> Have broke their backs with laying manors on 'em
> For this great journey.'

1

THE OLD ARCADE

AN old tea caddy stood on the corner of the mantelpiece in my mother's kitchen. It has stood there since 1900, the year when she was married. The measuring spoon was father's idea. It was more natural for mother to throw the tea leaves into the pot by the fistful.

Her lavish notions—it was the same with soup; half the town, father declared, could have been fed from her large black pot—were partly temperament, mainly habit.

For before her marriage mother was used to catering for a very large household. She did most of the cooking for her eleven brothers and sisters, and besides that, most of the kitchen work in a hotel and restaurant run by my maternal grandmother.

There was nothing fancy about Grandmother Greig's hotel. Scotch broth and Saturday night suppers of piping hot tripe and onions were its specialities. It gave good helpings at low prices.

The week-ends were its busiest times. It was then that young miners from the surrounding villages, eager for a bit of fun to break the monotony of the workaday week, made Cowdenbeath their centre.

A number of them would crowd into the restaurant, happy and carefree for an hour or two, making an unholy clatter with their laughter and banter.

My mother, the second eldest of Grandmother Greig's twelve children, was then a girl of nineteen. When people tell me that she was well liked by all the customers I can easily believe it. I can see her bustling around, quick moving but seldom flurried, making everyone feel comfortable, even a bit pampered. And the boundless goodwill she radiated around her kept everyone in a good humour even on the busiest of Saturday nights.

In 1899 one young miner began to appear in the restaurant suspiciously often. Grandmother Greig was not too pleased when she saw him come in. He was too ready to play practical jokes. And her tongue, which could bring most people to heel, had not the least effect on him. The more tartly she scolded, the more he seemed to enjoy himself.

By all accounts he was also a bit of a dandy. My mother still talks of the blue leather button boots he wore. She admired too his neat navy blue double-breasted suit. But there was one thing about him that rather disturbed her. No one could tell by looking at him whether it was the Sabbath or a weekday. He always wore the same neat navy blue double-breasted suit.

That was not as it should be. He ought to have had an ordinary shifting suit for weekdays and something different for Sunday best. It made it not so bad when she discovered that he achieved his nattiness by having two suits exactly alike and wearing them alternately. But all the same a lurking feeling remained at the back of her mind that it was a bit disrespectful of the Sabbath not to make some sort of distinction.

Her interest in the good-looking young collier was practical and direct. She was hoping he would ask her to marry him. And so he did. In 1900 these two became man and wife and set up house together in the traditional Scotch but and ben.[1] They quickly assembled four children around them. I was the third of their children and know these early days only from hearsay.

They sound endlessly strenuous. At four o'clock in the morning the alarm-clock would ring. Before five the young husband had left for his work in the pit. A few hours later the young wife had set her house in order, washed and dressed her babies and was off with them to Grandmother Greig's hotel.

My father came to detest this hotel entanglement. He hated coming back from his work to a meal of odds and ends hurriedly assembled from the hotel kitchen. The day came when he laid down the law. His food had henceforth to be bought with his own wages and cooked under his own roof.

[1] Two-roomde cottage.

That was a blow for Grandmother Greig. She depended a good deal on the help of her married daughter. But it never occurred to her to accept defeat. Her daughter was not coming to the hotel so often. Very well, the hotel must go to her daughter. So, piling all the hotel wash into the back of her old buggy, she drove off with it to her daughter's cottage. She had a very simple plan. Once at the cottage she dumped the soiled linen outside the door and let it be known that she would call again later in the week when it had all been nicely washed and dried. This scheme worked splendidly for a time. Then once again matters came to a head.

One day Grandmother Greig drove over as usual, the dirty linen piled up in the buggy behind her. But this time my father's mother was on the doorstep waiting for her. Grandmother Lee was also of a masterful disposition. The battle was pretty evenly drawn. In the end, however, Boadicea's buggy had to retire with the dirty linen still piled up inside it.

My mother, who then and always would do anything to keep the peace, remained indoors while all this was going on. She has told me since that she was 'heavy footed' at the time. That is her reticent way of saying she was with child. Her second son was born soon afterwards. He died while still an infant.

All these things happened several years before I was born. My maternal grandmother had become bedfast and was dying when, as a very small child, I first remembered seeing her. She lay in a large canopied bed in a darkened room and had a way of putting her hand under the pillow, then fumbling for a long time until she found her purse and slowly extracted a halfpenny which was given me for sweets.

Her illness meant that my mother had once again to do most of the work of the hotel. Ultimately my parents were persuaded to make the hotel their home. Then when my grandmother died they took over the business in their own name.

In these years Cowdenbeath was rapidly changing from a straggling village into a compact mining town. Old property was being pulled down. New buildings were going up everywhere.

Right in the centre of the town an arcade had appeared with shops on either side, a hall at the foot, and a hotel above the shops. The entrance to the hotel was half-way down the arcade.

Grandmother Greig's place of business had had to change with the changing town. Her old quarters were demolished and from 1902 onwards she rented the hotel above the grand new Arcade.

If modern advertising had been in fashion and the Arcade proprietors had been entirely immoral they might have given themselves a puff something like this:

'See Scotland where the past and present meet. The Arcade Hotel, High Street, Cowdenbeath, is on the Great North Road to the Highlands. Loch Leven with its good fishing and romantic memories of Mary Queen of Scots only five miles to the North. Dunfermline toune, the ancient capital of Scotland where Bruce lies buried and where Malcolm Canmore and his gentle Margaret reigned, six miles to the west. Excellent cuisine and all modern conveniences.'

It is very comical to think of the Arcade Hotel in these terms. Loch Leven and Dunfermline might just as well have been a thousand miles away. Especially in these days when there were few trains, no buses and the tramway line from Cowdenbeath to Dunfermline was a new-fangled novelty. Then, even more than now, the mining community was a world in itself. But no one could have been gaoled for a bogus advertisement of that kind. The location given would have been approximately right.

Actually the Arcade was a rickety structure of cheap red brick with a grey cement facing. Almost as soon as it was built it began to need heavy repairs and to look grimy and old. The most startling feature about it was the 'pug' engine from the pit that went shunting to and fro at all hours of the day and night immediately below the hotel windows. The hotel was built where the level crossing cuts across the main street of the town. Strangers unaccustomed to the noise of the pug had small chance of an unbroken sleep.

But from my third to my eighth year (while it was my home) that second description gives no more idea of how the Arcade looked and felt to me than the first does.

From a child's angle it was a superb place. All kinds of exciting things were always happening. Particularly in the hall at the foot of the Arcade. I could never be sure what new magic I would find there.

At that time touring companies were much in vogue. These were the great days of melodrama. East Lynne was drawing oceans of tears all over the country. The mining folks enjoyed a good cry as well as the next. They crowded into the Arcade Hall and by their patronage made it just worth while for companies travelling between Edinburgh and Perth to make Cowdenbeath an irregular place of call.

Between the visits of the theatre companies the hall was let to any organization that could pay the rent. It sheltered with equal readiness religious meetings, bird shows, wedding parties, funeral suppers, trade union lodge meetings, temperance lectures, the Clarion Scouts and the then active Social Democratic Federation. I patronized any of these gatherings that took my fancy. My mother was busy in the hotel upstairs. My father who had leased the hall was equally busy downstairs. No one had much time to pay attention to my comings and goings. I was able to run about pretty much as I pleased; and to collect a most dazzling range of acquaintances.

There was, for instance, my first love: a pleasant memory in spite of the grief he caused me. He was taller than any other man in the world and could carry me on his shoulder from room to room. He was not afraid to carry me through the kitchen to the back scullery where I was forbidden to go; and there he pilfered at my command small tin pastry shapes with wriggles all round the edge that I wanted badly as playthings.

One day I was hanging out of the dining-room window looking on to the main street of the town waiting for him to come along. I saw him. He was seated on the top of a tram-car that was rumbling past. I waved, I shouted to him. But got no response. He did not even look my way. I collapsed in tears. The world had come to an end.

At the time that was all I knew. Since then I have learned that he was one-half of a variety turn called 'The Long and the Short of It'. He was the long half. They were travelling theatre people who were staying in the hotel. On the day in question my friend was nowhere to be found when the company assembled to prepare for the evening's performance. The short half went around frantically seeking for his partner. I was discovered damp and forlorn. From my story they decided that he had been dead drunk when he passed on the top of the tram-car and was riding blindly on towards the Dunfermline terminus. A rescue party was sent off post-haste to Dunfermline and there, indeed, they found him.

Another special friend of mine about this time was the Chinaman with the long pigtail. I refused to believe that the pigtail was real. Then one evening I was permitted to enter his room and watch his wife brush and braid it in readiness for the evening performance. As a final test I was allowed to pull as hard as I could. That settled it; I agreed it was real.

He was a splendid Chinaman, tall and benevolent and smiling. Someone told me that when Chinamen died they were buried face downwards so that their God could pull them straight up to Heaven by their pigtails. I cherished that bit of learning and have liked the Chinese ever since.

I am suprised how vividly I remember some things from these early days. There is no proper sequence or continuity about anything; just an assortment of odd bits and pieces. Tommy Torrance, trailing onto the stage of the Arcade Hall with his toy dog dragging behind him and singing 'I'm happy for Life, I've lost my Wife and found a rare wee dug'.[1] Sam Tamson playing his penny whistle and making us all laugh when he piped 'I'm the saftest of the family, I'm the Simple Johnny Raw'. Dr. Body terrifying us with his tricks. His adopted daugher, Dolly, who, in the deepest woman's voice that ever was, sang 'Don't go down the mine Daddy'. (It was only later that we thought of parodies.) At that time we all cried.

Harry Lauder and Florrie Ford came to the Arcade along with the rest, but at the age of seven I could see nothing special about either of them. I preferred the ventriloquist with his doll. The doll was almost a young man in size. It could answer absolutely any question it was asked. Sometimes in the dressing-room behind the stage I had a special audience with it all to myself. Once I tried to pull it off its master's knee on to my own, but its weight nearly knocked me over and it mumbled in an affronted tone of voice, 'Don't do that'.

I remember very little about my mother in those early hotel days. She was always busy. One day there was an extra stir in the kitchen. I suppose an unexpectedly large number of people had

[1] Dog.

come into the dining-room and were clamouring for food. The bread supply ran out so I was bundled off to the baker's to bring back as much as I could carry. I bought delicious bread. It was still steaming hot straight from the bakehouse and had an odour that would have melted the heart of a stone. It got a bit squeezed on the way home but that could hardly be helped for the loaves were large square ones that doubled in like concertinas when I tried to make my arms go round them. I carried them home as best I could so was confused by the way I was raved at when I reached the kitchen door. My mother gave a cry of angry dismay. She was standing beside her bread-cutting machine at the large kitchen table. New bread somehow was no use to her. She wanted cutting bread, she said.

I took her at her word and, summoning my baby brother, retired to a corner with the steaming loaves. Nobody wanted them, so they were ours, I reckoned, to do whatever we liked with. We put one each on our knees and hollowed out the soft warm hearts. That seemed a much nicer way of eating bread than having it handed you in monotonous slices.

The success of our little spree was short-lived. Someone was shouting around the kitchen for the extra loaves. We were located in our corner and again somehow in disgrace. Apparently the loaves were wanted after all. But I had distinctly heard mother say that they were not what she wanted, that they were too new. It was all very perplexing and painful, not least the queer sensations in our insides. No one had ever told us that new bread eaten in hot chunks kept on swelling in your stomach until you felt like the whale with Jonah struggling about inside.

Another confused memory of the Arcade Hotel was the day when we thought our cat had been roasted in the oven. There was a sudden loud crack, then what looked like blood and entrails flowed out beneath the oven door. Mother flew forward, opened the door, and oh! what a relief! It was only Jam-jars up to his tricks again. Jam-jars was the name everyone gave to one of the hotel boarders who refused to eat any food cooked in the ordinary way. He prepared his own meals, cooking everything in jam-jars. This day his jar had burst. I have not the slightest recollection of what Jam-jars looked like, but I remember very plainly our large, slow-moving

black cat and the agony that seized us when the bursting of the
jam-jar made us think we had sent it to an awful death.

There was little time or place for domestic pets in that busy
hotel household. Rats were the animals I saw and heard most about.
A trap used to be set for them under the sink in the back kitchen.
They were both terrible and irresistible. When I knew there were
dead ones lying on the scullery floor, I wanted to run to the other
end of the building—and I knew I would have to creep near
enough to see their ugly faces and glassy, bulging eyes.

I probably remember the rats so well because of a fight I once
saw between my father and a live one. It was upstairs on the bedroom floor in a small turret box-room. There was no furniture in
the room. My father was standing in the middle of the floor with a
long stick in his hand. The Devil incarnate in the body of an
enormous rat was glaring at him with all Hell in its eyes. I had
heard a scuffle and looked into the room in aimless curiosity. I was
not prepared for this terrible sight. Father lifted the stick. The rat,
cornered by now, crouched and glared, ready to spring at his
throat. Then it leapt!—leapt right over his shoulder and out of the
one small window quite high up in the room. When anyone talks
of a cornered rat the picture that lives in me is quite definite and
clear. I see the old Arcade, the small turret room, the window, my
father, and that leaping grey embodiment of evil and of the disease
that lay in the stinking burn at the back of the hotel. The rats, I was
told, came from the burn. I hated and feared both.

There was quite a lot that was gloomy and threatening in that
grey, ramshackle building. The smoking-room, for instance, had
only one window and that looked out on a blank wall. It let in
almost no light. The gas had to be lit even during the day. But it
was important to go into the smoking-room sometimes for there
was a huge dark sideboard there and in a glass case on the top of
the sideboard three most wonderful dolls, as large as life. No one
was allowed to play with the dolls or even to touch them. They
belonged to my grandmother who had bought them at a sale and
had given them (nominally) to her youngest daughters. But that
was long ago and these daughters were now too old for dolls, so it
seemed hard that they should stand there out of reach of all the
grandchildren who were itching to get at them. It was only after

my grandmother died that the case was opened and the dolls distributed. I got one of them. But after it ceased to be untouchable it must have impressed me much less. I can remember no more about it.

People used to say that if ever fire broke out in the Arcade it would be a death trap. There was no fire-escape. There was not even a back stair. This infuriated my mother. It meant that all the refuse had to be carried out of the main entrance. Also the roof was continually leaking. So any little profit she had for all her hard work was eaten up in repapering the bedrooms, and other essential repairs.

But none of these worries weighed on my six or seven years. In spite of damp and rats and gloomy corridors and the bad smell from the burn, the odds and ends I remember from that time have a pleasant colouring. It was my parents who had all the worries; my mother in particular, who had to be up at dawn and rubbing and scrubbing and cooking and serving without rest for a single hour during the whole long day. She always worked much harder than anyone she engaged to help her. Her fatal defect was that she was much quicker and better at doing things herself than at ordering anyone else to do them for her. She almost killed herself with the work, but the only one who made any profit out of the place was the landlord.

The Arcade belonged to one of Grandmother Greig's many brothers. He paid us a visit once a year to fish in Loch Leven and collect his rent. Rather to our consternation, he was in the habit of kissing us all when he arrived and departed, an alien custom he must have picked up among the English. Scottish folks are not given to greeting their relatives so demonstratively.

In other ways this uncle was unlike any other member of his family. Starting life, quite literally, as a bare-footed boy peddling shoe-laces from door to door, he accumulated quite a comfortable fortune. His single-minded interest in money-making gave him an advantage over most people. Over Grandfather Greig, for instance, who loved his fiddle and loved his dram but had not the least scrap of business capacity. It was probably just as well therefore that he should have been induced to sign over his share in some property my great-grandmother then possessed for five shillings, the price of a drink or two.

Grandfather Greig spent the last years of his life roving about the countryside, usually sleeping in model lodging-houses. His children tried again and again to salvage him. But he had no liking for their settled, respectable lives. That they could never understand.

My mother, who had an invincible gift for making excuses for everybody, made them for him with more than her usual warm-heartedness. He was nobody's enemy but his own, she would say. He had no bad in him. He would not have hurt a fly. And, clinching every other argument, at sixty she could still tenderly recall how, when they were all young children at home together, Grandfather Greig would make them happy by playing his fiddle to them. Sometimes, for their very special delight he would make his fiddle say 'Ma-ma, Pa-pa'.

Before I was quite eight years old my parents moved out of the hotel into a small private house. There was no inducement for them to remain in the business. It had become quite clear that the uncle proprietor had no intention of modernizing the place. Also, although my mother was in her familiar environment, my father must have been about the strangest business 'gent' it is possible to imagine. He was not then, or at any time, a gloomy spoil-sport. But he had strong social and political convictions which he clung to with dogged persistence. For one thing, he insisted on the business remaining a 'Temperance' Hotel. That was considered a great hardship by jaded commercial travellers and thirsty theatrical people. And, on top of that, to be met by an eager landlord anxious to sell them a copy of 'Merrie England' or 'Britain for the British' was more than ordinary mortals could be expected to stand.

It is customary now to decorate nursery schools, and the infants' department in ordinary schools, with gaily coloured toys and pictures. There was little or none of that when I went to school. That was in the years just before the war. School was a drab, grey routine of unexciting tasks. But the stern old gods that frown down from our northern skies were cheated in my case. The Arcade was my real nursery school. Its actors and actresses, rats and ventriloquist's doll, its toy shop and Chinaman with a real pigtail, form in my memory a frieze of as grotesque and brightly coloured pictures as any child's artist could devise.

If we had gone on living there it would no doubt have looked different as I learned to see my surroundings with older eyes. But from eight years onwards, there was no more hotel life. Instead there was the usual routine of a small working-class household.

The hotel world faded entirely out of the picture. I do not remember even recalling it. We were caught up and completely absorbed in my father's life, which was entirely that of the mining community to which he again unequivocally belonged.

This incursion into hotel-keeping, so far as my father was concerned, was purely accidental. After an absence of a few years he went back to the pits where he had begun to work when he was twelve years old, where his brothers and his friends were working and where his father had worked for twenty-nine years. Grandfather Lee had, by that time, ceased working underground but he would have been very indignant if anyone had said he was no longer a miner.

His workmates had elected him a full-time official of the Fife Miners' Union.

2

THE OCTOPUS

THE great thing about moving into a four-roomed private house was the discovery that we now had a garden. There was none at the hotel; only a large, dreary piece of waste land with the stinking burn at the foot of it.

When I first saw our strip of garden it was glorified by a patch of white blossom. I thought it would be a fine thing to pluck all this loveliness and carry it off to school. Just as I had finished, my good-tempered mother, so seldom angry, came rushing out, scolding vehemently. It seemed that I had ravaged the strawberry bed, that every flower would later have been a large red berry, but that now, because of what I had done, we would have no strawberries that year. I liked flowers; but I liked strawberries too. It was a sad beginning.

Our home was now one of a monotonous row of houses in a typical working-class side street. There is no subtlety about the way such houses are designed. A narrow lobby ran through the centre of the house with two doors on either side. The two front rooms overlooking the street—there was no front garden—were used as bedrooms. One of the back rooms was the kitchen-living-room, the other a bedroom and sitting-room combined. The lavatory was always a source of annoyance to my mother. It was at the inside end of the lobby. If the door was left open it looked out directly on to the street. She did her best with it by draping a curtain over the entrance.

A still bigger nuisance was that once again we had no back door. All ashes and refuse had to be carried out on to the front pavement, then down a long draughty close to the back garden. The coal cellar and washhouse were also at the back of the house. This was doubly hard on mother for her eyes troubled her. Each time she went hurrying through the draughty close, the cold biting winds kept them reddened and sore. But for all that, by the time we rushed home from school in the middle of the afternoon, our kitchen was a very pleasant place to run into. There was sure to be a bright fire burning in the open grate, a white cloth spread on the table promising that tea would soon be ready, and, if the kettle was not already singing, we thought we had a grievance. Sometimes there was also the pleasant odour of scones and pancakes freshly baked for tea.

The only time we were really uncomfortable at home was Saturday forenoons. There was no school on Saturday. Mother did her extra week-end cleaning then and we were expected to lend a hand. I was not a great success. It would be too much to say that I disliked housework. I was just negative about it. So negative that I usually forgot what I was about and settled down on top of the large chest-of-drawers with the glass-doored bookcase on top. That was where our best and biggest books were kept. Right in front of me would be *The Arabian Nights, Das Kapital, The Family Physician, Ingersol's Lectures and Essays, The Count of Monte Cristo, Science History of the Universe, The Brass Check, White Fang, The Three Musketeers*. Before I quite realized what was happening I was the Count of Monte Cristo tapping away desperately in an effort to establish communication with the prisoner in the next cell. Or I was Liza fleeing from slavery across the broken ice and carrying a child in my arms. Or Burning Daylight swaggering into town, the toughest and whitest man in all the North.

Once having started a book I hated to lay it down before I had read right through to the very end. But, on Saturday forenoons, I was handicapped by a most inconvenient conscience. This kept telling me, to my infinite irritation, 'There's work to do, work to do, work to do'. If my mother had been in any sense a martinet I rather think I would have fought back at her and enjoyed it. But, supposing you should want to defy mother, there was no way of knowing where to begin. She had not the slightest idea of how to be exacting or stern. I knew that if I did not speedily hop down from the top of the drawers and rub and dust for dear life to make up for time lost, she would simply do the whole of the week-end cleaning herself without even being sulky about it.

Sometimes I came near to breaking her temper (a considerable achievement) in the early part of Saturday afternoon. It was then that the special week-end shopping had to be done. Mother always declared that she preferred doing this herself. But there was so much for her to do at home that most Saturdays she had to depend on me.

I would be sent off to go through one department after another of our local Co-operative, and bring home the week's supplies. Always I was told to be careful with the eggs. Always I told myself that this time there would be no accident. But at least one (sometimes more) had a miserable habit of getting itself broken. I never quite knew how it happened. I was too absent-minded, mother would storm. I must stop day-dreaming and remember what I was about. It astounded me that there should be so many mishaps, particularly as I had my own illegitimate reason for trying to remember not to swing the basket with the eggs in it. For, when shouting across the store grocery counter 'a pound of ham (must be lean), a packet of matches, a tin of creamola, half a pound of the best Ceylon tea, a packet of self-raising flour, two pounds of sugar', what harm was there in adding—'and twopenny worth of candy mixtures'. No harm that I could ever see, especially as there were large boxes of sweets propped up on the counter that kept staring at me all the time I was waiting to be served. But mother's view about that unauthorized twopence worth was different. The only hope of getting off with it was for the rest of the groceries to be in ship-shape order. If the eggs were broken, then you could be sure there would be a double fuss; one for the eggs, and one for the mixtures.

Truth to tell, her scoldings were never very terrible. But if sorely tried she would add—'and if you do that again I'll tell your father'. That was disturbing. There was always the possibility that one time she actually would. And what then? Our father never bullied and never used baby talk. He had a way of treating us as if we were responsible grown-ups. That was very flattering. We liked it. But the other side of the account was that we were anxious not to fall into his 'black books'. A talking to from him occurred only once or twice in a lifetime. It was a serious affair not to be met with lighthearted banter in the way we treated our mother's scoldings.

If Saturday forenoon was stormy and strenuous, the rest of the

week-end made up for it. By teatime at the latest, we could settle
down to real luxury. Everything at home, the fire and the firearms,
and the brass trays and candlesticks on the mantelpiece above the
fire, were dazzling to look at. Not that we bothered about that sort
of thing. We had more important business on hand. For it was then
the great moment came when we were given our Saturday pennies
and could dash off to buy our weekly quota of one penny fairy-tale
and two comic-cuts. I chose the fairy-tale, my brother the comics.
We each devoured our own, then eagerly swopped.

In a southern country, life, I imagine, must turn outwards a great
deal towards the sun. In this dreary, industrial north our life
turned inwards instead. There was not much to attract us out of
doors. For months in the year a grey drizzle fell dejectedly from an
uninviting sky. There was seldom even good, clean snow; just dirty
sludge, part snow, part rain, part coal-dust. Even in the summer
evenings we usually clustered around the fire. For in Scotland the
summers are short and precarious; winter weather takes up most of
the year.

During all my schooldays our kitchen fireside was the centre of
the world. We were very contented when we were allowed to
sprawl on the rug in front of the fire with our story-books spread
out around us. 'Tell me a story,' my small brother would demand.
That was easy. We had only to look into the flames and very soon
giants and hobgoblins and weird animals paraded in front of us.
We had to be on the alert to see them for they stayed only a minute
fraction of time, then vanished again down the sun-coloured caverns
behind the rocks of coals. We were fire-worshippers, and never
grew tired of it.

Sometimes at home in the evening it was very quiet outside with
only one sound breaking the stillness; the beat of the ventilation-
fan at the neighbouring pit. That regular beat, beat, beat, invaded
our fireside. It got tangled up with the giants and ogres we were
reading about. We invented stories in which the pit was a monster
and the rhythmic noise we heard, the beating of its heart. This
monster dragged all kinds of victims to their doom. It imprisoned
them in its gaunt dungeon. Then brave knights would ride to the
rescue. At first every knight met with danger and defeat. The faint-
hearted turned back. Even the bravest were disheartened some-

times. But, in the end, we always allowed them to set the captives free.

One day we found our father reading a book called the *Octopus*. He explained, when we pestered him, what 'octopus' meant. We promptly decided that the pit was an octopus. It had arms stretching in all directions. It sucked in everything around it.

In these days our father was the all-wise and infallible one. He taught us our sums a year ahead of school schedule. Without ever preaching at us, he taught us a great deal more besides. His critical socialist outlook influenced our attitude to everything around us. We knew that beyond our sheltered fireside there were evil spirits abroad. And we knew that he was one of the good knights and true who would one day slay all the dragons and set poor people free.

This 'we' I keep talking about was not a large company. I ought to have had three brothers, but two died before I was old enough to remember much about them. The third was two and a half years younger than I was. We were inseparable. He was a gentle and loving child. Our mother had a habit of humming and singing out of tune as she went about her work. One day, for some reason, she was worried and low-spirited. He always noticed that sort of thing. Tugging at her skirt, he tried to find out what was the matter. To satisfy him she had to start humming and making cheerful faces. He was just as foolish about animals. There was almost always a stray dog or cat sheltering in our back garden. The mangiest-looking creatures, they usually were. But you could be sure he would wait on them as if they were visiting Royalty.

Our mother strictly forbade us to bring dogs and cats into the house. Dogs, she said, brought dirt and smells with them. Cats were forbidden because of our canary. That bird was the drabbest, most rickety-looking little proletarian it was possible to behold. It was brought from the pit one day in a minute, coal-blackened prison of a cage. I remember my father plomping it down beside the kitchen sink and saying, 'Poor devil, it deserves to live'. Greatly marvelling, we listened to its story. Six times it had been sent into working places in the pit where the air was bad. Each time, by dropping off its perch, overcome by gas-fumes, it gave warning to the men that it was time for them to move out. The seventh time, when our father was pumping oxygen into it to revive it, he decided that it was time for the little collier bird to go into honourable retirement. At the end of the shift he brought it to the surface with him and home. That same evening, before the shops closed, we went out together and bought it as large and fine a cage as our small funds would run to. We were always proud when our friends remarked on how gaily it sang. And, prejudice apart, it really did sing remarkably well.

Although indoor pets were banned, one day my brother was allowed to invest his whole fortune—he had four shillings and sevenpence in his money-box—in a rabbit hutch and a small rabbit. He was in heaven. But as the days passed strange things began to happen. His pet's appetite was enormous. We trespassed over every garden in the neighbourhood searching for dandelion leaves for it. We made it immense helpings of a mixture of oatmeal and old tea-leaves that rabbits were supposed to like. It never seemed to stop eating. And the strong stench from its hutch that we were in honour bound to keep clean, was distressing. Worst of all, when we brought it out beside us on the green, hoping to stroke it and watch it scamper gently about our feet, it raced off at lightning speed and jumped over every garden wall and fence within sight. We had to chase after it as best we could. A growing suspicion began to haunt us. At last it could no longer be denied. Our rabbit was a whacking big hare. In spite of that, my brother clung to it tenaciously and would never admit that it had a single fault.

Some time before this he had his fifth birthday. It was time for him to go to school. And it was my job to take him there. That term nearly all my class seemed to be dragging younger brothers and sisters to their first days of schooling. Some yelled, others walked along quite trustingly. The great thing was to see whose charge would be at the head of the line when the infant class assembled in the playground ready to march into school after the forenoon interval. We older ones, each clutching a hapless infant of five, would eye one another suspiciously, then fight and push for position. It took careful generalship for we were not supposed to be in the infant's playground. As soon as the teachers appeared in sight we had to fly off to our own part of the grounds. In those school bouts I usually won. I was not fair and gentle like my brother. I was dark and stubborn.

After having started the child at school, my next concern was to make sure that he would one day go to heaven. At nine years old I was devoutly religious in a very concrete and primitive way. Hell was Hell and I saw it vividly, exactly as it was described to me— as a great big burning fire. Scotland, especially the Scotland of the older generation, is prone to take its religion gloomily. We talked of God-fearing men—very seldom of God-loving ones. The punishments lying in wait for the sinner loomed much larger on our youthful horizon than any pleasure that might be the reward of virtue. Hell always seemed a much more tangible and likely proposition than any conceptions we had of Heaven. My anxiety over theological matters was deepened by the fact that my parents were not church-goers. I secretly envied one of my little playmates whose father could be seen every Sunday walking solemnly to church wearing a tall silk hat, a tailcoat and gloves. He was a deacon. I had no idea what that meant but I felt that somehow we lost caste by having a father who had a tail-coat and a tall hat hanging at the back of the wardrobe but who would not wear them even to funerals.

Those social problems were important; but small enough in comparison with my concern as to what would become of us all in the next world, especially my brother. At all costs I was anxious that he should be saved. I did what I could by seeing that he never forgot to say his prayers both night and morning.

I remember one night, after we were both tucked up in bed, waking with a start, for prayers had been forgotten. I can distinctly recall kicking him out of bed, tearful and protesting, and not allowing him back again until he had prayed long and thoroughly. His tears had no effect on me for I saw the Hell flames leaping in the background. It was all for his own good. I was resolved that there should be no mishap where he was concerned. For myself, I mumbled all the words of the prayer but remained inside the blankets, knowing that was not so efficacious as kneeling on the cold floor but hoping it would do.

Apparently I succeeded in instilling into him a wholesome fear of the Almighty, assisted, about this time, by a terrible accident. One of the few things that were strictly forbidden in our household was bathing in the Netherton Burn. The Netherton was a small

winding stream more than a mile from home. We were told it was
dirty and dangerous. It looked shallow and clean enough, and on a
really warm day could be quite inviting. One day my brother ran
off with a group of other boys and succumbed to temptation.
Against strictest orders he went dookin' in the burn. I knew
nothing of this until after I had been in bed some time and all the
lights were out. A shivering bundle of misery woke me by creeping
into my bed. He was sobbing pitifully. God had punished him. One
of his boots had been lost in the burn. Worse than that, it was a
new boot worn that day for the first time. He had searched for it
desperately as long as the light lasted, then slunk home, leaving the
odd boot behind the outside door and hurrying straight to bed so
as not to be found out.

I don't know how such a thing would seem to a child in a well-
to-do household. For us it was the end of the world. Much more
than disobedience was involved. There was the cash side as well.
Boots cost a lot of money. I could hear what mother would say:
'Your father has been down the pit all day knocking his soul-case
out to get you boots and this is what you do. Two day's work
thrown into the burn'. That was how we reckoned money. It was
a sombre form of reckoning. Certain things cost half a shift. Others
a whole shift. Some even more than that. Boots were one of the big
items that had to be 'saved' for. They had to be treated with respect. And here was a brand-new boot—it might as well have been
both—lying at the bottom of the burn.

I comforted the sinner as best I could, telling him I would make
it all right with his father and mother, that God had already
punished him enough. I was lying valiantly. I could hardly see
how any mercy could be hoped for. They were very good boots.
The best quality the Co-op stocked. It was terrifying to think of it.

When morning came I did my diplomatic best. But there was
no way of putting it that did not come at last to the hideous, inescapable truth—one of the new boots was buried in the burn.

Mother gave a sharp moan. I could see from her face that it was
as bad as I had feared. Half begging, half bullying, I extorted the
promise that father was to know nothing about it. We arranged
that, immediately school was over, we would both go with her and
have another search for the boot. We went, but it was useless. All

our rummaging and plunging failed to bring up anything except old tin cans and a drowned cat.

That same year, or perhaps a year later, another boot incident darkened the world. It was Christmas Eve. We had written our letters to Santa Claus, hung up our stockings, and gone confidently to bed. I woke in the middle of the night and peered out to see what could be seen. There, clear as could be, was my stocking with a bulge in the middle of it and a new box lying beside the fireplace. I got up at once and found in the stocking one miserable and lonely orange. In the box there was a new pair of brown long-legged boots. Mad with resentment I strutted back to bed and wept bitter, scalding tears of anger. This was an outrage. Boots indeed. Everyone had to have boots, Christmas or no Christmas. To palm off boots as a Santa Claus gift was contemptible. Santa Claus was supposed to bring things you wanted, not just things you had to have anyway. To bring boots of all things was mockery and theft. It was an unjust world. A harsh malignant world. I wanted to sleep and not wake up again unless perhaps to slay people. On Christmas morning I woke late, dazed and stupefied. It was difficult piecing things together. What had happened during the night ? What was happening now ? For there, clustered all around the fireplace were stacks of boxes overflowing with toys and story-books. Gradually I saw what must have happened. I had frightened off my parents when they were just beginning to lay out our gifts. Now it was morning and everything was as it should be, and yet not quite everything. That Christmas day was less carefree than others I remembered. The bitter tears at dawn had left their mark. They made a difference when I walked off to school with the pick of my presents under my arm. I was not so jaunty and noisily boastful as I had sometimes been on these occasions. With a *Chatterbox* under one arm and a double-jointed doll under the other, I ran full tilt into a meek little girl who always hovered about the foot of the class. We compared notes. Once I had gone through my list of presents, not leaving out even the new, brown, long-legged boots, I asked for hers. Santa Claus had brought her an orange and a penny and a miserable squirt of a cotton handkerchief with rabbits in the corner. I was appalled. Her home was one of the poorest in the town. There was a large family of young ones. Their clothes were always shabby and worn. They never seemed to have any toys of their own. I looked at her warily. Had she been raving and storming earlier in the morning as I would have done? There were no signs of rage or bitterness or envy. She fingered my new doll in a quiet, gentle way. I could not even be quite sure she would have liked to have had one like it. I was afraid to ask her in case she said yes or cried. I don't think she would have shown much sign of feeling even if I had inquired. She was one of the meek who, I had heard somewhere, were to inherit the earth. She did not look like an heiress.

This encounter worried me. There were many others at school who had received little or nothing for Christmas. I was one of the plutocrats. The only others who had more imposing loot than myself were the children of business people whom we thought very rich. It worked out like a lesson in arithmetic. The richer you were the more you got. If you had nothing at all, you got nothing. I knew Santa Claus was partly one's parents but, in addition to that, there was a mystical glow about the season of Christmas and the hint that some other spirit was abroad. I developed a mordantly critical mood towards this other spirit, this spirit of Christmas. So Santa Claus was what the men in the pits would call a belly-crawler. The old gentleman with the red gown and white beard and benevolent air liked to keep in with the gaffer. He toadied to those who already had most and left out in the cold those who hung up their stockings with the biggest emptiness needing to be filled. He brought me, who already had a share in one penny fairy-tale and two comic-cuts every Saturday afternoon, several fat volumes of stories and other things as well. He brought this pale, inoffensive little schoolmate, who had no story-book, no best quality Co-op boots, no doll, no anything, a tawdry handkerchief, a penny and an orange. There was something wrong somewhere. I felt I must have a consultation with my father, who knew everything and was always just. I can still remember fragments of that particular talk. Capitalism, I learned, had 'neither a body to kick nor a soul to save. There would have to be a Revolution'. I felt blown-up with all this information, but not much wiser.

There was a great variation in the home-life of the children I grew up beside. Some, like myself, had comfortable homes, never had to go hungry, and, in addition to weekday clothes, had a special set of everything to be worn only on the Sabbath. Others lived in dismal, smelly, overcrowded quarters, never saw a freshly-starched white tablecloth, had poor food with little nourishment value, and sometimes in winter time came to school with no soles to their boots or wearing cheap canvas shoes that drew water like sponges and gave them chilblains.

Ours was a mining community and we were almost all miners' children. But, if there were six or eight in the family and all too young to be earning anything, it made an unbelievable difference to the kind of shelter and food that the family could afford. Even where there was a small family, it needed steady work, careful spending and some extra money coming in from somewhere before there could be any real comfort.

From a miner's wages there was little over for such flippancies as, for instance, filling Christmas stockings. My brother and myself got more than most. We ran a regular racket at Christmas-time. Weeks, sometimes months, before we badgered a young jeweller who lodged with us, to write our letter to Santa Claus. At that time he was a lonely bachelor and so an easy prey. We reckoned that if he wrote the Christmas letter he would not be able to make a mistake about what we wanted; and we were unblushing in our demands. He never failed us. He drew out the list of requests in the order of their urgency, blew the letter up the chimney and we found it politic to pretend we believed in the old man in the reindeer-sledge years after we had discovered the truth. I doubt if he was seriously taken in by our ruses, but he played up—and paid up—handsomely all the same.

3

INTO BATTLE

WHEN I was nine years old I must have known every word of *Robinson Crusoe* off by heart. I had a very special reason for this. Our father had told us that Lower Largo was the birthplace of Robinson Crusoe. Our mother had booked a room in Upper Largo for the miners' holiday week. The whole town knew of these goings on. We babbled for months beforehand of this coming holiday by the sea.

Then came the deadly warning. We were cautioned not to build our hopes too high. There were rumours of a strike that was to be the biggest ever known in the history of mining. Every pit in the whole of Great Britain was to be brought to a standstill. If there was a strike, there could be no holiday. For days longer than years we hung around in an agony of suspense. As children it seemed a matter of life and death to us that no strike should take place just at that time. We pleaded with our parents, trying to make them understand that the most important thing in the world was that we should go to Robinson Crusoe's birthplace. We badgered all we dared. When our tongues were silenced our eyes went on campaigning.

Eventually the family conference was held where our fate had to be decided. Our mother looked inquiringly towards father. It was his place to give a lead. Two disconsolate children were hanging on his every word. He went on smoking his pipe in a slow, tantalizing way he sometimes had, then began very slowly and deliberately: 'As likely—as not—there will be—a strike. But nothing—is definite yet. —We might—as well risk it.'

Oh, the relief! That was all we wanted to know. We could run off now and prepare for our ascension straight into heaven.

39

I can always return to Largo Bay with a special feeling of intimacy and pleasure. Its old grey harbour is quite lovely. It is peaceful in the uplands behind the sea.

But that is not the Largo we knew as children. That Largo was a place of pure magic. The fishermen down by the harbour in their great blue jerseys filled us with bashful hero worship. Sometimes they let us sit in their boats. Once or twice we were taken a little way out to sea.

Then there were the Pierrots. Such Pierrots. We never willingly missed a performance. We liked the funny songs and we liked the sentimental ones. We liked everything. One day the favourite comedian caught sight of our parents. Without stopping his songs and patter, he lifted his hat and called, 'How are you, Mr. Lee ?' A minute later in the midst of his fooling he sang out again, 'And how's Mrs. Lee ? I am coming round to see'. No one in the audience except ourselves knew that these words had any meaning. But we knew. My brother and I nudged each other with pride and pleasure. Later, jingling the collection bag, he made his way to our part of the crowd. He really was a special friend of ours. He had stayed in the Arcade Hotel years before we were born.

On the second day of our holiday we got the news from somewhere that quite definitely there would be no strike. A settlement had been reached. That same day, trailing down to the beach together, my father and I stopped to buy a newspaper. He read it when we reached the shore, then stared gravely out to sea. So gravely that I knew something was seriously wrong. I was filled with dark misgivings. Perhaps there was going to be a strike after all. Perhaps we would have to return home that very day. Even if we could stay our whole week, perhaps there would be no pennies for ice-cream and everyone would be looking gloomy. I asked what was wrong. Would there be a strike ? No, there would be no strike but the Germans—the German Fleet. Now I could breathe again. There was to be no strike. We could finish our holiday in peace. That was July 1914.

When the war began we collected all the broken dolls we could lay hands on and played at hospitals. Those with limbs missing were in special demand. And, of course, it was not possible for us to attend to our wounded until we had uniforms and white headdresses like other nurses. When our mothers were not looking we confiscated old white towels and handkerchiefs and improvised magnificently.

We had lots of fine war games. But as the weeks passed I began to feel disquieted. My parents were not cheering with the rest of the crowd. They were opposed to the war. This was awkward. It was worse than that, it was frightening. I dared not confess it, but secretly I felt ashamed. Children are sticklers for convention. They hate their family to seem in any way 'queer'. Yet here we were meeting each Sunday in the open-air miles outside the town because the local authorities and someone called D.O.R.A.[1] refused to give us permission to hold meetings in the usual places like ordinary people. Then one Sunday evening I became happy and proud, spiritually at one with my family. It was one of those rare Sundays in Scotland when it is gloriously warm even in the evening. I had walked out to the Netherton Burn, where our meetings were usually held, along with my parents and two visiting I.L.P. propagandists. They were to speak to us about the war. I don't remember a word of what they said but I recall very vividly a conversation I was holding with myself while the meeting was in progress. That week in school our history lesson had dealt with the persecution of the old Covenanters and their secret meetings on lonely hillsides. True, we were meeting at the side of a busy main road and beckoning to all who passed to come and listen. Nor had any of our members been put on the rack or tortured with thumbscrews. But the parallel was near enough. Were we not a persecuted minority ? Were not some of our members in prison ? Were we not forced to meet in the open country miles outside the town ? Were not terrible things done to some of our men while they were in gaol ? I had just overheard some talk about a conscientious objector who refused to wear khaki, so was stripped naked and left like that. When he still refused to wear soldier's uniform, he was laid on a table and scrubbed from head to foot with a wire-brush until his flesh was torn and bleeding. That decided it. We were the modern Covenanters, we were fighting for conscience' sake. There were only a few of us, but it was we, not the multitude, who were right. That conclusion made things much easier. Nothing could

[1] "Defence of the Realm Act".

now make me feel ashamed. Indeed, I was now ready to go forth to battle and to slaughter everyone who stood in our way.

During the war years, Duncan Beaton, a local miner, Mrs. Watson, wife of the Member for Dunfermline Burghs, and Mr. Garvie, the blind bookseller, conducted a flourishing socialist Sunday School. I learned to recite with great gusto a poem called the 'Image of God'. It went something like this:

> *I slaughtered a man, a brother,*
> *In the wild, wild fight at Mons,*
> *I see yet his eyes of terror,*
> *Hear yet his cries and groans.*

Every one of us without exception was made word-perfect in the ten socialist precepts. I thought the one about war very reasonable. 'Do not think that those who love their own country need hate or despise other nations or wish for war, which is a remnant of barbarism.'

Mrs. Henderson, a miner's wife with a strong, sweet voice, attended every Sunday forenoon to help us with the singing. We learned to sing after her:

> *O beautiful my country,*
> *Be it thy nobler care;*
> *Than all thy wealth of commerce,*
> *Thy harvests waving fair.*
> *Be it thy pride to lift up*
> *The manhood of the poor,*
> *Be thou to the oppressed*
> *Fair freedom's open door.*

After that we all joined in the chorus:

> *We are children, but some day,*
> *We'll be big and strong and say,*
> *None shall slave and none shall slay,*
> *Comrades all together.*

We shall up and march away, march away, march away,
We shall up and march away, marching all together.

Another important part of my wartime training was a cartoon I picked up among my father's papers. It showed a monkey sitting in the tree-tops and looking quizzically down on a vast plain where men were fighting, maiming and killing one another. The caption underneath read: 'Thank God civilization missed me'. I thought that very fine. I was now a politician and one with very definite views.

When the war had been on for some time and food rationing was at its strictest, my brother became ill. He needed more nourishment than the ration-cards allowed. My mother went to the Town House and applied for a permit for extra rations of meat and eggs. She was told that she must first get a doctor's certificate. The doctor called the following day. After a long examination he looked grave and said there was a small spot on one of the child's lungs. That way of putting it did not help. I knew that meant an early stage of consumption. The doctor then advised sending him to a sanatorium. I felt sick and panicky.

For the next three months the war was not important. I learned no more poetry and didn't care whether we were the Covenanters or not. All that mattered was our weekly visits to a small boy lying in the bed fifth from the door in the children's ward of Thornton Sanatorium. He was made to wear a grey flannel nightshirt. I was angry and sad every time I saw that awful garment. It made me think of gaols and poor-houses. Why couldn't he wear his own clothes ? I petitioned the nurses about it. They answered me civilly but firmly. It was a hospital regulation. And hospitals will be hospitals—when poor people are the inmates.

Each Saturday I walked through the field to the sanatorium. The bus went only part of the way. When the snow was on the ground it was a bleak, tiring journey. I discovered that the best way of carrying parcels was in a net bag slung over my shoulder. I was too proud to arrive carrying it that way so, when the last corner was in sight, I swung it down and hung it nonchalantly over one arm. Once round the corner I could see the sanatorium and the glass door at the end of the ward. It was usually open. With any luck I could tip-toe right to the bedside without asking anyone's permission. And, knowing how I hated cold, my brother would thrust my hands and head beneath the blankets on his bed, and would have to be satisfied that I had thawed before he would even look at his parcels. To our great joy, three months later he was home again looking comically round and red and greatly improved in health. I could now go on with the war.

Shortly after this the war became almost real. My mother's youngest brother was killed in action. We all sat down together and wept, then, about a week later, the socks that had been knitted for him were sent to another uncle who was in the trenches. It became still more real when my closest friend at school arrived with red swollen eyes and wearing a black dress. Her father had been killed in action. All of us in the class tried in clumsy little ways to show our sympathy. I thrust before her all my answers in the arithmetic tests, although in the ordinary course of things it was arithmetic I depended on to pull me above her in our battles for first place in class.

But we were young and soon forgot those things.

The meetings held by the I.L.P. to explain the causes of the war and how to end it made a much more lasting impression on me than anything else I remembered from those years.

One evening, greatly daring, it was decided to attempt an anti-war meeting some miles from home, practically at the gates of a military camp. David Kirkwood was the speaker. My father was in the chair. Before the meeting could begin a great hulking brute of a fellow caught my father in the ribs and threw him right over the heads of the crowd. Kirkwood immediately jumped on the chair that served as a platform and, brandishing a stout stick in the air, roared out: 'If there is a better man than me here, let him come and take this platform.'

Both soldiers and civilians in the audience enjoyed that kind of pacifism. Order was soon restored. A roughhouse of that kind seldom occurred when the audience was made up exclusively of miners. Experience varied in different coalfields. Here I am recording simply moods and circumstances as I recall them in our corner of Fife And I am referring to public meetings, not to miners' lodge meetings.

Within the union, Grandfather Lee, then Disputes Agent for the Fife Miners' Union, was almost the only official who stood out against the war. I have heard since how the other officials, led by the late Mr. W. Adamson, who were all violently pro-war, did everything in their power to make life Hell for him.

When the war began I was not yet ten years of age and when it ended I was barely fourteen, so its tragedies and controversies sat lightly upon me. But it made our home a very busy place. The few active local socialists who were campaigning against the war were constantly coming in and out for odd meals and discussions.

The week-ends were crammed with events. Very often we had a visiting I.L.P. propagandist staying with us. Usually he came from Glasgow, occasionally from London, and sometimes he was a young fellow on the run from place to place, wanted by the police for his anti-war activities.

Those Saturdays when the speaker's train was due to arrive before father could be home from work, washed and changed, it was my job to go to the station. I liked that. It was always a tense moment waiting for the train to draw into the platform. If it was someone who had been with us before, then he was a friend and sure of his welcome. If it was a stranger arriving for the first time, it was a different, but equally pleasant kind of excitement. It was like putting your hand into a lottery bag and drawing out a ticket. You never knew what was going to turn up. Sometimes at first sight I was a little bit nonplussed. But I cannot remember a single one of those visiting propagandists who did not quickly become a friend we enjoyed having with us.

I think most of our guests enjoyed themselves as much as we did. Mother would bustle around, serving us all with unquestioning cheerfulness. Father sat by the fire explaining the local situation. The armchair on the other side of the fireplace was for the visitor. My brother and I were quite satisfied with this arrangement. It left for us the corners of the fender-stool where we could sit with our backs to the warm grate and our eyes glued to the stranger. Very occasionally he would ignore our existence and the room would echo with strange, exciting words—Nietzsche, Dietzgen, dialectics, Engels, Hegel——. But more often he would turn to us with all the usual wiles of a grown-up trying to make friends with children.

I can recall only one serious misadventure in our attempts to make our guests feel at home. The redoubtable Dick Wallhead had arrived for a series of meetings. He was an ace among propagandists and we were delighted to have him. We had also heard that he was fond of music. My parents felt, therefore, that he must have the pleasure of listening to me play the piano.

I could play 'Poet and Peasant', 'Tannhauser', 'Il Trovatore', 'Rigoletto', and at least a score of other pieces with deadly accuracy. I swear to the accuracy, for Mr. Garvie who was blind and had a bookseller's shop in Cowdenbeath High Street, had given me special facilities for practising.

In the parlour above his shop he had two pianos, an ordinary one and a mechanical one just like those in the ice-cream shops. He and I were very good friends and read together several volumes of *The Story of the Working Class throughout the Ages*. A group of Cowdenbeath Socialists had clubbed together to buy the series which at that time had quite a vogue. The books were stored in Mr. Garvie's book shop. He was an eager, intelligent man, with a great faith in education. I enjoyed reading to him and hearing his sharp questions and criticisms. As an exchange in courtesies he invited me to use his pianos. I would wind up the mechanical one and, while it drummed out the scroll, keep perfect time on the other.

In preparation for Dick Wallhead's visit our mother moved the piano from the best parlour bedroom to our kitchen-living room. All was in readiness for our guest. After supper was cleared away, my parents mildly announced that he must hear me play. I was egged on to begin.

Wallhead sat by the fire looking more and more gloomy and disgruntled. I could feel antipathetic currents of feeling swirling around the room, Finally, able to bear it no longer, he spluttered out in his cracked croak of a voice: 'That girl can't play the piano and never WILL be able to play.'

I don't remember what happened immediately after that. My parents must have felt a bit damped. To pay for piano-lessons, examinations and all, was a big drain on their tiny income. They had very great faith. My own sympathies were divided. I dimly realized that Wallhead was right. And I hated practising. Anyhow, before the end of his visit we were all good friends.

In fairness I must say that that was the only time when a guest had that kind of entertainment thrust on him.

When visitors were due, our mother had us carefully warned to sit quietly by the fire and go on working at home-lessons, or reading our story-books so as not to be a nuisance.

But there were regular old-timers who were special favourites with us and would not allow us to be quiet. James Maxton, for instance, would saunter in with a jaunty air and at once look challengingly around for someone to play with. At least that is how it seemed to us. His brother-in-law, the Rev. J. R. Munro, was another disrupter of the peace. Before he had been more than an hour in the house he had even my shy little brother on top of a chair shouting out Burns' poems. I was sorry he insisted on teaching him 'Fair fa' your honest, sonsie face, great chieftain o' the puddin'-race', for I thought the 'Address to a Haggis' the dullest poem Burns ever wrote. But my brother enjoyed it. 'Tam Samson's Elegy' was more to my liking. Munro enchanted us for ever by the gusto with which he used to recite it, especially the way he intoned the last three words of every verse—'Tam Samson's deed!'[1]

A less boisterous, but painstaking guest was the Rev. Campbell Stephen. He had no gift for stories but, as we grew older, we found that he was hot stuff on quadratic equations.

As I changed from childhood to adolescence I looked forward with increasing eagerness to these week-end visitors. I was grateful to those who did not try to talk down to us; to those who answered our questions with the same gravity with which we asked them. Maxton would never do that. Always urbanely charming, and with a delightful sense of humour, he would answer nothing seriously. I would tenaciously stick to my point as long as I could in spite of the charm and the humour. But in the end I was always turned away hungry and made to feel a fool for being so clumsily importunate.

As I grew older (I am now thinking of the years just after the 1914-18 war) it seemed a matter of life and death to have all sorts of questions answered.

The coalfields were in a ferment. The union had never been so strong and its morale was even stronger. Miners returning from active service joined in with the rest to demand better conditions. Hadn't the Government said that that was what the fighting had

[1] Dead.

been about? To make life more spacious and gracious for the ordinary man? Lloyd George knew all the words. Our people were now bent on packing some content into them. Now was the time, father said. The sidings were empty. The returning soldiers were not in the mood to be played with. Every advantage lay with the miners.

The coal companies were in a state of funk. They knew the men were in a position to dictate terms. They saw themselves being compelled to disgorge some of the excessive wealth they had piled up during the war.

At this point the Government intervened, offering the Sankey Commission. The miners were to appoint half the commissioners, the coal companies the other half, and Sir J. Sankey was to act as chairman. It was a tempting offer. The more so as, in the same breath, the Government let it be understood that, if there was a national stoppage, soldiers would be drafted into the coalfields and any subsequent bloodshed would be upon the miners' own heads.

Our home, like thousands of others, rang with the controversy. To accept the commission and abide by its findings or to strike without delay and put the issue to a contest between the naked strength of miner and coal-owner?

Most of our lot were for striking. They did not trust Lloyd George. They did not trust any of the Government. They felt they would be tricked and they knew that by virtue of their own strength they could at that moment have wrung solid concessions from the coal companies.

The most powerful voice for accepting the commission was that of Bob Smillie. Bob we loved, trusted and respected. We knew he was incapable of deceiving us. Every phase of his life had been marked by lion-hearted endurance. At that time he was president of the M.F.G.B.[1] and at the height of his power. By the narrowest of margins the coalfields finally voted in favour of accepting the commission. Hurriedly an interim report was got out and the growling of the suspicious was drowned in promises of an immediate reduction of the working hours from eight to seven and some advance in wages. In addition, it soon became evident that Smillie, in his evidence before the commission, was putting an unanswer-

[1] Miners' Federation of Great Britain.

able case for the miners. Nationalization, a six-hour working day, pithead baths, improved wages, were just around the corner. The miners, to clinch matters, received the following letter from Bonar Law:

11, *Downing Street,*
Whitehall, S.W.,
21*st March,* 1919.

Dear Sir,

Speaking in the House of Commons last night I made a statement in regard to the Government policy in connection with the Report of the Coal Industry Commission. I have pleasure in confirming, as I understand you wish me to do, my statement that the Government are prepared to carry out in the spirit and the letter the recommendations of Sir John Sankey's Report.

Yours faithfully,
A. BONAR LAW.

We were getting on famously. It was an alive, bracing time. The union was strong. The I.L.P. was growing rapidly in numbers and influence. In our part of the world it was a close cordial fellowship proud of its anti-war record. It was succeeding so well that we forgot to remember, unless as good yarns to tell around the fireside, the harsher side of war-time treatment. It was quite true that many of our best people had been in gaol, that many more, such as my father, burned their calling-up papers and were not sent to prison by the mere accident of their occupations. There had, too, been many ugly incidents at meetings. But war memories faded very quickly. We were growing too fast to have time to look behind. Very soon now we would revolutionize the world. Our socialist hymns seemed to me to give a pretty good idea of what it was all about. I could never sing in tune, but I mumbled fervently to myself the words of the songs we were taught to sing every Sunday forenoon in our socialist Sunday school.

'We are children but some day we'll be big and strong and say, none shall slave and none shall slay, comrades all together.'

One of our favourite hymns seemed to me to contain the whole of history, and everything about the present and future that really mattered. It went something like this:

Lift up the people's banner, now trailing in the dust,
A million hands are ready to guard the sacred trust;
With steps that never falter and hearts that grow more strong;
Till victory end our warfare we sternly march along.
Through ages of oppression, we bore the heavy load,
While others reaped the harvest from seeds the people sowed;
Down in the earth we burrowed, or fed the furnace heats,
We felled the mighty forests, we built the mighty fleets.
But after bitter ages of hunger and despair
The slave has snapped his fetters and bids his foes beware.
We shall be slaves no longer, the nations soon shall know,
That all who live must labour and all who reap must sow.
So on we march to battle, with souls that shall not rest,
Until the world we live in is by the world possessed.
And filled with perfect manhood, in beauty it shall move,
One heart, one home, one nation, whose king and lord is love.

That sort of thing is not meant to be read in cold blood by grown-up people. They can see all its inadequacies. But our blood was warm, we were young, infinitely impressionable. Every line was real to us. 'Down in the earth we burrowed' meant our fathers working in the pits right under our feet. We had lots of friends working in the shipyards along the Forth and Clyde. It was they who 'built the mighty fleets'. And some of our cousins and uncles and brothers who had emigrated to Canada were sure to be among those who 'fell the mighty forests'.

I was now completely captivated by the socialist movement and well on the way to becoming a youthful socialist edition of Colonel Blimp. I had my prejudices. I had no doubts. I had not the slightest inkling of what went on under the skin of people who did not see things exactly as I did. Idealism, ancestor worship and a happy feeling that we were the people who would one day revolutionize the world so that 'none shall slave and none shall slay' seemed to me just about everything in philosophy, religion and economics that anyone need bother about.

One day, shortly after the war ended, my father announced that Clifford Allen was coming to stay with us. That was staggering news. Clifford Allen, a leading figure in the I.L.P. and in the No

Conscription Fellowship, seemed to us the very embodiment of the martyrdom that some of our members had suffered during the war.

Before he arrived father told mother that he must be given most-favoured-nation treatment. That meant having a fire kindled in his bedroom. For husky young fellows, mother thought that unnecessary. But when the propagandist was elderly or not too robust, this extra little privilege was arranged. Clifford Allen, we were gravely told, had had a severe prison sentence and as a result was very, very ill.

I curled up as usual on the corner of the fender-stool and waited tensely for the stranger to appear. A hero was visiting our home. Everyone said that he had not long to live; that his health had been ruined by prison. I had to wait a long time. The local I.L.P. Committee had met the train and they had all gone directly to the hall. Half-way through the evening someone came in with the news that the meeting was a complete fiasco. Something had gone wrong with the timing or advertising and, anyhow, it was a Saturday evening, the hardest of all nights to assemble a crowd. I was wrung with pity. To think that a dying man had dragged himself all the way from London to Cowdenbeath only to be met by such callous indifference.

I settled myself for another long wait. At last I heard the front door opening and knew that the speaker, my father and the rest of the I.L.P. Committee were treading along the lobby towards the kitchen door. By the time the door opened, my eyes were hazy with excitement. I shall never forget the tall, ascetic face and figure of Clifford Allen framed in our kitchen doorway with half a dozen squat dark-looking miners grouped around him. I should not have been surprised if he had suddenly sprouted wings and a halo.

Later in the evening, when everyone else had gone, he won our hearts all over again by telling us how in prison he and another conscientious objector played an intricate game of chess, one move being made each day by signing to one another when as prisoners they were assembled and marched round and round the exercise-yard. It was all very elevating. Ours was a wonderful movement. All knights in shining armour who would never rest until the words in the songs of our socialist hymn-books had indeed come to pass.

I was wild with impatience when I thought of how much of this struggle I had already missed. I had been born so late that I could not even be a suffragette.

Mrs. Helen Crawford, one of the old militant group, sometimes stayed with us as a visiting I.L.P. propagandist. Responding to our eager prompting, she would talk for hours about her window-breaking adventures and prison exploits. I longed to have broken windows and been sent to prison for the greater power and glory of the suffragette cause, and wondered ruefully if anything at all would be left to do by the time I had finished with school.

It was Grandfather Lee who cheered me most when I was in this mood. 'Lass,' he would say, 'there will be plenty left for you to do. It takes longer than you think.'

4

REBEL STUDENT

I FOUND it a great nuisance when I had to begin to think about earning a living. I felt no special urge to stand behind a shop counter all day or to sit typing in an office or to join the early morning rush of girls waiting for the tram to take them to the Dunfermline factories.

But my father and mother were quietly insistent. I was fourteen. The time had come when I must prove that my feet were on solid ground, that I knew what I wanted to do.

There was a vague notion floating around the family that I ought to take a course in 'business training'! I was not enthusiastic.

In the end we agreed that I might remain at school for one year more. But, as a gesture to a wage-earning future, I was at the same time to attend night-school classes in shorthand and book-keeping.

When my fifteenth birthday arrived I had quite definitely decided that I did not want to leave school. That was awkward for my parents. They were willing enough for me to continue; but fearful about incurring expenses they could not meet.

The examination results decided the issue. I had taken first place in class. Mother was determined that I should go on. Blindly determined. She, who always liked to plan her way so carefully, embarked on this grave undertaking without the least idea as to where the money was to come from. She would carry me on as far as she could. She was game. Something might turn up.

That year, with a view to assisting Providence, she put a shilling each way on the Derby. We teased her mercilessly when we found out about this. My father was strictly opposed to gambling in every form. Mother knew this and, as always, agreed with him. But she was bent on helping me to do the things I had set my heart on. Somehow or other I had to be put through secondary school and then through college. She was willing even to risk sinning a little if that would help.

The following year I found it not so easy to keep grinding away at school work. I did only indifferently well. I was at the age when you parade arm-in-arm along the school corridors with one eye on your books and the other on the look-out for mischief. Beath Secondary was a large mixed school. I should have hated it to have been anything else. Schools exclusively for girls struck me as silly; especially when later on we had to compete against men students in University classes. It was more reassuring to have to scramble for your place in a mixed examination list. We, at least, knew where we stood.

And I rather imagine that there was less furtiveness and romanticism among us than appears to haunt adolescent school life where boys and girls are educated entirely apart. We were just ordinary, healthy youngsters reaching an age when to be shyly flirtatious was as inevitable as breathing. Sometimes when we ought to have been entirely preoccupied with conjugating *amo*, *amas*, *amat*, we were wondering instead what it was all about.

That was one cause of indifferent examination results. The other, and the obvious one to my father and mother, was that I was giving too much time to socialist activities. On Sunday forenoon there was the socialist Sunday school. On Sunday evening there were the great public meetings. On Saturday there was the arrival of the visiting propagandist. And, at least two nights during the week there were the I.L.P. dues to collect. It was my particular job to go from door to door every week, visiting each member of the Cowdenbeath I.L.P., collecting his or her membership dues and stamping the membership card. I loved doing this. Almost every house of call made me one of the family. Sometimes I would stop and have tea. Much too often we would argue for hours when I ought to have been more business-like and hurrying on to the other doors.

Besides politics I was greatly concerned at this time about religion. My grandfather was a devoutly religious man of simple unquestioning faith. My father held that religion was an exploded myth. I loved and respected both men so had to turn and wrestle with the question for myself. The bookshelves of my friends were loaded with explosive material. I picked up Ingersol, Tom Paine, Joseph McCabe, a score of tracts written by the pamphleteers of the rationalist press and even that monstrous Big Bertha among this kind of literature, *Li Hung Chang's Scrap Book*. Stunned and overborne by the pressure of these polemics, I thrust all the books aside and told myself I had better think things out for myself.

I became violently anti-sectarian. I wept for Hypatia, torn limb from limb by the early Christians. I could see with horrible visual precision the tortured bodies of victims of the Inquisition. I could hear the screams of harmless old women burned as witches by the Kirk Elders in my own native Scotland as recently as 1722. That was bringing it very near home. It seemed to me that the original Christian had had some sense of pity, but that the sects that later on used his name had none at all.

I did not get much beyond that. Even in my childish gropings I rejected the simple anthropomorphic view of God. At five I had been able to visualize Santa Claus with red gown, white beard, reindeer sledge and all. But at fifteen, I could not quite see God as a benevolent bearded gentleman living above the clouds and made in the image of man. It had to be something a little less concrete than that. Perhaps there was something in the pantheistic view of the universe. I discovered Wordsworth's 'Tintern Abbey' and took what refuge I could from a bleakly mechanistic view of life in the lines:

> *And I have felt*
> *A presence that disturbs me with the joy*
> *Of elevated thoughts; a sense sublime*
> *Of something far more deeply interfused,*
> *Whose dwelling is the light of setting suns,*
> *And the round ocean, and the living air,*
> *And the blue sky, and in the mind of man:*
> *A motion and a spirit, that impels*
> *All thinking things, all objects of all thought,*
> *And rolls through all things.*

After carefully looking up the dictionary to confirm that agnostic meant 'I do not know', I decided that so far as I could label myself

I appeared to be a cross between a pantheist and an agnostic.

I was a bit sensitive about the untidiness of such a position especially when arguing with those of my friends who were bright clear Marxist materialists, but I could not for the life of me see my way through to anything more presentable.

My mother was always uneasy when we discussed religion. I could never quite make out whether piety or prudence accounted for her reactions. At no time would she allow us to use God's name lightly. Why go out of our way to make another enemy, seemed to be her point of view, when we were already exposed on every front in our fights with coal companies and political time-servers.

Going from door to door collecting the I.L.P. dues, I could have arguments about politics and religion in every other household. But I could not hope to make much headway with school work. I had to choose between arguing about God and the Devil and Engels and Joseph Dietzgen, and passing my school examinations.

I cannot imagine either of my parents being harsh or nagging. They left me entirely to my own devices. But I knew they were worrying. No tyranny could have been as effective as that. In a violent reaction, after a period of slacking, I made a foolish vow. I made a pact with myself that I would be ready to leave for the University at the end of my fifth year and that I would become Dux of the school before leaving.

Lord, how I worked: every night, cram, cram, cram. Every other thought and activity banished. There was no more reading for fun, or dreaming or debating from door to door. The world, as the school year dragged slowly on, became one long nightmare of examinations. I had my little triumph and took first place in school, then, a few weeks later, broke down completely.

We had reached that waiting time at school when all the examinations are over but the end of the term still some weeks ahead. The teachers were mercifully easy on us. Only the minimum of routine tasks were imposed. But even that had become too much for me. One warm day in the Latin class I found I could no longer see. The words were all blurred and made no sense. I always hated Latin. I was bad at it and it never, at the best of times, made much sense to me. But now my strength was spent. I lurched forward on the desk weeping uncontrollably.

That last year at school I worked harder than at any other time in my life. It left me with a sour distate of cramming. I made up my mind that when I went to the University I would allow myself to sprawl a bit. I would have to be careful to get through my examinations. But I was determined not to get strung up on the rack of competing for first place in any of my classes.

Actually what happened was that in the early part of the University term I did very little work, but, as examination time drew near, I crammed with the best. I was too scared of failing to maintain my cavalier attitude right through. This got me a first-class certificate in all classes except one. The exception was economic history. I had blithely decided that as I was doing more general reading on that subject than on any other there was no need for me to memorize, parrot fashion, the lectures read out to us in class. That was a mistake. I got only a Second and had all my cynicism about the examination system confirmed. It just didn't do to get interested in a subject. That tempted you to read too widely. The recipe for successful results was very simple. Find out anything your lecturer had written, memorize copious notes of lectures, and cultivate the art of emptying out on to the examination paper everything you knew from these sources grouped in some sort of order around the actual questions asked.

The novelty subject for me in my first University year was psychology. I was fascinated by all the new words. Nothing like it had happened to me since the time I sat on the corner of the fender-stool listening to my father's friends discuss Dietzgen, Nietzsche, dialectics, eclectics, the proletariat and the bourgeoisie.

I broke my usual rule and in addition to the prescribed books read everything of Havelock Ellis and of Freud that I could lay hands on. Considering my erudition, I am bound to laugh at two incidents that occurred that same year.

One day, going along Princes Street, I caught sight of a familiar face. I recognized a girl from home and ran careering along the street to catch up with her. She was a very great swell, fur-coat and powder and paint to the eyes. I knew her home people. They were one of the poorest miners' families in the place. I was a little bit surprised by her grandeur, but she was a girl I had always liked and I was glad to see her and, anyhow, I did not get things connected up any more than that. She seemed taken aback for a moment when I grabbed her arm, but I hauled her along towards the nearest tea shop and said we must have a cup of tea together. That would be fine, she said, 'but if you will just wait here I must go round the corner first.' I waited and she came back quite soon, smiling radiantly.

We had tea together and she insisted in paying for both. I met her several times afterwards and always enjoyed her company. I had not the least inkling what must have been so plain to the rest of the world. Her profession was exactly what you may have guessed it to be.

Years later, when she was dying and there could be no more dissembling, I met her again. Rallying some of her old verve, she sat up in bed and began to laugh. It was then she told me that when I had first run after her in Princes Street, she had not had 'a penny to bless herself with', so she had dashed round to a familiar pawn-shop 'to raise the wind'. She was not going to be affronted by having a 'kid' pay for her tea.

Another time, as I was walking towards my lodgings rather late in the day, a rather good-looking man of about fifty lifted his hat and said 'good evening' to me. I at once said 'good evening' and we fell into step. I had no idea who he was, but I would on no account have hurt his feelings by telling him so. I had often been in this predicament in Fifeshire. All sorts of people knew my family and would greet us as we passed. I was hopeless at remembering faces. But this was Edinburgh, not Cowdenbeath. When we reached the quiet of the Meadows behind Edinburgh Infirmary my friend began to be demonstrative in his affection. I quite suddenly realized what was happening. I had been 'picked up ' and had not known it. I was abjectly apologetic and sorry for making the man look so foolish. Then it all seemed so funny that I almost choked as I hurried away. I was trying not to laugh out loud.

So much for my worldly wisdom. I had not recognized the most obvious type of street-walker (not that it would have mattered; I liked the girl), nor known when I was being 'picked up'. But from my text-books I had assembled a most unholy collection of words. They stood me in good stead when examination time came around. I got a first-class certificate in psychology.

The following year—my second in Edinburgh—some of us had little time for study until the term was well begun. We had a rectorial election on hand. Bertrand Russell was Labour candidate. We had invited him, nominated him and now had to see the thing through.

I was overawed by the thought of what we had undertaken; but reassured by the worldly air of one or two of the older students. The only thing to do, apparently, was to put one's best foot forward and try to look as wise as the rest.

Our biggest effort was the production of a paper which we were bound to sell instead of giving away in the traditional manner of the richer student parties. After much heart-searching, the name we found for the paper was *Rebel Student*. We thought it a pretty distinguished production, but had difficulty in selling a sufficient number of copies to clear the printer's bill.

An emergency meeting had to be called to consider the financial crisis. Stacks of *Rebel Students* looked up at us inquiringly from the floor of the committee-room. We had exhausted our market among the student population. There was only one thing left to do. We must each take a bundle of papers and go out into the town and sell them. That sounds easy, But have you ever tried selling papers for the first time ? I felt my legs unaccountably weak. I put it off as long as I could. But postponement did not help. There lay the papers; they had to be sold.

I taunted myself with my cowardice. What was the use of pretending to be a revolutionary if I was afraid even to take a bundle of papers under my arm and go out into the streets and sell them ? After all, it might be worse. Think of our socialist hymn '. . . come dungeons dark or gallows grim . . .' In the end I took up my post outside Pringle's Picture Palace, hoping to catch the crowd that poured into the great Sunday-night meetings that the Communist Party held there at that time. And I found it was true what everyone had said. Getting started was the worst. There seemed dozens of other newsvendors shouting their wares: '*Sunday Worker*, one penny'—'*Labour Monthly*, sixpence'—'*Russia To-day*, twopence'. I got started at last: '*Rebel Student*, twopence; *Rebel Student*, twopence!' The more nervous I became the louder I shouted. I had a disagreeable sensation of tears in the offing. That would have been a fine thing for a revolutionary. So I shouted louder still, and began to do good business. Many of the crowd stopped to buy. They were a rough-and-ready, sympathetic lot. Some smiled to me; some smiled at me. I was too tensely poised to notice much. But for one moment, I happened to look behind. A shy, gentle-natured girl student had been told off along with me to sell papers at this same stance. I caught sight of her, a bundle of papers under one arm, clutching a brass railing in the hall entrance with the other, head thrown back, white to the lips, mutely repeating '*Rebel Student*', but never a sound coming out, and no customers!

Socialist activities were once again taking more of my time than I could afford. I was drifting into the same sort of dangerous muddle that I had got into during my fourth year at school. And again I was blackmailed into a bout of hard work by the gentle tolerance of my home people. I knew that although I went back to them with a wasted year behind me there would be no reproaches. That made the prospect too terrible. I decided I had better have an orgy of 'swotting'. My prize for good behaviour was the winning of £100 in a competitive examination in Roman Law and Constitutional History and Law.

The money was badly needed. I was beginning to see signs of strain at home. My mother was up to every dodge to keep me from noticing anything. I was bookish and absent-minded. But there was a limit even to *my* blindness.

I have often been asked how it was possible for a working miner to pay for university training for his daughter. That makes coalmining sound a very profitable occupation. It worked out something like this. I leave you to judge for yourself.

Under the Fife Education Authority, I had more help given to me than I would have had almost anywhere else in Great Britain. That was one of the by-products of a lively socialist movement in the industrial parts of Fife. Years before I was born, Grandfather Lee and a handful of others of his generation were already members of the old school boards. Steadily they pressed for free books, better schools, free secondary education, maintenance grants for all. 'Education', Grandfather Lee was fond of saying, 'was a grand thing'.

We laughed lovingly at some of his dreams. He himself was

taught to read and write by his sons. He had great faith in what a younger generation, able to recite the principles of Archimedes and to speak bad French, would one day do for their people.

By the time I was old enough for school, a small part of the socialist programme had been won. At eleven years of age we finished with the elementary school; those who did sufficiently well in the examinations had the option of going on to the secondary school.

If our parents could manage to feed and clothe us, the education authority did the rest. Free books and schooling were provided right to the point when we were ready to leave for college or university. Those pupils who had to travel any distance to the secondary school had their bus or train fares paid for.

When I was ready to leave for Edinburgh University, Fife Education Authority presented me with a maintenance allowance of forty-five pounds per year. In addition, the Carnegie Trust paid half my class fees. I was left to find the other half, money for essential text-books, lodgings, meals and clothing. There were a number of hostels where it was usual for women students to live. These were too expensive for me. For which I was thankful! I hated regimentation and much preferred a room I found for fourteen shillings a week.

Paying for a warm midday meal was the thing I grudged most. My total living expenses had to be kept under thirty shillings a week. I would rather have had no lunch than do without coffee in the middle of the morning, and, if any good movie or show came to town, I liked seeing it. There was only one way of budgeting for that kind of extravagance. I made my main meal most days of soup, fourpence, apple dumpling, or any other sweet that was sufficiently filling, another fourpence. Sometimes, for variety, I cut out the soup and had a fourpenny meat roll instead. I did not mind much what I ate and could digest almost anything.

In the morning and evening I concocted a meal in my lodgings. These too cost very little for every week a hamper arrived from home with tea, home-made cake and scones, sometimes eggs, sometimes home-made potted meat and always, even at times of economic depression at home much greater than I realized, funny little packets stuffed in the corners with chocolate or cheap sweets.

I was enjoying life and had no complaints. I was well protected too against the sharp, biting Edinburgh winds by an adequate supply of warm clothing. I was not exactly a model of fashion, but what of that! Considering the *tour de force* with which I had been assembled, I was mighty well pleased.

Even the simplest college outfit costs an unconscionable amount of money. My mother had been almost at her wits' end to know how we were to clear that particular hurdle. We had no reserves in the bank. We traded almost exclusively with the Co-operative Society, where no credit was allowed.

Then, one day, inspiration came. Greatly daring, mother made up her mind. Clothes I had to have and clothes she was going to get for me. With the light of battle in her eyes, she marched down Cowdenbeath High Street towards Forrests, one of the best drapery stores in town. During the war years, when money had been a little more plentiful, Forrests had developed a less blatantly shoddy line of goods than has usually to be stocked in mining communities where cheapness above all must be considered. 'Their stuff was dear,' mother said, 'but good.'

So, pocketing her pride and the habits of a lifetime she went to Forrests and asked if she could be allowed to 'take on'. She need have had no fear. Tradespeople in that size of town know their public. She was cordially invited to help herself to whatever she wanted. Payment could come later.

Every day for about a week she came staggering home with her parcels. I got two costumes, two blouses, a jersey, an overcoat, stockings, handkerchiefs, and even a bright blue velveteen afternoon dress with silver lace draped over the skirt.

One of the parcels I opened gave me a violent shock. I wondered if my good, sensible mother had gone stark, staring mad.

On top was a voluminous white nightgown of the best Irish linen, elaborately embroidered, complete with long, tight sleeves and a cape. Underneath there were bloomers drawn in tightly at the knees and adorned with frills and pale-blue ribbons. There was also a chemise and a camisole of equally elaborate design. The stuff must have cost a fortune. But this was 1922, the very height of the pyjama age. I would rather have died than be caught by fellow-students floating around in an outfit of that kind. I was staggered and didn't know whether to laugh or cry. My mother's face was the last straw. She was looking at me in a non-committal kind of way, veering towards a smile.

This, she explained, was her special present to me. No, it had not come from Forrests. It had come from a box beneath her bed. It had been sent to her from Dublin by Dr. Body and his wife (friends of the old Arcade days) as a wedding present. But that, I protested, was twenty-two years ago. Yes, she agreed, so it was. But I could see for myself that the stuff was as good as new. It had been worn only once, then laid away for a rainy day.

By such varied means I was ultimately launched. The worst time was towards the end of my third year. Someone told me that if I could produce a respectable array of class certificates and prove need as well, I might be able to get an extra grant from the Carnegie Trust. I was not very sanguine about that but did as directed. In reply, a letter came asking me to call on a certain Mr. Burns in his Dunfermline office.

I went to the appointment in a highly-strung, defiant state of mind. What sort of questions would I be asked? Would I be humiliated more than I could bear? Perhaps make an ass of myself by breaking down during the interview. We were proud people. It was my parents' code that they had never begged nor borrowed and had always paid their way. That was before mining families had been humbled by long years of unemployment, means tests, and public assistance committees.

I decided to stand for just so much and no more. But I need not have feared. A courteous official shook hands with me, sent to the next room for a file where, apparently, he had all the particulars he needed, then, within a few minutes, was again shaking hands and I found myself leaving the office with twenty brand new Scotch pound notes stuffed into my handbag.

Soon after that I got another windfall. I won the £100 prize in the Law examination. Then, in my fourth year, I got a half share in a £20 prize in the Education class. As the Fife Authority did not reduce my yearly grant of £45 because of prize money (for a bit I lived in terror of that happening), in my last few terms at Edinburgh I was comparatively opulent.

Another change at home still further reduced the strain. My

brother was now seventeen and eager to be allowed to go to Australia. A Government agent had been touring the mining district with a magic lantern show, illustrating the glorious life that awaited young men who were prepared to emigrate.

My brother was fascinated. He plunged into a romantic fantasy in which he was already riding a horse in the wide open spaces and driving the cattle home to the ranch.

My parents said he was too young to go so far away from home. They were strongly against the idea. But he had set his heart on it. One term, when I came home from college, he was waiting for me to intercede for him. Could I not persuade father and mother that it was a good idea? I thought about it a great deal. We were passionately attached to one another. The thought of his leaving for the other end of the world was like the wrench of losing a limb. But what was there for him to do if he remained at home? He had not wanted to continue at school and had no special liking or talent for school work. We all of us regarded work down the pit as a last resort, the thing he must be saved from if at all possible.

For almost three years he had been working in the office of a linen factory in Dunfermline. He earned £1 a week and had heavy travelling expenses deducted from that. What was left for the sort of things for which a young fellow likes to have money to burn? How could he have enough in his pocket to take a pretty girl to the Palais de Danse on a Saturday night? Or to join sports clubs, or to do anything at all? He was a bundle of wants and discontents. Once when we were both clamouring for the impossible in the thoughtless way of seventeen and twenty, our mother turned on us, almost angry. 'I wish you were still bairns,' she said. 'I could manage you then. That was your happiest time.' Father, hearing this, looked up from his paper with a twinkle in his eye and retorted, '*Your* happiest time, you mean.'

Every Monday evening a regular pantomime worked itself out. My brother, home from work and ready to go out to meet his pals, would stand in the doorway, making signals of distress towards mother. His Saturday pocket-money was spent. He was again broke. Mother would make angry answering gestures whose meaning could not be misunderstood. Not a word would be spoken. My father and I, reading quietly by the fireside, would wink at one another. The rules of the game were that we were supposed to be entirely unaware of what was going on. In the end, mother would follow my brother to the outside door, thrust a sixpence into his hand, muttering fiercely as she did so that this was the very last time that she would give it to him. The following Monday the same pantomime would be staged with entirely the same results.

I wondered how it was all going to end. The decay that had begun to invade the mining industry had already overtaken the linen trade.

Australia was a younger country. I knew very little about it. But going there was at least a gamble that might lead to quite a good life. My brother's health was what finally decided me. He was now a husky young fellow chafing at the restrictions of an office-stool. But, after the sanatorium period in his childhood, we never felt quite certain about him. Ours was a damp, cold climate. Australia might give him a better chance of a healthy life. Our decision had to be made quickly. We had no money for steamship passages. The Government was offering to send boys out to Australia for £2, provided they were under eighteen years of age.

Mother, looking very sad, at last had to yield to him. She began to prepare for his departure. Her son must not go out into the world without a good stock of durable clothing. Once again she had to ask Forrest if she might 'take on' a little. She hated asking for credit. It always worried her, and it was against her principles. But our needs came before everything else.

One day during term-time I saw my brother leave from Edinburgh station. He was a great, hopeful young fellow, the rest of his luggage off in advance but hugging his violin. He never would practise much but he had a certain facility for playing and was boastfully pleased with the name inside the instrument. It had been made by Alexander Greig, his own great-uncle. My good-bye present was a canvas and leather outside cover for his fiddle.

We made a pact with one another that no matter what happened he would write regularly to our mother saying everything was fine, but that he would write under separate cover to me saying bluntly and truthfully, just exactly what was happening to him.

5

1926

IF I could have afforded it when I left school, I would have gone to Oxford or Cambridge. That seemed the dazzlingly splendid thing to do. But now I know the south I am rather glad that I had to choose either Edinburgh or St. Andrews. The southern counties are very lovely. But in such a flat, enervatingly peaceful kind of way! There are no Pentland Hills within easy reach of Oxford or Cambridge, and no Arthur's Seat dumped right at the College gate.

I liked living in Edinburgh. It has lots of slums like the rest of our cities and no one could call it a gay, colourful place. But, for all that, in its own sober, northern way, it has great beauty and distinction. At eighteen, with the drab unloveliness of colliery districts as my standard of comparison, I found it very pleasant to be living there.

I liked trailing around the town. I liked still more the times when we were free for the whole day and could go off on tramps over the hills. And I am undyingly grateful to the Carnegie Public Library on George IV Bridge.

But of the University itself what is there to be said ? It was the least important part of student life for me. In saying that I am not trying to be smart or facetious. I am too anxious to set down as candidly as I know how the influences that formed my point of view and selected my subsequent activities. Why I feel driven to do this will, I hope, become clear in the later chapters of this book. But, for the moment, I think I had better resist the temptation to argue and simply describe incidents and impressions as I happen to recall them.

I spent term-time in Edinburgh and the long College vacations at home. Crossing from Edinburgh to the coalfields on the northern side of the Forth was, in a physical sense, like moving from a brightly-lit room into semi-darkness. But, emotionally and intellectually, it was for me exactly the other way round. At that time there was a vigorous socialist movement in the industrial parts of Fife. In odd corners of this movement there were men whose knowledge of industrial history, economics and philosophy made me ashamed of how little I knew. Theirs was an eager, questioning, purposeful kind of knowledge; in exhilarating contrast to the dead, disconnected, parroting that earned us our University degrees. Of course, the comparisons I made were grossly biassed. I contrasted the average University student with the exceptional collier. I am not pretending otherwise. But at the time that never occurred to me. I was too exuberantly partisan, and too elated at the thought of what our socialist movement stood for and what it was going to do.

It was a dull business returning from heated arguments on how to make the whole world anew to the factory routine of swotting for examinations. Each term I returned to Edinburgh with increasing reluctance. The novelty of the place had worn off. It did not answer or even ask any of the questions that I was most concerned about. But I was in honour bound to plod steadily on until I had collected the certificates I needed as a preliminary to earning my living.

The strictly utilitarian part of University life consisted of going in droves to one class after another, taking down copious notes of lectures, memorizing these and reading the prescribed books.

At certain times of the year we poured out all we could remember on to our examination papers. Given a reasonable mixture of industry and luck, this process earned us pass certificates. Once these were safely netted we could comfortably forget all but the vaguest medley of what we had memorized and settle down to 'swot-up' some other subject.

At the end of four and a half years of that sort of thing I had assembled an M.A. degree, a teacher's certificate, a diploma in education and, as final flourish, an LL.B. degree. That was considered pretty good going so it was probably foolish of me to have a feeling of guilt about it all. But it did seem an awful fraud to possess for life a barrow-load of certificates, knowing all the time just how very little the whole performance signified.

I don't quite know what I expected from a university. Certainly something a little less reach-me-down than the degree-collecting process turned out to be.

One or two of our professors lectured with a freshness and enthusiasm that, looking back on, I can appreciate now better than I did then.

Old Professor Grierson of the English Department, for instance, had a warm, infectious intensity that few of us could resist. Apparently undismayed by the rows upon rows of us, he would abandon himself to a favourite author, declaiming from selected passages for a solid hour on end with all the ardour of a young lover for a new-found love.

We were all on our best behaviour in the old man's classroom, for we liked him, and those who by temperament were unable to share his enthusiasms, at least marvelled at them. I boggled a bit over some of his Wordsworth, but otherwise was one of his most impressionable disciples.

Professor Harvey Littlejohn was another of our lecturers who was never dull. His subject was forensic medicine. He talked of crime and criminals with a relish that, if we had been older and less grateful for any kind of entertainment, we might have been inclined to deprecate. Certainly his was a very extraordinary personality. As he lectured he dramatized each crime, acting now the part of the murderer, now the victim. It was like being back in the old Arcade Theatre watching a rattling good melodrama.

But most of our lecturers were dreary and circumspect. I suppose they had to be in order to survive. Edinburgh is not the sort of place to encourage any kind of unorthodoxy.

Only one of them during the four and a half years I attended classes made any attempt to break away from the mechanical routine. This incident, so far as I was concerned, blew the gaff on the whole business.

I was then in my fourth year and had enrolled for a post-graduate course in education. This class was intended chiefly for those of us who expected to earn our living as teachers.

Professor Godfrey Thomson, newly-appointed to the Chair of

Education, had just arrived in Edinburgh, apparently bringing with him a rather high opinion of Scottish standards of education.

We trooped into his introductory lecture, produced our note-books and pencils, and settled down as usual to an hour's industrious note-taking.

Straight away the professor gave us an uncomfortable jog. We were to put away our note-books and pencils. They would not be needed. He did not intend reading aloud to us at dictation pace. It really was not necessary. The material we may have expected to have read out lecture by lecture was at our disposal in book form. This said, smiling in the friendliest way, he paused for a moment. The poor devil may even have expected some sign of approval. Instead there was mutiny in the air. Not noisy mutiny. Just sullen anxious dismay. No notes ? What did that mean ? How then could we memorize our pieces in readiness for examination time ? His next announcement was a degree worse. We were to form ourselves into groups, each group doing a special piece of reading and research and, later in the term, reporting to the general class.

That was too much. That was taking the ground from under our feet altogether. That made the range of possible questions when examination time arrived too dangerously varied and unpredictable.

A few of us were flattered by the new professor's expectations and disgusted with the timidity of the bulk of the students. A fine showing we made, it seemed to us. Final-year students, most of us already in possession of at least one University degree and frightened out of our wits when a University class threatened to become anything more serious than memorizing set pieces taken down to dictation.

For once in my life I found myself on the side of authority. And, of course, I had to choose an occasion when authority was hopelessly outnumbered. The rebels won. The proposed scheme of work was modified substantially to give a much larger dose of formal lecturing than had been originally intended.

As far as I could discover the explanation of all this was simply fear. Economic fear. We were mostly poor students. We could not afford to take risks. We wanted to be left to plod along after the manner of the ancient Chinese in a kind of memory marathon race. We wanted the old familiar well-established system that enabled us, by sheer donkey work, to graduate successfully in the shortest possible time. Not to mince matters, our degrees were primarily our meal tickets.

Into this dim little, trim little world crashed the General Strike of May 1926. Very few students had any idea of what it was all about. Only a handful (at the outset) had any active animus against the miners.

But the University authorities, wasting no time about it, wholeheartedly began the task of turning each and all of us into bellicose class warriors. Students were encouraged (and bribed with the offer of easy money) to enlist as strike breakers.

Inside twenty-four hours I began to hear normally goodnatured young fellows talk with unholy glee of the pleasure it would give them to run a tank through some of our mining villages.

I noted this, taken by surprise a bit. In theory I had always claimed that moods change rapidly, and in pretty much the same way, and to pretty much the same degree everywhere, when working people make any serious organized attempt to improve their economic position. I was impatient with people who argued that the British were different from the rest of the world; more goodnatured and easy-going. It seemed to me entirely a matter of the degree of provocation. But, although in theory I knew all these arguments, emotionally I was unprepared. That is a common failing among socialists.

Apparently members of the General Council of the Trade Union Movement had not realized what they were up against any more than I had. Under their leadership, the working-class blundered into a General Strike. During the whole of 1925 the coalowners and the Government had been preparing elaborate strike-breaking machinery, the coalowners enjoying a special subsidy the while. Everyone knew these preparations were being made. Everyone knew a clash was imminent and inevitable. But the socialist movement, as it has done so often before and since, took its leaders on trust. It assumed that they had some sort of plan and knew what they were about. Actually, the Government and the coalowners, as in 1919 and 1921, found us easy game. Once again we had simply plunged blindly forward; and under such leadership, or lack of it if you like, disaster inevitably followed.

Rank-and-file workers all over the country proved magnificent scrappers. That always is true and always will be so, but of itself is not enough to win a war.

When the Strike began a few of us from the University rushed down to the trade union headquarters to ask how we could help. I was given the job of receiving and dispatching orders for strike bulletins. We supplied the whole of Edinburgh and most of the surrounding districts. By the third or fourth day everything was going with a swing. We settled down for the duration and were blissfully pleased with life.

Then came the terrible news. The strike had been called off. Nothing had been won, yet the strike had been called off. Our leaders had run away. Ordinary men and women all over the country were standing their corner. But what good was that? Our leaders had intended perhaps only to make a mild industrial demonstration. Or had hoped that the mere threat of a General Strike would be enough. The Government had called their bluff.

That evening, while the Central Strike Committee attended to the last funereal rites on the floor above us, we younger ones were huddled together in a corner of our improvised office, stunned and listless, demoralized by the utter, absolute fiasco of it all. We ended the day with a cursing competition. I was shocked at the language I suddenly discovered I knew.

Over the wireless, Baldwin, then Prime Minister, promised there would be no victimization. That was another joke. Such government assurances meant nothing at all. Men and women were victimized in every corner of Great Britain. Some of them were never reinstated.

In the next few days I discovered that, although in Edinburgh the Strike was over, in Fife my home people were still holding out. So were the miners everywhere. They were not running away. They were standing their ground even if they had to stand alone. I was torn between pride and pity. I longed to go home. But I dared not leave my books. In June, the following month, I had to sit my finals for my M.A. degree and for my teacher's certificate.

That was a nightmare time. I worked with what seemed to be a dark veil all round me. What was happening? Why had the other unions deserted us? How were they managing in Fife? What prospect was there of winning with such odds against us? Was it going to be a long battle? Would the women be able to stand it? Always when there are rumours of a strike but nothing is as yet definite, the women in the mining towns are more fearful than the men. But, invariably, once the battle is joined their staying power puts all waverers to shame.

At last I could go home. It was June. Examinations were over. I was qualified to teach if I could find work when the schools re-opened in the autumn. But, for the present, there were more important things to be done.

That summer was one unceasing round of meetings. At all hours of the day and night we would dash off to corners of the coalfields where there was any sign or rumour of weakening morale. A group of boys or young men would go from street to street ringing a bell or beating a drum then shouting out their message: 'A meeting—will be held—in the Welfare Hall—at three o'clock—this after-noon—speakers are——' and so on.

I enjoyed it all. In Edinburgh before I was free to go home I had been moody and dejected. But, once in the fight, there was no more time for moods. It is always that way. People's spirits rise once they get into action. Melancholy is very much the emotion of the onlooker.

The last months of the 1926 Strike (lock-out we were meticu-lously careful to say) was a time of mounting anxiety. Our minds knew what our emotions refused to admit. The guns were all in the hands of the enemy. None of *their* women and children had to starve. They could hold out indefinitely. On our side, there was a limit to the food and funds we could collect. And beyond that, what?

One day some of our old friends and neighbours from Cowden-beath (we had moved two miles to Lochgelly, to be nearer my father's work) made a proposal to me. They wanted me to go to Ireland to collect money for their soup-kitchen. All the surrounding districts had been bled white. More money had to be got from somewhere. I was doubtful about Ireland. Miners' bands had already gone there and were not doing too well. But I was willing enough to try, so I crossed Scotland to Stranraer and set sail for Belfast.

Once there I found that the only way of raising money was by street-corner meetings. There was terrific opposition. We bawled ourselves hoarse shouting above the din of the drums that the Orange Lodges brought out against us.

The authorities would not allow collections to be taken, so I auctioned my stock of miners' lamps and, when these gave out, my friends raked in their cupboards and under their beds for every old pamphlet they could find on politics, economics, religion, or anything else under the sun. Those we sold at the meeting. No one wanted the antiquated pamphlets but many wanted to help the miners. It was an open conspiracy with the crowd to keep within the law.

In Dublin I got on better. But only after a difficult start. I had been told to go to Liberty Hall and present my credentials to Jim Larkin. Before ever I had time to produce them, this great towering figure of a man looked over the counter at me and snorted his contempt. No, he would not fix up meetings. 'All right, all right,' I said. 'You have had your chance. You won't get it again.'

Out I stamped. I had as hair-trigger nerves as he had. If we had been carrying revolvers, we would probably have shot one another on sight.

I went now to the headquarters of the postal workers and was immediately on good terms. They would co-operate with other unions and fix up meetings. Straight off, as a token of their fraternal feelings, they signed a cheque for twenty pounds.

In my anger I had left my suitcase at Larkin's office. I went back for it and was astonished at the change in the atmosphere. Larkin's assistant—he never had colleagues; he did not understand the meaning of the word—came forward at once to receive me. There had been an awful mistake. They did not know I had official credentials from the Fife Miners' Union. Larkin did not know that I was the granddaughter of his old friend, Michael Lee. No, sir, there was much too much, I told them, they did not know, and I was not playing. They begged and expostulated. They now had plans for meetings. They invited me to accept the hospitality of one of their members. Larkin came in as we were talking. He left his henchmen to do the explaining and apologizing and stood with his back to us. But I could see that he was listening attentively. I looked again at the big, powerful, helpless-looking figure and

softened. All right. I would do their meetings. Larkin and I became good friends. He even unbent so far as to invite me once to
go with him to a concert. It was an amateur affair held somewhere
in the rear of his office buildings. We had been seated barely a
quarter of an hour when my host took a violent dislike to a little
slum girl who was parading across the stage bawling a sentimental
song. To mark his disapproval, he stamped noisily out in the
middle of the act. I was used to his whims by this time and quietly
slunk out after him.

But I did not stay with his friends. I had grasped that in Dublin
there was a very divided working-class movement. In the interests
of our soup-kitchen I would have to try to lie down at one and the
same time with both the lion and the lamb. Neutral ground was
what I must find. So I followed one of our miners' brass bands
home to its lodgings and asked if there was room for me.

They were living in a broken-down hotel with a lot of glittery
decoration around the door; and an army of flies struggling to
capture every bite of food that was put on the table. Yes, there was
room for me. I was pretty tired and dropped asleep as soon as my
head touched the pillow. But soon afterwards I woke, wondering if
I had caught scarlet fever. My skin was itching from top to toe. I
scratched sleepily. It got rapidly worse. I was obliged to get up,
fumble towards the gas-jet and turn on the light.

The bed was a moving mass of fleas. I was convulsed with horror.
I stripped and stood on a chair out of their reach. I wanted to fly to
a bath but did not know where to go, or if there was such a thing in
this primitive place. As best I could I extricated myself and my
clothes and fled to the bleak dining-room downstairs. The chairs,
turned upside down on the tables waiting for the morning cleaners,
looked unfriendly enough; but these things are all a matter of
relativity.

In just over a week I was home again with £100 to hand over to
the Cowdenbeath soup-kitchen committee and promises of more
to come. The promises were not kept, but as (apart from the postal
workers' donations) I had been collecting penny by penny from
bitterly poor people, we felt that Ireland had done reasonably well
for us.

My father's position in the first weeks of the 1926 lock-out was a complicated one. He was a fireman. Firemen are known in some parts of the coalfields as deputies, in others as inspectors. As children we had listened enthralled to his stories of the time when firemen were given their name because they went into the pit ahead of the rest of the men, wrapped in wet blankets and carrying a naked light. The light tested the air for gas. If there was an excess accumulation, it was just too bad for the firemen!

In modern mining the official duty of the fireman is still to warn the men if a dangerous percentage of gas is present and to see that ventilation and other safety measures are properly attended to. The relations between firemen and other workers ought to be close and cordial. But it is usually exactly the reverse. Coal companies favour 'yes' men as firemen. Men who can be bullied into scamping safety work and concentrating instead on speeding-up output.

In some coalfields, notably South Wales, the miners have so despaired of receiving loyal co-operation from the firemen that they exclude them from the miners' union. In Scotland, firemen, if willing to accept the obligation of union membership, are welcomed into the general ranks.

The test of the fireman, as of every other mine worker, comes when strike notices are served. Will he stand with the men or blackleg for the coal company?

Trade union loyalty was not something apart in our family. It was our very life. There could be no question of my father's attitude towards the stoppage. But he himself was expected to go on working. The Miners' Federation of Great Britain instructed him to do so. The pits had to be kept free from flooding and from dangerous accumulations of gas. The argument of the union was that unless this was done there would be needless danger and delay once the lock-out ended and the men (presumably victorious) were ready to resume their work. No coal must be produced but safety work must go on.

That may sound reasonable. But coal companies are never reasonable. In our district they took advantage of the presence of safety men underground to attempt to bring coal to the surface. A trickle of blackleg labour began to return to the pits. No one underground was mad enough to ask my father to handle coal. But it served the purpose of the coal company equally well if a few safety

men of honourable name and reputation could be kept underground. These they hoped to use as a cover for blacklegs.

One evening in June an unofficial conference took place around
our fireside between my father and two other firemen from the
same pit. What were they to do ? Blacklegs were being allowed to
work in their pit. If they continued acting as safety men, they would
be keeping the pits safe for the blacklegs. On the other hand, if they
left their jobs, they would be acting contrary to trade union
decisions. I watched their serious faces. One was a man of sixty. If
he left the pits now, he feared he would never be given work
again. The other was a middle-aged man with a large family of
young children. They had not the clear black-and-white position
of the miner working at the coal face. All three were socialists and
loyal trade unionists. If the union had ordered them to stop work,
they would have been relieved, even happy, to do so. In the end,
they decided that safety workers or no safety workers, they could
not stomach being in the same pit with blacklegs. They hoped too
that their action would call attention to what was happening underground and help to put an end to the blacklegging.

One consequence of this decision was that when the lock-out
ended, the colliery where my father had worked had no further use
for him. After the stoppage there was supposed to be no victimization. Men were to return to their old jobs. But coal companies
never keep their word to colliers unless their employees are
strongly enough organized to compel them to do so. Why should
coal companies be more scrupulous than governments ? In 1919
Bob Smillie was used by the Government to break the resistance
of the miners. He did not know he was being so used. For Smillie
was a great and honourable man. When he made a promise he
meant it and stuck by it. Therefore, when Bonar Law sent him a
signed letter from 11 Downing Street, promising that the recommendations of the Sankey Commission would be kept in the spirit
and the letter, he believed a great advance for the miners was as
good as won.

The Government knew differently. Their pledge had been
merely a manoeuvre to divide and disarm the miners until the coal
companies, and the Government, were in a stronger position to
fight them.

The same sort of warlike ruthlessness was now practised by the coal companies. They re-employed or blacklisted men entirely as they thought fit. A man blacklisted at his own pit had no chance of being engaged elsewhere. His bad reputation preceded him where-ever he went.

The lock-out lasted from May until December. Four months after the general resumption of work my father was still idle. Each week he appeared at the colliery office asking if there was a job for him. Each week he got the same reply. The manager told him without any subterfuge about it, that he wanted 'safe' men as safety men. My father replied as you may well imgaine. Then, at last, he was sent for. But he was not reinstated as a fireman. He was told off to do casual labour.

After being idle so long, pit work would have been trying even to a muscular navvy. To a man of my father's delicate physique it was crucifixion.

We watched him each day trailing his limbs homeward at the end of the shift. Our mother was more than usually careful to see that hot water was ready for him to wash and that a light milk-pudding with the white of an egg whisked on top was waiting to tempt him to eat. He could not digest anything more solid until later in the evening after he had rested. And, even then, he ate very little.

No word of complaint was ever spoken and no word of sym-pathy ever offered. To have done either would have been a viola-tion of my parents' ways. But I could see our mother's eyes follow his every move, ready to anticipate his slightest wish, and she, like me, knew that he was not able to walk upstairs to bed. He had to hold on by the banisters and drag himself up step by step.

We had fought and we had been beaten. The coal companies now had the whip hand. They were driving home the lessons of defeat.

All over the country men were victimized. The unions in most districts were too enfeebled by the long struggle to be able to pro-tect them. Then there was the wonderful alibi—unemployment. Oh no, there was no such thing as victimization. It was simply that trade was bad and there was not enough work to go round.

Under cover of that kind of talk—where the unions were weak

the coal companies did not even trouble to disguise what they were doing—the fight to break the spirit of a proud people went savagely on. Some miners who were active during the stoppage became permanently unemployed. Others were re-engaged, then, once underground, subjected to every conceivable hardship and humiliation.

Still others were driven into exile. Told quite plainly that they were not wanted, they felt there was nothing else for it but to sell their bits of furniture and migrate, usually to the dominions. There were some sad partings. We were loath to see them go. Some of our closest relatives and friends joined the outward trek. Not Jews persecuted by Hitler's Germany. One hundred per cent Aryan British colliers driven into exile by one hundred per cent Aryan British coalowners. And all because they thought miners should be paid more than starvation wages and had had the courage to say so. You can find such family records in every colliery village in the British Isles. Poverty, atrocious working conditions, intimidation, victimization, exile; yet there was no such thing, I was told, as a class-war. All the polite people said that to talk of such a thing was ignorant hysterics. All the popular papers and famous preachers denied its existence. Then what in God's name, I wanted to know, were they doing to our people? I wanted an answer to that. I wanted to get to the bottom of this thing more than I wanted anything on earth.

6

TREACHERY AND DECAY

IN 1927 my father was blacklisted from the pits. My one
brother was hoboing across Australia. I was earning my living
as a schoolteacher. My income kept the family going. Most of
our neighbours, from one cause or another, were worse off than
we were. Many of them much worse off. There was nothing unique
about what was happening to us. If there had been, these things
would not be worth recording. Ours was the ordinary history of the
times and place we were living in. Our circumstances were similar
to thousands of other families around us. Unemployed fathers,
brothers shipped off to the dominions like so many surplus head of
cattle; what was there out of the ordinary in that ? Nothing at all.
Every other house in our street had some member unemployed
and, as likely as not, other members in Canada or Australia. But
that did not make it any easier for each of us. We missed my
brother. The house was sadly quiet in the evening. There was not
even the beating of the pit engine to break the silence as there had
been when we were children.

The mining industry was progressing, so they said! The ventilation fans at the pits worked silently now! Everything seemed
strangely silent. In 1926 we had shouted and protested, we had had
our meetings and our marches. In 1927 we had time to notice how
shabby and disheartened everyone looked. Essential food and
clothing got on credit during the lock-out had now to be paid for.
So had arrears in rent; bit by bit, week by week, in instalments that
left everyone bare to the bone.

The year 1927 was the one when charity organizations made it
fashionable to collect old clothes and send them to the miners. Old
clothes! The very idea made me fighting mad.

79

I was teaching in a school about two miles from my home. One day in December I suspected by the grey-blue complexion of one of the girls that she was particularly poorly clad. I say 'suspected' for she was wearing a pinafore as top garment with a torn jersey showing through. I set the other children to work and took her along to the staff-room. There, in front of the fire, I found she had only a thin cotton rag of a vest under the jersey and, below the waist, no knickers or anything else. Her thin young limbs were naked to the December weather.

That was an extreme case. But almost everyone, children and adults alike, looked shabby and drab. The faces of the older people were listless and grey. There was no money for even the simplest repairs and replacements. Women sat at home patching and darning and counting over and over their few shillings, planning and scheming to see how they could make them go just a little further. Sometimes losing heart altogether. You could tell from the children in school, from their carefully washed and mended clothes and from their general demeanour, those whose mothers were still putting up a fight. It was miraculous how many still were. There were the others, of course, who had simply given in.

Our school building was in keeping with the rest of the place. It looked more like a prison than a place for children. The walls of my classroom were colour-washed in a bilious shade of pea-green. A coal-tip blotted out the view from the window. Huddled together in this cell, were forty to fifty children. They were restless, nervous and not inclined to settle down quietly. It was my job to keep them interested and orderly. Every morning at nine o'clock we valiantly began the day. The first hour went quite well. But, before the end of the afternoon, I was hanging on for dear life in a losing struggle to maintain some semblance of order.

I had no bent for this kind of teaching. I was too impatient; too much at war with my whole environment. I did not believe in what I was doing. I did not believe that there was any good reason why either the children or myself should come to terms with life as we found it in that bleak mining village.

Most of the misery I saw around me in school, in the streets and in private homes had its roots in the poverty of the place. I did not see how, within the four walls of a classroom, I could ever hope to change any of that. The world seemed to me full of excellent craftsmen. People who spent themselves in teaching, in mining, in ploughing, in making bricks, in making furniture, as well as any one of these jobs could be done. It was not this individual work that was at fault. It was the general social design. The bone structure of society shows through in colliery districts with appalling obviousness. All the old moral injunctions about being honest and hardworking, thrifty and civil and you will prosper just have no relevance. You can be all those things and still starve. Fancy telling a collier to work harder! Or that he can grow rich by being thrifty. Of course, if he is ambitious and industrious he may go to night school and begin to study for a mine manager's certificate. Yes, he may do that. But although a student in the evening he is still presumably earning his living as an ordinary collier during the day. Then the occasion comes when strike notices are served.

Some workmate has been wrongfully dismissed—or perhaps the company are attempting to dock wages already woefully low—or maybe the men are insisting on some slight improvement in their working conditions. What happens then to the young collier and his ambitions? Coalpits make no provision for any sort of no-man's-land of blurred, comfortable compromise. It has to be one thing or the other. Will he stand in with his workmates or scab for the company? That may be a bitter moment for a studious young fellow, one of real anguish and full knowledge of all that is involved. I have known young colliers, scholarly and imaginative, for whom it has been all that and more. But these are the exceptions.

Much more usual, hot young blood is the first to cry out against injustice done, and there is no struggle at all. Right is right, wrong is wrong. Besides, a strike is a holiday in the open air, and mother at home will manage, somehow, as she has had to do so often before. And so the pattern is set.

It was in 1927 that with a sudden shock of recognition I realized that the woman approaching me on the main street of the town was one of my old playmates of secondary-school days. In 1917 she had been a pretty, intelligent spirited girl. Now she had a baby in her arms, another clinging to her skirt and a slightly older child walking by her side. Ill-health, lack of proper food, hopeless poverty were written all over her. Later I saw where she lived. A wretched insanitary but and ben with hardly a stick of furniture in it. She had not been brought up like that any more than I had. But she had fallen in love with a young miner, married him and children had begun to arrive just when the slump years came catapulting down on our defenceless villages. He was unemployed most of the time and when working, earned almost as little as when on the dole. We, in these days, flared up if any outsider used the word 'dole' and were quick to retort unemployment insurance if you please, and remember we pay for it; but among ourselves we tolerated the word as a kind of shorthand.

The evening my old schoolmate came to supper with me, we talked of local politics and of this and that and mother chimed in in a friendly, cheerful way. But when I had said good-evening to our visitor, closed the front door and returned to the living-room I found her crumpled up in front of the hearth having a good cry. The contrast between the pretty rather spoiled schoolgirl I had brought home ten years ago and the ill, anaemic, overburdened woman who had just left was more than her tender heart could bear. In the unwritten laws that govern family relationships I had the status of eldest son rather than a daughter. I was the opinionated, self-reliant one. It was not for me to sit down beside her and weep. I made an excuse for going out and wandered wrathfully around the town. This colliery world I had returned to after four and a half student years in Edinburgh seemed grimly different from my earlier memories of it. That was partly, of course, an illusion caused by our mother's gift for putting the best face on things. Because of her a great deal of the sorrow and the squalor of the district had been veiled from us as children. I really believe that if you set her down in the middle of the Sahara with only a bucket of water and an umbrella to help her she would somehow have contrived to make a home out of it.

Also between 1914-18 and 1921-26 (the decline began sooner in some areas than in others) the coalfields of Great Britain had caught glimpses of less savage living than ever before or since. Glimpses, that was all. The most monstrous lies are told about the earnings of miners during the 1914-18 war. An occasional contractor made a fancy income. The average worker earned roughly twice as much as in pre-war days. But as prices had also more than doubled the

margin of improvement was nothing like as great as it was afterwards made out to be. Our father, who was a skilled craftsman,
averaged a pound a day while wages were at their peak point.
Keeping in mind wartime prices that was by no means a princely
salary.

My mother's finances were always a mystery to me. At long
intervals when she took it into her head to jot down exactly every
penny she spent they became a mystery to her too. She would sit
on the fender-stool in front of the fire with a note-book and pencil
on her knee and a look of consternation on her face while my
brother and I, if she had been rash enough to tell us what she was
about, would dance around bubbling over with delight. We knew
what to expect. She would count and recount, add, subtract, begin
all over again and then again and end up by throwing the paper
angrily into the fire. On paper, she never once was able to reduce
her expenditure to her income. We though that very funny. But in
practice she managed miraculously. If there had been a dozen of
us instead of two, as she was fond of repeating, we would not have
had anything like so comfortable a life.

Anyhow, for those various reasons of time and family circumstances, my brother and I during our growing years were saved a
good deal that the miners' children I taught during 1927 and 1928
were exposed to. We were fed on a diet consisting mainly of starch
that would shock the modern dietician, but it tasted fine and was
ample. Our boots were the best quality the Co-op could supply.
Our Sunday coats were made of the best Galashiels tweed. Mother,
a bit aghast at the price, would defend herself against an invisible
assailant with her famous maxim about it never paying to buy
shoddy; that the best was always the cheapest in the long run.
Incidentally, she was not such a stickler about quality when it
came to her own shoes and clothes. Even in medicines a distinction
was made in our favour. We got sweet cascara, our parents the
bitter stuff. It never occurred to us that the reason was that the
bitter stuff was cheaper. Indeed, father gloried so much in retailing
without slurring the minutest detail how grandmother had brewed
senna tea for him when he was a boy and the other horrible con-
coctions he was made to swallow, that we may even have supposed
they liked it that way.

The high-water-mark of prosperity had been our Saturday evenings. There always seemed to be a shilling or two available to flood the house with a small quantity of fruit, a bag of cheap sweets and luxury beyond all, our penny fairy-tale and two comic-cuts. What else in the world was left for anyone to want ? Nothing, so far as we were concerned. Unless, and that too we got, an occasional jaunt to Dunfermline to see Grandmother and Grandfather Lee and to watch the squirrels in Pittencrief Glen crack and eat the nuts we threw to them.

On one occasion, how we had the courage I don't know, we decided to do what all stylish people did when they visited the Glen. The band was playing and the open-air restaurant beside the band-stand was thronged with chattering worldly people. My small brother and I were due to leave all this gaiety and go off to have tea with our grandparents.

I decided that instead we would walk right up to a table, sit down and be served by a waitress. We had fourpence each in our pockets which seemed enough to pay for at least one cup of tea and one cake. It was the glory we were after more than the food. We knew that in the mere matter of eating we could have all we wanted later at home.

After stalking round and round the tea-rooms at least five times we screwed up enough courage to approach. Then the embarrass-ment and the misery of it! There was no table vacant and we had to keep walking in and out of a maze of tables with eyes staring at us, or so we imagined, from every direction. At last two people got up and we guiltily grabbed their places. Now it was all glory again. A queenly but motherly waitess came and stood over us, seeming to shield us from a world that had suddenly become rather too much for us. Somehow she knew we had only fourpence each—I forget how we got through that part of the business—but she loaded the table with currant bread and sandwiches and cakes, and every little while she would dart back to where we were sitting and whisper, 'Eat your fill now; eat your fill'. Bless her and bless her again.

But as we grew older unpleasant changes occurred. The sense of well-being that pervaded our childhood became exceedingly brittle. By the time we reached the secondary-school age, our wants had become expensive. It was no longer possible for our parents to buy us contentment for a few pence. Some classmates had bicycles. Please could we have bicycles ? Some class-mates had joined the local tennis club. Please could we have money to join the club and money to buy a racket and tennis-balls ? Next it was golf or dancing lessons or a special outfit for gymnastics. In short, whatever we saw anyone else having we came home and clamoured for. Unhappily for us at the very time when our wants were mounting the family income was declining. Everything seemed to be declining. Partly, of course, we were beginning to look at the world more critically and with wider standards of comparison. But in addition there was a very real scaling down all round. We had moved from a four-roomed house to a three-roomed one. We hated that. It meant too much furniture cluttering up every corner and a much smaller living-room. But the heart of our discontents was that we were suffering from a kind of rash that breaks out sooner or later on most children from working-class homes who are given higher education. That is, we had become bitten with small-town snobbery. While this phase lasted we made life for our mother one long punishment. The family income was incongruously inadequate to meet even a quarter of our demands. Our mother peered at us anxiously over her spectacles and scraped and scrambled to meet us as far as she could. One day she came in beaming, carrying the much-coveted tennis-racket and an elegant net-bag holding six tennis-balls. The racket was presented to me. My brother borrowed it and in his enthusiasm straight away smashed it. The family fortunes never again enabled us to replace it so that was the end of our tennis careers.

About this time an itch took possession of us to change round all the furniture in the house. We wanted to make it look smarter. The kitchen dresser was an obvious target. The shelves of the dresser were laden with useless ornaments climaxing in the inevitable 'China dogs'. I announced that I really must have these shelves for books. Mother was devoted to her miscellaneous crockery. Every week it was lovingly taken down, dusted or washed, and put carefully back in its place again. That week, reluctant but anxious to meet us as always, the china dogs, the remains of her wedding tea-service, weird shepherdesses, pink angels posed on sea-shells and all the other bric-a-brac, were taken down and not put back. I had

won. Books, chiefly my father's and of not the slightest use to me
for school purposes, arrogantly lined the dresser shelves. The
household gods they had deposed were laid to rest in a large clothes-
basket thrust out of sight under the bed. Next we turned our
marauding eyes towards our father. He was no longer hero and
superman. Why, if he had anything to him, did he remain a simple
colliery fireman ? Why did he not make more money ? We measured him against the fathers of some of our friends who were
richer than we were and decided he had more brains than they had.
That just increased our exasperation. Why, why, did he not use
any gifts he had to make more money so that we could become
small-town swells ? We had no patience with him and his socialist
theories and the poverty we were condemned to by his obstinacy.
Money, make money, lots of it, that was what counted.

With me this silly season lasted less than a year. My brother was
smitten rather more severely. One day he helped to cure me by
adding to our usual impossible demands on our mother a tone of
bullying and contempt that was something new. I found myself
flying to her defence, mad with rage. Henceforth I stood guard
over her, waiting to tomahawk the boy if he should again forget
himself. Not that she took his lapse as stormily as I did. Whatever
we did she had a happy knack of finding a reason for or at least a
good excuse. We were tired, overstrung, working too hard at
school, just thoughtless.

Soon after I had recovered from this phase, I noticed something
on coming in from school one day that stabbed me to the heart.
The shelves above the kitchen dresser presented a droll sight. Two
tiny clearances had been made in the midst of the books and a pink
angel had been timidly inserted in each. Mother must have been
under the bed looking at her china and had been tempted to re-
instate these two pieces. In the quick-changing adolescent moods
that young people go through, I for the moment no longer wanted
to have everything my own way. 'Let's put all the dishes back,' I
volunteered. 'I think they look much nicer than books.' She knew
I was lying and although bewildered as to the reason, sensed that I
genuinely detested those pink angels on their fatuous sea-shells. As
quick as quick, she turned down the proposal and stoutly insisted
that she thought the books looked much nicer than dishes and she

would rather that they were kept where they were. I knew she was lying just as she knew I was lying, but there the matter ended. The books remained on the shelves and the next day even the pink angels were again slumbering in the basket beneath the bed.

By 1921 there was no longer any doubt that the post-war slump had marked the colliery districts down for heavy punishment. The coal strike of that year meant that everyone had to exhaust any small savings that might have been assembled when wages were higher. And the following year I had somehow to be financed to begin life as a University student. How that was done I have already described.

But in 1927, looking back on even our worst times, we seemed to have been living in a golden Eldorado compared with what was now happening. The year 1927 was like living in a beleaguered city. You felt that relief must come soon or you die. If anyone had tried to say that more than a decade of this grey death in life lay ahead, we would have laughed unbelievingly. 'There will be bloody revolution sooner than that,' the average collier and his family would have told you. And meant it, too! 1927 was a year of bitter political controversy and recrimination. Almost every evening we held meetings. These were mostly stormy, acrimonious affairs in keeping with the temper of the times. After the fiascos of 1919, 1921 and 1926, the Communist Party had a rich arsenal of material with which to attack the Labour Party.

According to the gospel as preached by the spate of Communist orators who were let loose during those years in the advanced industrial area, all Labour leaders were traitors, fakirs, twisters and parasites sucking the blood of the poor. I detested the harsh, mechanical vocabulary and the insensitive indiscriminate abuse that characterized Communist Party utterances. And I resented bitterly the virulence of the attack made on those of us inside the Labour Party who were doing our utmost to destroy the right-wing MacDonald, Thomas, Henderson influences.

One day in Cowdenbeath High Street I listened to a young Communist orator declaiming in the usual fashion. Some hours later I passed him in the street and on a sudden impulse went up and demanded he should come home with me. I was determined to have this thing out. I wanted to know whether a goodly portion of the abuse he had been scattering around him was grounded in ignorance or deliberate malice. Did he really believe that the MacDonalds, Thomases, Hendersons and the rest were as deep-dyed villains as he had made them out to be? And more particularly, did he seriously contend that families like my own representing the left-wing point of view inside the official movement were actuated by anything other than a burning desire to end poverty and establish socialism?

By the end of the evening I had dropped my hectoring tone. My friend, the enemy, took the wind out of my sails by a very simple line of argument. The trouble with good little idealists like me, he retorted, was that we were for ever concerned with motives, intentions, subjective states of mind. That was territory better left to the psychologist. As for himself, as a Marxist, scientific socialist, he was not interested in what went on inside the heads of Ramsay MacDonalds and James Maxtons and Jennie Lees. He was solely concerned with the objective results of their political behaviour. Looked at objectively, was I prepared to defend leaders who had thrown away the revolutionary opportunities of the immediate post-war years, who had given us Black Friday in 1921, the disastrously ill-planned General Strike of 1926 and who showed every symptom of going on to further fiascos and betrayals unless they could be ruthlessly got rid of?

I jumped in impatiently at this point saying he could cut out all that line of talk. The issue between us was something quite different. I no more supported the right-wing leadership of the Labour Party than he did. Only by working inside instead of outside the party, I was making my opposition a hundred times more effective than his could ever be. Also, he had better remember that the Labour Movement was something much bigger than a handful of leaders. There were devoted, disinterested men and women campaigning for socialism in every corner of Great Britain and managing to do so without sickening the general public and degrading themselves by descending to filthy, slanderous attacks on individuals every time they opened their mouths.

'Quite true, quite true, Comrade,' he came back sarcastically. 'The Communist Party is kept outside the Labour Party, but the I.L.P. is allowed to remain inside. The I.L.P. is the darling of the

Labour Party. For how could the Jimmy Thomases and the Ernest Bevins and the Hendersons get away with it if they had not the James Maxtons to whitewash them in the eyes of the ordinary worker ? Nice, kind, sentimental, witty speeches from Maxton that slide down as easily as an ice-cream wafer and make everyone feel what a happy family the Labour Party is at bottom. I tell you, Comrade Lee, your kind are the worst of the lot. Romantic revolutionaries like you have got to be discredited. You are a drug blinding the masses. Without you the right wing gang would be seen and exposed in their true light. Without you they could not survive a single day. And so you see, Comrade Lee, I shall go on denouncing you and your slavering, sentimental I.L.P.' At this point, mother, with an overcoat thrown over her nightdress, put her head anxiously round the kitchen door and asked if I knew it was two o'clock in the morning and that the alarm-clock would be ringing for father to go off to work in less than three hours and that we were making such a din, no one could get a wink of sleep.

Hastily, we said good-night and shook hands and agreed to meet and finish the argument another night.

I went to bed and lay awake for some time with two words jumping and tumbling around me—objective, subjective, objective, subjective, subjective, objective. Was it true that socialists like myself were merely giving a false front to the Labour Party behind which leaders I neither trusted nor respected could the more easily mislead and betray ?

The following week there was a much advertised Communist Party propaganda meeting in the town and I went along to it determined to be 'objective'. After three hours of Communist oratory I crept home feeling dirtied and dejected. Whatever I was looking for, this certainly was not it. I hated the nauseating reiteration of the words traitors, fakirs, applied indiscriminately to all and sundry: I was impatient with the cheap quackery of infallibility that all Communist Party spokesmen laid claim to. I found nothing warming, sustaining in this diet of hate and mechanical Marxist clichés. This was at best a barren caricature of what I believed a revolutionary socialist party should be. I turned back with a feeling of going home to the broad Labour Movement. There, quite plainly, was where I belonged. There were fewer people claiming in-

fallibility in its ranks, there was room for a vigorous exchange of
views, there was the hope of turning this vast powerful organization that three generations of my family had loved and laboured
for, away from the damning influences of MacDonaldism and
forward to socialism.

My natural bent, although I hated it when anyone else said so,
was evangelical. MacDonald himself was not much better at
painting the sorrows of the poor, the beauty and dignity of the
Promised Land of socialism—and of trusting to Providence somehow to jump the gap between the distressful present and that
beatific future.

I had endless opportunities for exercising my talents. Every
week-end, sometimes week nights as well, I was off on a round of
socialist propaganda meetings. At first it was hard going. I would
carefully prepare and write out a speech with a beginning, a middle
and an end. Once on the platform I forgot most of what I had
written. I was no use at reciting from memory or reading aloud from
a manuscript. My temperament made speaking a hit or miss affair.
I had to know beforehand what I wanted to say, then trust to the
inspiration of the moment for the right words and imagery in
which to say it.

I had, or imagined I had, when first I began to attempt to speak
in public, one grave handicap, and, also an advantage I was not
entitled to have. A great, husky collier in the Lothians (most
miners are small) made me conscious of the first; my grandfather of
the second.

I had been booked to speak at a meeting in one of the mining
villages near Edinburgh. That was back in 1925. The local secretary wrote that he would meet me when I arrived and take me to
the hall.

On arrival, I jumped off the train and looked around hopefully
for my escort. The platform gradually emptied until I was sure
that one particular man who was scrutinizing all the passengers
must be looking for me. I went up to him and announced myself. He
looked down at me and said just these two words, 'Great God!'
But they were eloquently spoken. I was nineteen. My round, red
face and snub nose made me look even younger than I was. He was
plainly filled with panic. Had he chalked the streets and booked a

hall and made all arrangements for a really important propaganda meeting with only this to see him through the evening ?

I trailed miserably along by his side, now in a bigger panic than he was. I was trying to repeat to myself the speech that I had so carefully prepared. But my mind was a complete blank. We reached the hall. It was packed and impatient. I was rushed through the central passage, thrown on to the platform, introduced in thirty seconds and left to it. Somehow I staggered through. When I sat down I had not the faintest idea of what I had said. I wanted only to escape. Yet no one had laughed at me. That was the incredible thing. No one had laughed! They had sat quite still. At the end they even applauded.

That was in 1924. For several years that 'Great God' rang in my ears. The effect it had on me was that always when I had platform work to do I did everything I could to make myself look older.

One spring day in 1927 Grandfather Lee paid one of his rare visits to Lochgelly. We went often enough to Dunfermline to visit him, but it was not often he found time to come to us. That happened only when there was something special afoot. I arrived in from school just after four o'clock. Tea had already begun. The table had been drawn over to the fire so that he could sit in the most comfortable armchair.

As I came in, he got up from his chair and came over to meet me. We shook hands which for an undemonstrative family like ours was in itself unusual. Then he said, very proudly, 'Master of Arts, Bachelor of Laws.' I had just completed my LL.B. degree. I had not taken the work seriously. For me it had meant six months' cramming after I finished the M.A. degree and thus earning the second half of the £100 law scholarship that I had won the year before. The conditions attached to the payment of the second instalment of £50 was that the holder must complete the degree examinations.

I was pleased that he should be so pleased and, at the same time, felt what a fraud it all was. The universities were turning out ten-a-penny graduates in large droves several times a year. Most of us remained largely illiterate. For some months before examinations, we crammed to the teeth. A month or two afterwards, we had forgotten all we had learned. All that remained were our certificates, and in the case of those who were particularly obtuse, a feeling of superiority over people who had not been initiated into these mystic rites.

But often at my meetings I saw the faces of elderly and middle-aged colliers looking up towards me from the body of the hall, reconciled to my youth because of the letters after my name. It is part of Scottish working-class pride to deny any respect for University degrees, but part of its practice, particularly inside the Labour Movement, to pay far too much deference to them.

I knew how my grandfather's, even my father's, generation felt about education. They were very romantic about it. They thought of it as a kind of lamp to light the feet of their children, so that we need not stumble and hurt ourselves as they had done, or as armour buckled around us so that we could meet in fair fight all who stood in our way. They never doubted that our fight would be anything other than their fight and with them and of them and for them.

Through long, difficult years, men who felt limited by their own lack of formal education fought that we should not be so handi-capped. That fight was all part of the struggle to build a self-confident working-class. Jude the Obscure, fearful of his own limitation and impressed by the training of his superiors, vowed that his children should be numbered among the initiated. But the pity of it is that only one in a thousand of those who have benefited from his efforts have any idea of their immediate social and political antecedents.

In a very direct sense those of us who are graduates from the industrial parts of Great Britain are the children of the Labour Movement. Our education has been wholly or partly paid for by the public authorities. On those public bodies it is always the socialist members (with an occasional Liberal) who press for free schools, free books, access to high schools and maintenance grants to help us through training-college or university.

It is very hard on the old idealistic socialist when he sees gradu-ates from the working-class homes turn into small-town snobs. He had counted on them to be his invaluable allies. He cannot under-stand what has gone wrong, for he seldom realizes the limitations of the educational processes they have been through.

I do not remember either in elementary or secondary school a single history lesson in which I was given the slightest idea of the life of ordinary working-people, still less of their distinctive organizations.

At home, from my father's books, I read a great deal about the year 1848. I read about the potato famine in Ireland, of the Chartist agitations all over Britain, of starving children sent to gaol for stealing food, of miners working for two and sixpence a day, of boatloads of helpless Irish labourers dumped in the Larnarkshire coalfields to prevent any successful agitation for an improvement in wages—and much of a similar kind.

At school, believing it to be history, I was taught a great number of fairy stories about kings and queens and warring nobles. When children read, they identify themselves with the characters they read about. I was always a king or a queen or, at least, a great feudal lord. I was never a collier stealing from hunger and punished for stealing.

I am not really complaining about how history is taught in schools. That would be a mere waste of time. I do not expect education in England, Scotland, Ireland, Russia or Germany, to be anything other than propaganda in favour of whatever happens to be the controlling power in the State. Some day the world may be run on something other than the murder and plunder principle. But until then, no one country dare allow its schools to be anything except propaganda factories. Russia is a case in point. Within its own frontiers it has overthrown the plunder principle, but the Soviet Union is conscious of enemies all round it. It does not feel safe. All teaching material is, therefore, subjected to the most rigid kind of censorship. The young Soviet citizen, like the young Britisher or German, is carefully drilled in that version of history and of current affairs that is best calculated to help forward whatever happens to be the immediate purposes of the State.

Caught up in that kind of tangle, there is only one thing that a serious socialist movement can do. It is bound to regard working-class education, quite independently of the ordinary school system, as one of its key activities. It is bound to train advocates who can teach adult audiences the history and objectives of the organized working-class movement. That is how any reputable socialist propagandist sees his job. That, at least, is how I saw mine.

That day in 1927 when my grandfather came specially to Lochgelly to show me how pleased he was, I did not start any argument. I was happy to see him and tried to show him so in every way I could. But I felt hopelessly out at elbows with most of his values and expectations. He was still at bottom a gentle, civilized, nineteenth-century radical who believed that socialism would be brought about mainly by Acts of Parliament and would come in gradual, inevitable stages.

His outlook was more representative of the Labour Movement than mine was. It was not so much what he said as what he assumed. He took it for granted, for instance, that whenever the public should choose to return a majority Labour Government, large chunks of socialist legislation would be passed through the House of Commons, obstructed a little by the House of Lords, but would ultimately become law and, as such, be universally respected and enforced.

Respect for the Law, for Parliament, for public opinion were to be sufficient to restrain anyone who might feel like obstructing or resorting to extra-constitutional methods.

It is remarkable how many socialists of that generation, even those whose industrial experience should have protected them against such lavish assumptions, clung to this simple faith.

All his life, in the disputes between colliers and coalowners, my grandfather had been familiar with lies, double-dealing and crude victimization. Coalowners don't hesitate to bring soldiers and additional police into the mining towns to be used against the miner if they think that, by doing so, they can better gain their ends. My grandfather had seen policemen's batons used against his workmates. In 1921, then barely seventeen, I got caught in the middle of Cowdenbeath High Street in a fight between policemen and miners. I was cycling home from Dunfermline library with a bundle of books tied to the back of my bicycle. The pressure of the crowd forced me to dismount. They went surging past me, growling and cursing at the police. I had no room to turn my bicycle or I would have run too. My sense of property must have been stronger than my sense of fear! I clung to my bicycle and my books and stood my ground, dazed by the quick, backward flow of the crowd. Still bewildered, I found a line of policemen with drawn batons literally towering over me. Some of the younger miners were throwing stones at them from closes at the side of the High Street. One was beautifully aimed. I saw the blood trickling down the side of a policeman's face. Everyone was beside himself with rage. Tempers had snapped. There was a 'free for all' for a few minutes, then, quite suddenly, it was all over. I had to walk home the rest of the way for the frame of my bicycle had been twisted in the general mix-up. I felt pleased and excited and angry all in one. For me this was a childish adventure without any serious risk. But I did not forget it. Miners, it seemed, when they set out to improve their wages and conditions, had to reckon with the physical forces of the State as well as with the money and influence of the coal-owners.

In that same 1921 strike, soldiers had been quartered at the pits. That was two years after Bob Smillie and the miners had been tricked by the Sankey Commission. Lies, batons, broken promises, soldiers' bayonets, all these we were familiar with in the coalfields. Yet, by some strange alchemy, our socialist movement still trusted, still believed in peaceful evolutionary change provided only a Labour Government sat at Westminster.

I was bothered by those inconsistencies. But not too deeply. After all there were plenty of others beside myself to do the thinking and the worrying. And, anyhow, I was too busy to have much time for thought. There was always an endless stream of meetings to be addressed.

7

WESTMINSTER

WHENEVER a telegram arrived in our house mother ripped it open at once and steadied her trembling eyes as well as she could to read what it had to say. Letters were private affairs and as such respected and left untouched. But a telegram was a calamity. She had better be the first to know, so that she could break the news. As I got myself more and more involved in political activities and telegrams began to arrive quite frequently, she relaxed a bit; but never quite. She never entirely lost that little tremor of fear whenever she saw the post-office message-boy jump off his bicycle in front of her gate and waited for him to call out, 'Telegram for you, Mrs. Lee.'

One July day when I came in from school she handed me the usual pink telegram-form and I read, 'Labour Movement in Shotts desires to nominate you for Parliamentary Candidature of North Lanark under I.L.P. auspices reply per return as to your considering same. Dewar Secy, 5 Benhar Rd. Shotts.'

I must have looked startled or upset or something, for immediately I laid it down, mother lifted the wire and read it for the second time, then puzzled, inquired, 'It is nothing serious, is it ?' She had been quite at her ease after glancing over it when it first arrived, for no one was dead; no one in trouble.

'No, no, mother, nothing serious. Just I.L.P. business.' That kept her from worrying. I could settle down to the meal she had prepared for me and decide what to say in reply.

I was in a mild kind of panic. It was one thing to address propaganda meetings, to take part in local affairs, even to steady your nerves sufficiently to carry your feet to the rostrum in national party conferences when there was some issue before party members about which you were so violently agitated that you felt you must speak or bust.

But a Parliamentary candidature ? And in a constituency where the sitting Tory Member had a majority of only 2,028. That meant that when the election came our people ought to win. Ought to. But supposing I was candidate and made a hash of things. I thought of the great May Day demonstration I had addressed in Shotts less than two months before. That thought was warming. It had been an entirely working-class and mainly collier gathering. What a cold windy place that public park of theirs was! But there was nothing cold about the people themselves. Why should I be afraid of them ? They were almost identical in outlook and needs to the Fife people I had grown up among. Yes, yes, after all, the telegram only asked consent to nominate me along with others to go before a selection committee. Yes, all right, it was their suggestion, not mine. They surely knew what they were about. I had no money. Every penny for the organization work of the division and the election campaign itself would have to be found by the local movement. And I was dismally young. But I smiled when I remembered that young women between twenty-one and thirty would have the vote for the first time at the next general election. The Tory Party would be bound to throw bouquets to this new section of the electorate. It could hardly at the same time attack me on account of my age!

The following February the sitting Tory Member for North Lanark died. A by-election was precipitated. I found myself elected to Parliament with a majority of 6,578.

The by-election caused great excitement throughout the constituency and more than the usual national interest. For everyone knew it was only a matter of months until a general election must take place. Socialists everywhere were delighted with the result. It confirmed the high hopes they already held that their party was soon to become the government of Great Britain.

Even in the rush and splutter of that first contact with North Lanark, I was appalled by the poverty of the place. I was at home in colliery districts. I thought I knew exactly what to expect. But this was worse than anything I had ever known. In some of the smaller villages living conditions were such that one might have been back in the time of the Chartist agitations and the hungry

4

forties. Everywhere there was a housing famine. For years I had
been repeating from public platforms the statistics of Scottish
housing conditions. Half the population living in one or two-
roomed houses, seventy-five per cent of the people of Lanarkshire
living in one or two-roomed houses. I was now learning in all its
unforgettable squalor what that Lanarkshire figure meant. Unemployment was another torment. Desperate men and women packed
those 1929 meetings clamouring for work. And those in jobs were
equally dissatisfied, for wages and working conditions throughout
the county left them little better off than the unemployed.

I dubbed the eighth hour underground of the collier's working-
day 'Baldwin's hour'. A feature of the election was the promise that
the Labour Party empowered me to make that one of the first acts
of a Labour Government would be to reduce the working hours of
miners from eight to seven without any corresponding reduction in
wages.

After Lanark came London and initiation into the ways of the
House of Commons. The Trevelyan family probably saved me
from making a too ungainly entrance. I was living with them during
my first few days in London. An hour or two before I was due to
leave for the House, Lady Trevelyan had a sudden inspiration. Did
I know exactly what I was expected to do when the Speaker called
on me to take my place ? In walking down the centre of the Chamber towards his chair, three times I would have to stop, keeping in
step with my two sponsors, and bow neatly. 'Now', she said,
striding to the opposite end of her long drawing-room, 'imagine
I am the Speaker and let me see you bow.' I bent my back but
made the expected mistake of keeping my head sticking into the air.
That was not at all graceful. I would have to try again and this time
incline my head properly. This all seemed to me rather a fantastic
way of fighting the class-war, but as I was a novice sprawling
around in an unfamiliar environment, I was glad enough to be
saved from making any unnecessary blunders.

In the inner lobby of the House of Commons, Bob Smillie and
James Maxton were waiting for me. I had chosen them as my
sponsors. Maxton, leader of the I.L.P. and friend as long as I could
remember. Our beloved Bob Smillie, my grandfather's mate and
miners' leader and family friend even before I was born. Incident-

ally, this choice of sponsors was my first disagreement with the
Labour Party officialdom. The head office had selected Margaret
Bondfield and Tom Kennedy to introduce me, but in facing
Parliament for the first time I wanted to have those other two
whose texture I had been familiar with all my life, within touching
distance. I was a good deal more nervous than pride would allow
me to show.

Not that there was any need for me to be so apprehensive. I
found my colleagues in the House of Commons almost stiflingly
affable. That is, with the exception of a number of the Scottish
Miners' M.P.s whose faces, for reasons that at that time I was
totally unable to fathom, curdled up like a bowl of sour milk whenever we accidentally collided.

The real terror of my life during this first year in London was
the journalists. At that time I had no acquaintances among them
and did not understand them nor the compulsions that made them
act as they did. Also, before leaving Lochgelly, the first to invade
my privacy had made me mistrustful of the whole lot. I was still
teaching but was due to leave school and begin the North Lanark
campaign at the end of the week. On the Wednesday of that week
I rushed home as usual for a midday meal and found a strange-
looking creature embedded in the living-room sofa. Mother had
placed a small table in front of him supporting her ample bread-
scone-cake conception of what makes a hospitable forenoon tea. I
bristled up spying danger whenever I set eyes on him. When the
'story' appeared in the press my suspicions were confirmed. My
poor mother declared she was afraid to show her head outside the
door. What would the neighbours think of her for telling all those
lies ? For what either of us had actually said had been totally ig-
nored and a fantastic sob-story invented in its place. I was out-
rageously angry and decided that if that was journalism and
journalists, I wanted nothing to do with either. I brought this same
attitude with me to London. I simply could not understand why
what I looked like, what I wore, my favourite breakfast and
whether I thought whiskers should be curled upwards or downwards had anything to do with the serious political purposes that
engaged my working hours. And I was most particularly determined that whatever place I made my home in London should

remain inviolate. I laugh now when I think of the lengths that Annie and I went to to ensure that no press man, especially press photographer, should invade us. Annie was my charlady, six feet tall, muscular and blindingly blonde. She polished floors superbly and was in every way magnificent except that she liked to smoke and scatter tobacco ash around all the time she was at work. I was then renting 28 Dean Street, Soho, from Clifford Allen (later alas, Lord Allen of Hurtwood). Apparently one of the things about this minute top-storey flat in the heart of London that had attracted him, was that Karl Marx had lived and worked there for a number of years. Actually therefore the place had a certain legitimate 'news' interest. But I was totally blind to any other consideration except a stubborn determination not to be 'done' a second time. Several times when an incident in the House made the I.L.P. group 'news', Annie reported that these there people were knocking at the door downstairs and peering over the window; she would further report, 'Keep back, Miss, keep back. They got cameras.' We took it as seriously as a military engagement and when the knocking had died away, celebrated the victory. Annie's real ambition was to pour a bucket of water from the top storey window on to the heads of the enemy below but I thought that was going a bit too far. This was hardly a sophisticated approach to public life. But I had not been sent to London because I was sophisticated. I had been sent there because I vehemently resented the poverty and slums and unemployment that were sapping away the very life of the industrial population of Scotland. And had persuaded the majority of the electorate of North Lanark that these were not acts of God about which nothing could be done, but man-made evils that men could also remedy.

I was not likely to forget that Scottish background. But even if I had wanted to every post brought a torrent of reminders. Oh! those mails!

Ex-soldiers of 1914–18 too ill to work but somehow not entitled to pensions; men hurt in the pits, able at most for light work but no light work available and compensation being stopped. Women living in two-roomed cottages with one of the rooms so damp that the water made rivulets down the wall and the whole family had to huddle together, sleeping and waking, day and night, when they were sick and when they were well, all in the one apartment. Old people hungry because they could not spin out their ten-shilling pension even as supplemented by a shilling or two from the Public Assistance Board to cover food and fuelling to the end of the week. Unemployed men in areas where no work was available cut off benefit for 'not genuinely seeking work'. Lads stranded, workless, penniless in Australia or Canada and wondering how they could get home. Other lads unemployed at home and wondering how they could get out to the fine openings that the papers talked about in the Dominions. Women in new council houses, worried and frightened out of their wits as they made the discovery that it now took more for lighting, cooking, heating and the barest repairs than they had had to budget for in their old houses and finding themselves shorter on food rations than they had ever been in their lives before. Optimists who had acquired furniture, bicycles, wireless-sets on the instalment system and could not keep up their payments. What rights had they ? Could the firm carry the goods away and could they claim back any of the money they had so laboriously paid in ? One evening in the House of Commons I was working away at a pile of 'cases' on a side-table in one of the division lobbies. That was my dodge for getting on with correspondence and at the same time being on hand when the division bell rang. Maxton sauntered along the lobby. Looking quizzically down at me, he tapped with his long brown fingers the enormous bundle of letters I was ploughing my way through and said in his slow disarming drawl, 'You had better make up your mind, you know, whether you mean to be a socialist Member of Parliament or another bloody welfare worker like Geordie'—chuckling and nodding in the direction of his bosom pal, George Buchanan M.P. Only Maxton could sum up his friends so pointedly yet without giving offence. I laughed, seeing the justice of his remark. But all the same letters had to be answered.

Twice a day I looked apprehensively at the fresh pile of 'cases' that arrived for me. It seemed as if the floodgates had opened and all the pent-up sorrow and hopes and fears that had accumulated in North Lanark since the time of the Boer War were streaming down to London. Those letters haunted me. Some months later Roden Buxton passed along that same division lobby and found me drowning in letters at that same table. He stopped and helpfully suggested that I ought to have a secretary. I told him I agreed but that a Parliamentary allowance of £400 a year that had to cover living expenses in London, family commitments in Scotland and lots of other odds and ends besides left a margin that barely paid for the postage-stamps I needed. To pay a trade-union rate of pay to a competent secretary was just out of the question. The next day he persuaded me to meet Dorothy Hawkin who, as part of her service to the socialist movement, was apparently willing to work for me as a voluntary unpaid secretary. I was not keen. From my men colleagues I had heard a good deal about fancy people of independent means who volunteered to act as secretaries and turned out to be more trouble than they were worth. But soon afterwards, I found myself racing at a pace probably never seen before through the grey corridors of Westminster and reaching the secretaries' room, breathless and apologetic if I was so much as five minutes late. I hoped one day to arrive there first and be able to look at Dorothy in the superior way she looked at me. But it never happened that way. Always she would be there at her desk, the morning mail opened, read, routine letters answered and the rest waiting for me. I had a superb secretary and was very proud of her.

The actual time I had now to spend on correspondence was more than quartered. But 'cases' remained the bane of my life. My difficulty was that I had no gift for thinking in abstract categories. My mind reduced everything to the personal, immediate and concrete. An old man's letter, though I may never have met him, telling me how he was trying yet failing to live on his old-age pension, was my friend, John Garrity, appealing to me. John, with the great leonine head that I had taken so much pleasure in looking at. John, who was brave and gentle, and so proud; and such good fun too with his quick Irish wit and belligerence. Year after year he attended our Lochgelly I.L.P. branch meetings with religious regularity. He was branch treasurer for a long time and although he had no other income than his old-age pension, we knew we had the safest treasurer in the country. Nearing seventy the time came when John, who all his life had been doing for other people, himself began to need looking after. He had no one to keep house for him.

He had only his pension and the usual shilling or two allowed by the public assistance authority. The day came when he was no longer able to keep an independent fireside. They found him a place in a charity institution in Edinburgh. He was well enough treated there after the manner of such places. But he was not happy. He wanted to go home to Lochgelly. He wanted to be free to go in and out as he pleased. He wanted to be back among the people he was used to and liked best. John is only one of thousands. If he had had even as little as a pound a week in those last few years it would have made all the difference to him between independence and cold impersonal charity; between life and death in life. A pound a week is not a fancy income. We should blush to offer old people so little. But it is twice as much as John was allowed.

It was the same with letters about men stranded in the Dominions. Always it was my brother I saw. Mostly the letters came from districts in Scotland that I knew very well; letters sent by mothers aching to know if their sons could be found work or brought home again. I knew every minutest nuance of the grief such women feel. I had cause to know. Never a day in life passed that my own mother's thoughts did not go out to her son, wondering about him, always wondering. Was he well? Did he have a warm meal when he needed one? Had he a comfortable bed at night? Was he homesick or liking the new life? Not quite eighteen was so young to be sent so far away from home. And letters took such a long time. Six weeks going and another six weeks for a reply to come back. Anything could happen in that time.

It has been the same with Grandmother Lee as it now was with my mother. Always when I went to see my grandmother she used to ask me the same question. 'How old are ye noo, Jen?' 'Ten, Grannie,' I would say. Or as the years passed, 'twelve, Grannie,' 'fifteen, Grannie'. 'seventeen', 'twenty', 'twenty-seven'. 'Twenty-seven,' she would repeat (I was twenty-eight when she died), 'then it's twenty-seven years come Michaelmas since Charlie gaed awa'.' Charlie was her first-born. He left for Canada when I was three months old. I was my grandmother's calendar. Always from my age she told herself the unbelievable. Charlie had been gone all those years. Charlie, the quiet, corrie-handed, scholarly one; Charlie, who went out with a neighbour's lad star-gazing at night, coming home at dawn just in time to put on his pit clothes and be off to the pit. Charlie—and her pride and wrath would struggle in her voice—who saved up along with his neighbour thirty good Scotch pounds then spent it all, yes, every penny of it, on a telescope to look at the stars. What was he looking for ? What did he think he would find ? He was shy with strangers she would say. But mind you, Jen, never wi' you. It was a strange thing. You were just a wee baby. And he would lift you up and carry you frae room to room. My grandmother had another ten sons and daughters. You would think that in such a crowd one more or less would never have been missed. Yet all her life she thought about Charlie and kept wondering about him. For the first few years after he left he wrote regularly and sent home a pound whenever he could. Then, mysteriously, entirely out of character, letters abruptly stopped. There were rumours that he had been killed in 'labour trouble' on the west coast of America, but nothing definite was ever discovered. Just silence and grandmother left counting the years and never giving up hope.

As a child, always when I heard the Jacobite songs—'Will ye no come back again'—'Far over yon Seas'—'Bonny Charlie's Noo Awa' '—'A Wee Birdie cam' to our ha' Door', my grandmother's Charlie got mixed up with the Stuart Charlie. With her I am sure there was not even a mixing. It was her own Charlie that all the songs were for. After my brother left we waited long weeks for letters; and worried when they were delayed. If we had known definitely what was happening to him, when he had money in his pocket, when he was unemployed and 'broke', it would have been less wearing than the uncertainty. Those of our neighbours who had friends abroad felt and worried just as we did. I would hear a voice shouting to mother in passing, 'How is your boy getting on, Mrs. Lee ? I had a letter from our John last week.' Then the tongues would be busy, sharing news, finding relief in telling one another their hopes and fears, boasting joyously when the exile was prospering, sometimes confiding, sometimes hiding the worst of the truth, those times when parcels and postal-orders small in themselves but a harsh cut into a working man's income were being sent off to tide the immigrant over a particularly bad patch.

In the seventeenth century there was a considerable exodus of

population from Scotland and Ireland to the continent of Europe.
Men without property or prospects hired themselves as mercen-
aries to fight the battles of other powers for a few pence per day.
They came to be called the 'wild geese'. In the twentieth century
the wild geese are still on the wing. People without property,
without continuity, without a past. People who leave no trace
behind, who walk on water. Wild geese blown hither and thither
by circumstances over which they have so little control. Never
rooted for long in any one soil. Without property and therefore
with no enduring ties. Most of us need roots. But the continuity
is always being broken. A few links are forged, then once again the
chain snaps. We must start all over again perhaps at the opposite
ends of the earth.

You may want to say how morbid, how unenterprising! It is a
splendid thing to be an empire-builder. To go off and conquer the
world anew.

My experience is that those who talk in that way know nothing
of the iron compulsions of poverty. And still less of the suffering of
women who rear families only to lose them while they are still little
more than children. I have heard so many women say, 'If only I
could see him again—just once.'

Well-to-do people seldom know that kind of hurt. They can go
and if their heart is breaking, they can come home again. But ours
seldom come back. The awful finality of those long ocean crossings
is very hard to bear. Hope never dies that your own may be
exempted from the general fate but you know very well that the
majority of penniless immigrants have little chance of ever again
seeing their home people; as little as had murderers and thieves
sentenced for life in the old days and shipped off to Botany Bay.

When civil servants and soldiers are working abroad, it is made
possible for them, if they so wish, to return home from time to
time. No one has ever been able to convince me that to make provision so that lads from British pits, factories and farms persuaded
to emigrate by propaganda, mostly Government-controlled or inspired, that is at best a misleading tissue of half-truths, should even
once in all their after-life be given a similar privilege would impose
a strain upon the resources of the British Empire greater than it
could bear. But in 1929 I have already learned this curious fact about

national expenditure. A Conservative minister of the Crown can look you in the eye and quite solemnly assure you that to add even one shilling a week to the old-age pension is a financial impossibility. To do so would overburden industry; kill the goose that laid the golden egg. The old people would be the first to suffer. Such an effort to help them, however well intentioned (and of course your heart was never in question; it was your head only that was at fault) would produce disastrous results and might make it impossible to continue even their present allowances. You can switch round from pensions to the care of sick people, or children, or work schemes or housing and always the same formula is applied. The Government is already doing the maximum that the economics of the situation allow.

When first I sat in Parliament and heard Conservative Ministers talk like that I listened half antagonized, half admiring. It was obviously second nature for them to look at the world in that way. Super-tax payers and paupers existing side by side in no way discountenanced them. The earth and all its fruits belonged to a small group of the elect. Theirs the pits and shipyards and factories. Apparently they even thought it right that they should gobble up mountains and forests and great heather-clad commons. And their friends in Parliament could be relied on to defend every iota of their monopolies. The many, the ordinary people might be suffered to exist so long as they kept to the main highways and to the special compounds built to accommodate them—and tolerated even there only on condition of paying fabulous ground rent and other tribute.

It was too obvious to be worth saying that if the same Ministers of the Crown had had to find an additional hundred million or even a thousand million to pay for extra soldiers to police property, they would have been able to find the money. It was simply a question of what was thought to be important and urgent.

I prayed to my own particular gods that whenever working people should come to power they would have this same sublime sustaining sense of what was due to them. That they in turn would allow nothing to stand in their way.

8

THE 1931 DEBACLE

MR. STANLEY BALDWIN was British Prime Minister in 1926. That was the year of the General Strike. The year when the coalowners of Great Britain were able to call to their assistance, in their fight against colliers, the entire powers of the State, not excluding its soldiers and police. The year when the working people of Great Britain were taught that effective resistance to wage-cuts is a revolutionary act.

Mr. Stanley Baldwin won handsomely in 1926. The General Strike collapsed; the miners were starved into submission; the Trades Disputes Act was amended in a way that the Government hoped would permanently cripple the unions.

And the aftermath of all that was the defeat of Mr. Baldwin and his Government in the general election of 1929.

There was great excitement everywhere when it was found that a second Labour Government had been elected. Working people felt that they had scored a sensational victory. This was their answer to 1926. But the excitement did not last long. It was soon followed by bewilderment, disappointment and a good deal of despair. The external events of that time are well known. The year 1931 was one of exceptional economic depression all over the world. Labour leaders found they had to abandon most of their election promises. Wages, pensions, housing, education, yes, it was desirable to spend a great deal more money on all of these. But Mr. Philip Snowden, as Chancellor of the Exchequer, could not find the money. He consulted the directors of the Bank of England and the leaders of the Federation of British Industries. Very sorry, Mr. Snowden, he was told, we cannot find money for your socialist programme, and if you try to press your policy through Parliament

in spite of us, you will make nothing of it. You will simply pre-
cipitate economic chaos and collapse. Indeed we go further than
that. You must go back to your party and tell it that wages must be
reduced, social services restricted, unemployment benefits cut. And
if it does not agree, then the first effect of its obstinacy will be the
unparalleled disaster and disgrace of England going off the gold
standard.

No one seemed to know what going off the gold standard exactly
would mean. But the very vagueness of the threat made it all the
more effective. Mr. MacDonald lost his head entirely. At the height
of the crisis he rose to speak in the House of Commons, brandishing a German note of the early post-war inflationary period. If we
went off the gold standard our money would soon become worthless. Mr. Snowden apparently agreed with him. The bulk of the
Labour Party sulked. They did not know what to make of it all.
But there was one thing that they stuck on. 'If the situation was as
desperate as it was made out to be, then let those who could best
afford to, make the main sacrifices. Above all, don't ask the unemployed, already far below subsistence level, to accept a further
ten per cent reduction.' The next step was the formation of a
National Government, the country going off the gold standard,
instead of the predicted collapse, quite a revival in export trade,
everyone beginning to breathe more freely again, and the Labour
opposition coming out of its corner and boldly declaring, 'Bah! we
knew all the time it was only a bit of spooking. The crisis was
never half so serious as it was made out to be. This was the Tory
Party up to its usual tricks—frightening the electorate with highly-
coloured scare stories. And MacDonald is a traitor for having lent
himself to their infamous scheming.'

The main brunt of Labour's attack fell on MacDonald. Its
favourite explanation for the whole miserable fiasco of Labour's
period in office was, 'It was all due to MacDonald's vanity and love
of a Lord'.

Maybe, but that does not account for Philip Snowden. There
was no love lost between these two men. Yet, for his own quite
separate and sufficient reasons, Labour's Chancellor of the Exchequer also crossed to the ranks of the Tories. The spiritual bio-
graphy of Philip Snowden is a conventional one; youthful idealism

becoming gangrened in later years and ultimately degenerating into a harsh contempt for the general run of humanity. But to say that he was capable of deliberate 'betrayal' is just so much my eye.

When three Labour leaders of such widely divergent temperaments as MacDonald, Snowden and Thomas decide to abandon the party they have belonged to all their lives, serious socialists are bound to ask not what was wrong with their morals but what was wrong with their political philosophy.

All three men belonged to the 'Socialism by Consent' school of socialists. That is, they accepted most of the assumptions of nineteenth-century liberalism. Every day, in every way, the world was to become better and better. There was to be no sharp, distressful struggle to decide whether economic power should remain a monopoly of a small group of overlords, or pass to the representatives of the people. Nothing like that. Simply a world more and more able to raise standards of living and bit by bit won over to the acceptance of each item in Labour's programme of social reforms. Can the Labour Movement assume that a Labour Government will ever be allowed to function in an atmosphere of trade prosperity and 'confidence'? That 1929-31 was an entirely exceptional experience of a kind that will never again have to be faced? I don't think it can assume any such thing. But it does. Labour had a policy for calm weather; no policy for crisis, in a world that is now in a permanent state of crisis.

I am writing in 1939, eight years after the downfall of the Labour Government; eight years in which fascism has come to power in Germany, Austria, Czechoslovakia, Spain; but the British Labour Party sleeps on. It still looks at the world obliquely through a nineteenth-century mirror. It has not awakened to the dangerous challenge of contemporary things. Perhaps it is afraid to awake. Perhaps consciously or unconsciously it knows that once it wakes a lovely dream will be shattered for ever. The dream embodied in MacDonald's early socialist writings. The dream that official Labour still lives by. Belief in the possibility of Labour Governments being allowed to carry through one piece of social reform after another and so, gradually, step by step, forward to socialism. The belief that the ruling class of England will allow itself to be legislated out of existence. It sounds incredible after its

1931 experiences and all that has happened in Europe since, that any vestige of that early faith should still remain. But it does. And so far as it has died only fear seems to have taken its place, fear expressing itself in bitter hostility towards any socialist or group of socialists who attempt to present a revised version of socialist philosophy, strategy and economics more in keeping with contemporary realities.

After the collapse of the Labour Government I wrote to Sir Charles Trevelyan asking him about MacDonald in Parliament during the war years. His reply confirmed what the best of our local socialists had always maintained.

'As to J.R.M. I can't altogether disentangle my early and later feelings about him. I began very uncritical. I could not regard him as other than courageous. But I always found him avoiding straight issues. I was concerned with the U.D.C. He, Morel, Angel and I founded it. Certainly Morel and I did the chief of the work. Ramsay didn't hinder but didn't inspire. In the early part of the war he mostly lay low. In the House of Commons he took no part. During 1915 first Ponsonby, then I, then Snowden spoke. It required courage. I remember John Burns, a gallant, vain man, coming in and cheering me as if I were a popular leader, in a frigid house. It was a manly, human thing to do. And Asquith (quite justifiably) referred to the twittering of a sparrow in a hurricane.

'Such experience did not feed vanity in any way. Not till some time after did Ramsay speak. He thought he would be howled down. In that sense he was afraid. But I doubt if he was physically a coward. There were a few nasty meetings, and he at least went through with them. But he certainly hadn't the contemptuous indifference of Snowden, or Morel's challenging readiness to face contempt or death.

'Of course, his dominating anxiety was always not to make a decision. Every time our little band wanted to move and speak in the House of Commons he was against it. But Ponsonby, Snowden and I knew our minds and always got our way, and when the debates came he always spoke quite loyally and well. But we made the policy of peace by negotiation; he would never have ventured it. I think during the war he had a certain courage. But I always have had a feeling that he was caught and felt it. He had expected to lead

a big flock of Labour, perhaps international Labour, and there he
was with a miserable remnant of stern pacifists. He wouldn't perhaps have done it if it had been to do again. That is what I feel
about him.

'The vanity, which has now eaten away his soul, was in the first
beginnings protective. He clung to what worship of him there was
in those dark, cold days and got his solace there, where stronger
men got it in the sense they were doing a damnably unpleasant job
but less unpleasant than that of the poor devils in the trenches they
were trying to save.

'If *his* speech at Glasgow was an oratorical success he glowed.
If *mine* was a success, I could say "thank God there are some of the
people yet who are worth bearing the grim, political solitude for.
Thank their good hearts and sane heads."

'When fortune began to come his way, he knew himself for a
really great man, which was his undoing. I am sure he deteriorated.
For I cannot pretend to have had deeper doubts of him till I began
to see him at work in the Cabinet, and clashed with him over the
Zinoviev letter, and gasped at "easy, oozy fools".'

MacDonald's desertion was spiritual death to thousands of
Labour people who had worshipped him. That he should have left
them was beyond comprehension.

I was not affected that way for I had grown up in an environment intensely critical of MacDonald. Even his war record was
regarded sceptically by many Fifeshire colliers. They declared that
during the war Morel, Snowden, Trevelyan and others could be
got to take any risk, speak anywhere, but MacDonald preferred to
keep out of difficult areas until others had plunged in before
him and tested the temperature.

The general body of Labour voters cannot be blamed for having
trusted and adored the man. They saw only the fine actor declaiming his eloquent pieces. But those close to him and working within
the party machine knew a very different MacDonald. In the end he
was able to lead his party to disaster. For that the Parliamentary
Labour Party of 1929-31 must carry a very heavy burden of
responsibility.

Throughout the whole period of the Labour Government, a

handful of us tried in vain to rouse our socialist colleagues to some sense of their individual responsibility.

In the Parliamentary Labour Party it was not the shepherds who frightened me. Nor yet the plain, ordinary party hacks. Every political party has a percentage of ambitious people ready to do anything that carries the hope of promotion. You are a fool if you don't expect to find that sort of thing and to have to reckon with it. I was prepared for that. But what I was totally unprepared for was the behaviour of the solid rows of decent, well-intentioned, unpretentious Labour back-benchers. In the long run it was they who did the most deadly damage. Again and again an effort was made to rouse them from their inertia. On every occasion they reacted like a load of damp cement. They would see nothing, do nothing, listen to nothing that had not first been given the seal of MacDonald's approval.

The I.L.P. group to which I belonged was bitterly attacked by the rest of the Labour Party for opposing the Government on the floor of the House. We were told that if we had any criticism to make, the place to raise our objections was in the private meetings of the Parliamentary Labour Party.

These meetings were the crowning ignominy of that unhappy time. Day after day MacDonald and Snowden were dragging us nearer disaster. The I.L.P. group protested. Sir Charles Trevelyan resigned from the Cabinet and in his speech of resignation baldly, without trimmings of any kind, informed his Parliamentary colleagues that they would do no good until they got rid of MacDonald. Sir Oswald Mosley and a few bright young men he had gathered around him carried on a separate guerrilla warfare on their own. But none of the dissenters had the least success. Baffled and furious more than once in those private meetings of the Party I found myself muttering Joe Corrie's 'A' to Keep in Wi' the Gaffir'.[1] That was probably very wicked of me. The majority of my colleagues may have genuinely agreed with the policy of Mac-Donald and Snowden. But if they did, just so much more pitiful become their later denunciations of their leaders.

When the final collapse came the majority of Labour's suppor-

[1] A satirical poem after the style of the 'Vicar of Bray'. Written in collier dialect.

ters throughout the country did not see things my way. They refused to admit that MacDonald's crossing to the Tory benches was the end of a process. They preferred to regard it as an isolated and infamous act. In a howl of bitter execration, they called for MacDonald's blood. MacDonald's old henchmen obligingly stepped forward and led them in the burning of his effigy. That was the cheapest and safest thing for them to do. Much easier than facing up to a serious analysis of what had gone wrong, to a recognition that MacDonald's defection was merely a superficial by-product; that the causes of Labour's failure went much deeper than that. The first time I voted against the Labour Government I did so with the greatest reluctance. The I.L.P. group magnificently led by John Wheatley (whose death was a major political tragedy for the whole socialist movement, not just for the small group of us who were most closely associated with him) set itself up as a kind of unofficial opposition to MacDonald. It did so from the very first days of the Labour Government. I thought that unfair. 'Give them time,' I urged. 'Give them a chance. The Government is dependent on Liberal votes before it can pass a single piece of legislation. Its hands are tied. It is unreasonable to expect too much. Perhaps the Cabinet has some sort of plan and is manoeuvring for the right moment to bring it forward.'

But the summer months dragged on, winter came, the unemployed were as badly off as ever, no serious work schemes were attempted and we were all supposed to pin our faith to the increasingly tenuous utterances of Mr. Ramsay MacDonald.

At first I had voted against the Government rather gingerly and with considerable doubts as to whether or not that was the right thing to do. But I became increasingly convinced that there was no effective answer to those who claimed that what such a Government did not attempt in its first months of office, it would not do at all. I knew all the careful arguments that the party manager could muster for avoiding at all costs the defeat of the Government until it had had a run for several years. A second general election within a year or eighteen months of the last meant a terrific strain on the Party's finances. That was serious. But there were worse calamities. I believe in teaching by doing. The great mass of people are not politically minded. I wanted to see the Labour Party attempt something concrete and understandable. I did not mind which of a number of things it was—nationalization of mines, fulfilment of election pledges to the unemployed, or say, to old-age pensioners. The onus would then lie with the Liberal Party either to give the Government the necessary majority or explain to the country why it had refused to do so. I did not even feel certain that a quick, firm stand of that kind would have brought in profitable party dividends, measured in terms of votes, at the election that might have been precipitated. But again, it did not seem to me the job of a socialist party always to trim its sails so that it might in all circumstances win the maximum number of votes. People have to learn by experience. If another Tory Government got itself elected in the midst of the world-wide economic depression of 1930-31, I did not see that that need have been the end of the world or even of the Labour Party. The country would have been left with the memory of a straightforward, honourable effort on the part of Labour to fulfil its election promises. That memory would have stood Labour in good stead when people were once again in the mood to turn our way. There is no shame in fighting and being overcome by superior numbers. Shame comes when a party refuses to fight, however elaborate the reasons it may produce for running away.

If MacDonald had had a sense of humour, you might have thought it was some puckish whim on his part that made him appoint Mr. J. H. Thomas as a kind of emergency Minister of Action to deal with unemployment, giving him Sir Oswald Mosley and George Lansbury as his assistants. That was one of the Prime Minister's many stalling devices. Nothing got done, but the new appointment sounded fine, made a useful talking point for a month or two and kept the wolves of reality from the door. If J. H. Thomas had not been an important and influential Labour leader I would have found him good fun. He was a merry scamp. When I met him in the evenings bulging out of his dress shirt I could never help grinning. He looked so exactly like the caricatures of himself that you had to prod him to see if he were real. It would have been all very funny if there had not been millions of destitute people desperate for work and looking to him to make some serious effort to meet their needs. But that was something that neither he nor his Cabinet colleagues seemed able or willing to do. I watched Sir Oswald Mosley ably assisted by John Strachey try again and again to break through the Government's inertia. Failing to make any headway, Mosley next tried campaigning among private members of the Parliamentary party. He had not the least success. What MacDonald did not initiate or at least sanction, the Faithful would not even consider. Very likely Mosley's insane vanity would have attracted him towards the role of fascist *Führer* even without his experiences within the Labour Party. But I wish that the blistering contempt that he developed around 1930 for the 'yes' men with whom MacDonald surrounded himself, had had less to justify it. Mosley's wealth and arrogance fenced him off from the ordinary worthwhile dependable rank and file of the Labour Movement. He knew next to nothing of this, the Party's greatest asset. He knew everything there was to know about its liabilities, about the tired, cynical, profoundly reactionary elements that occupy an alarmingly high percentage of official posts. Mosley had no roots in the working-class movement. It was emotionally as easy for him to leave it as it had been for him to join it. There was nothing in his memories, values, traditional loyalties to prevent him buying himself a black shirt, a bodyguard and setting out to indulge his spleen against the whole socialist movement, and everyone and everything associated with it, to the last bitter dregs.

The small I.L.P. group with which I worked during the period of the Labour Government, had as little to do with Mosley as with MacDonald. We shied suspiciously at the approach of both. But we were keenly concerned to see the Labour Government make some attempt to keep its work or maintenance pledge to the unemployed. Private Members of Parliament and groups of Members deluged Mr. J. H. Thomas's department with suggestions for work schemes. Many of these proposals may have been impracticable. Mr. J. H. Thomas assured us all of them were. He negatived almost every suggestion. And put very little in their place.

It was this negativing propensity of the Labour Government that tried everyone inside the Parliamentary Labour Party who was energetic and concerned more sorely than anything else. It drove everyone under forty to the verge of madness. We all went off at a tangent. Mosley, Dr. Forgan, John Beckett to fascism. John

Strachey to Communism, Oliver Baldwin and W. J. Brown to positions as independents, myself to a disaffiliated I.L.P.

Anuerin Bevan was about the only one of the younger Members with a sound anti-inertia record who remained within the official machine. He argued day and night with John Strachey and myself in an effort to make us do likewise. At that time Strachey had committed himself to co-operating with Mosley in forming the New Party. Bevan argued vociferously against this course. 'Where is the money coming from ?' he demanded. 'Who is going to pay ? Who is going to call the tune ? I tell you now where you will end up. You will end up as a fascist party. I tell you——'

Then turning to me—I was bent on what I called 'keeping faith' with the best of our Scottish I.L.P. even to the point of remaining with them if they should decide to leave the Labour Party—'And as for you, I tell you what the epitaph of your Scottish dissenters is going to be—pure, but impotent. Yes, you will be pure all right. But remember, at the price of impotency. You will not influence the course of British politics by as much as a hair's-breadth. Why don't you get into a nunnery and be done with it ? Lock yourself up in a separate cell away from the world and its wickedness. My Salvation Army lassie. Poor little Casabianca. That was a hell of an intelligent performance now, wasn't it ? I tell you, it is the Labour Party or nothing. I know all its faults, all its dangers. But it is the party that we have taught millions of working people to look to and regard as their own. We can't undo what we have done. And I am by no means convinced that something cannot yet be made of it.' I had many other friends inside the Labour Party who made the same sort of appeal to me. I tried hard to school myself to respond. But a sick feeling in the pit of my stomach held me back.

It was true that some of those with whom I was asked to associate in rebuilding the public's faith in our *bona fides* were fine, honourable men and women with a self-forgetful devotion to the cause of socialism. But an uncomfortable number of the others seemed to me quite empty inside. They dared not disbelieve in public for believing was their trade. But in private their cynicism chilled everything they touched with the stale atmosphere of decay.

9

AMERICAN LECTURE TOUR

IN the November 1931 election when the MacDonald-
Baldwin 'National Government' was returned, I, in common
with so many other socialist candidates, was defeated at the
polls. I had to make up my mind what I intended to do next. There
was nothing I wanted to do. Nothing, that is, except read, take
time for reflection, renew contacts with the rank-and-file of the
Scottish movement, find out how much human material was
available for starting all over again. I still believed that we could
build a socialist movement that not only talked about winning
power, but really wanted power and would know what to do with
it once it had it. This 'nothing', therefore, was a full time, exhaust-
ing occupation.

But it did not provide any salary. It required me to find money
elsewhere to pay for food and lodgings. I had to unearth, therefore,
some kind of side-line so that my stomach might sustain me while my
convictions were trying to sustain the tattered remnants of our I.L.P.

It was under these compulsions that I first approached America.
Long before my time Labour notables, large and small, had established a regular trade route between Great Britain and the States.
Old hands put me 'wise' to the ropes. First, you find an agent who
will advertise your wares. It is the agent's job to approach the
infinite number of colleges, town forums, foreign policy associa-
tions, women's clubs, men's clubs, peace groups and the rest in
which America abounds, inquiring who wants to have you come
to lecture them and how much they are prepared to pay. The
agent deducts his commission, and you pay all your travelling
expenses and, if you are lucky—if—you return home with the
trade balance in your favour.

The fortunes of the American lecture world are, to say the least, varied. Socialists, anarchists, communists, liberals, fascists, conservatives and republicans from every corner of the globe jostle one another for the ear of the American public.

An agent's job is a highly-skilled affair. He knows how to build up the right kind of 'story' about each new prodigy in turn. Americans like piquancy and, if you go there to lecture, you are going to be made piquant whether you like it or not. I found, to my infinite embarrassment, that wherever I went I was resplendently introduced in terms that almost knocked me unconscious.

I had been speaking from coal carts at an age when other children are still in their cradles. I was Hypatia, Portia and Jenny Geddes all in one. I was the youngest woman ever to have been elected to the British House of Commons.

If I had been the fattest woman who had ever swum the Atlantic, or the saltiest sailor who had ever climbed to the top of the North Pole, I could not have been more highly acclaimed.

This phase did not last long. I rapidly deteriorated in market value and on the last occasion I visited America, was thrown around the country at cut-rate bargain prices.

No ordinary commercial agent could be expected to put up with me. I was constantly falling through the hoop and landing on my behind beside a group of striking miners, or in Uncle Tom's Cabin where he and I and all his coloured family had a grand old time together. But there was no money in it!

I loved the south. When you arrive in Memphis, the soft husky voices ask if you are going to the 'deep' south. The 'deep' south! I liked the sweet tang of that. It means down to New Orleans. And so I was. I was prepared to go down just as deep as they could make it.

Cortes, 'silent upon a peak in Darien,' was not more pleased with himself than I was first time I penetrated as far south as the Gulf of Mexico. It was February and, by all my northern standards, it ought to have been cold and disagreeable. Instead, the world was a festival of sunshine and flowers, scarlet and purple and gold, flaunting ones, gentle ones. I know very few flowers by name. But I know lots of them by their character. My idea of wealth is to have masses of flowers.

In the Gulf of Mexico in February, I felt like an illegitimate millionaire. I was rolling in wealth and all at the wrong time of the year too!

But I doubt if I should have loved the south so much if I had just regarded it as a spectacle. It was its people that held me most. It was the coloured people and their unaffected ways and their quick laughter and their brown skins and their plentiful piccaninnies and their voice and their songs. And, tying us in close fraternity, the pathos of their tentative first efforts to organize industrial unions.

At Mark Tree, about two hours' car ride from Memphis, I had my sharpest taste of the bitter behind the sweet of this deluding south.

In the early months of the year the cotton plantations are brown and bare. The only things that catch the eye are the tumble-down wooden shacks dotted about the fields, some of them hanging at such an angle that you hold your breath, waiting for them to fall over.

White families lived in some. Coloured folks in others. They were all share-croppers and all nakedly poor. We had come out to form a union and to invite black workers and white workers and workers of all the shades in between, to join together in the one organization. But the Sheriff and his thugs decided no meeting should be permitted. At the edge of the town we were met and warned off.

The group of poor, white share-croppers who were waiting for us were downcast at the news. We looked at one another, I trying to sense what to say. I was keen to go on with the meeting, but conscious of my safe British passport tucked inside my dispatch-case. I was just a passer-by. It was the local people who would have to suffer any consequences.

When labour trouble breaks out in the south, you can get shot and you can get beaten up. A young union organizer was killed in this area a short time after this. But those seemed remote possibilities. More likely I might, at worst, be gaoled for a night—that is nothing in America. It happens more often and means less than it would in this country.—But if gaoled or deported the story would be 'news'. It would be featured in the press. It would bring down on my head profitable invitations from well-to-do lecture organizations to come and tell them all about it. I could not quite put my finger on it, but there seemed to me to be something wrong in that sort of alignment. But America was like that. One-half was always anxious to pay me for lecturing to it about things that the other half wanted to gaol or deport me for.

When I explained my scruples to the local committee, they were jubilant. They had been hesitating only on my account. If I was game to speak then, somehow, they would fix up a meeting.

The compromise they made, in face of the Sheriff and his gun-men, was to drive a lorry into the fields just outside the boundaries of the town, then the word was sent round that it was there we were going to meet.

I stood by the side of the lorry watching the crowd assemble. From all points of the compass, the outcasts of the south came slowly towards us. At first in twos and threes. Then in larger numbers. Some were white. Most were coloured. Around the lorry they were jumbled up all together. It was time now for the meeting to begin. Presiding over our meeting, to my infinite delight, we had old Uncle Tom himself. He had on his frayed, black frock-coat and his benevolent air just as I had pictured him in my childhood's story-book.

He opened the meeting with prayer. He blessed the meeting and blessed the union and blessed the town and blessed the president. I think even God was given his blessing. He was followed by the union organizer, who briefly explained the purpose for which we had met.

Another stranger, who had blown in from somewhere, was Naomi Mitchison. Naomi, rather breathless, fervent and kind, as always, was asked to speak for five minutes.

I don't think those simple children of the south understood much of what she said, but they felt that she was all right and counted her in.

It was now my turn. What an audience! I had met nothing like it. We could easily have worked upon one another's feelings until we became a kind of political holy rollers. I held myself in check as well as I could. When I concluded, the audience, which had been standing all the time, seemed to rise. Raising its arms heaven-wards, it chanted in unison a hymn of union solidarity:

We will not be moved,
We will not be moved,
Like a tree, planted by the river,
We—will not—be moved.

That was the general refrain, repeated with infinite variations and going all the way up and down the keyboard. It was their own language. It was a negro-spiritual. It was their own inimitable way of saying that they would stand by one another and not allow themselves to be intimidated. And it was sung as only angels and negro plantation workers know how.

After that, the whole demonstration walking two by two, the platform party leading, moved slowly towards the town. We walked warily, singing the union hymn and watching for the Sheriff and his men.

That day they did not interfere. They let us pass. So I had to wait until I was among white workers, entirely and exclusively white, before I saw America's rawest side.

I had heard of Harlem County, the coalfield where no union was tolerated, where the coal companies openly employed armed thugs and where any man or woman who dared challenge their authority was shot or gaoled or beaten up and run out over the county line.

But in 1932 President Roosevelt was not yet on the map. The class war was being waged in the Kentucky mining-camps without even a loin-cloth around its middle.

Quite alone, a mere observer, I arrived in Harlem. Within an hour, two ruffians broke into my hotel bedroom. I was talking with the wife of one of the local miners' leaders. It was the miner himself I had expected to meet, but he had been beaten up and thrown over the county line shortly before I arrived.

One of the two invaders lurched forward, attempted to grip my wrist and snarled, 'I guess we'll keep you.' They were disgusting-looking toughs, and it was all so like a badly-acted improbable Hollywood production that my fury was tempered with disbelief. No, this was not real. This was a caricature of reality.

The voice of the outraged Britisher—it has its uses if you don't happen to be up against your own authorities—held them back. I ordered them to give me an account of who they were and what they thought they were doing.

One explained that he was the mayor of the town. The other that he was the chief of the police. Both chorused that they had been told I was another goddam reporter from New York and that they had had enough of other people nosing into their affairs. They were sorry, lady, but they had to keep the town in order. There were a lot of tough characters around.

Afterwards, with these two guardians of law and order at my heels, I went on a sightseeing expedition. At the local gaol I was able to get into communication with some of our organizers, a young Y.W.C.A. secretary and a reporter or two, who, sure enough, were all tidily locked up inside.

Next day I contrived to get off on my own to the mining settlements a few miles outside the town. There I found families living in a pre-Truck Act age, with the company store flourishing and a starving and terrorized community answering violence with violence, for nothing else was allowed it.

Later, I met the miners of Gillespie, Illinois. Compared with Kentucky they seemed peaceful and prosperous. But, if you go among them, they too can tell you stories of the class war fought out fist for fist and gun for gun.

I had no thought of going to Gillespie until the miners themselves sent repeated messages insisting that I must. Then, at last, I went—laugh if you like—because I heard that one of the Gillespie miners had worked beside my father in Lochgelly and others had emigrated from our part of Fife. We had a boisterous time together. A packed public meeting, a feast in the village hall, a presentation from the children, another from the grown-ups and, later in the evening, when we gathered in one of the miner's houses—there was no fireside to sit around, but everything else was homelike—what tales! what tales! Lochgelly battles, Gillespie battles, all fought over again, with the children listening-in as I in my own home so often had listened, to this, their own, superb and little recorded history.

There is a great deal more on the other side of the Atlantic besides mining-camps and cotton-plantations. Even I could not help but notice that. The eager, restless mood of great masses of

Americans is for ever sweeping them off in half a dozen contra-
dictory directions at once. But, at least, they sweep. They don't
stagnate. I could never quite make up my mind whether this was
the finest or the damd'dest country in the world. It has wide islands
of civilized living, then plomp, down you plunge into raging
currents of savagery.

I totally failed to form any coherent picture of America. I don't
think it can be done. And the more Americans explained America to
me, the more blurred the pattern became.

On the evening I arrived in New York, Maurice Hindus took
me to a party. Everybody who writes books in the whole of America
seemed to be there. It was probably all very pleasant but so hot and
crammed and noisy that I wanted to go home. Maurice was enjoying himself among friends. He had no intention of taking me
home. Instead he piloted me from one group of fierce conver-
sationalists to another, ending up in the corner of the room where
Sinclair Lewis had betaken himself. I was niecly introduced and
for at least the tenth time that evening had America explained to
me. But this time I got something to hold on to. I was interested
and entertained, for Sinclair Lewis talked about his country in the
way that a younger and more aggressive David Kirkwood used to
talk about Scotland: a kick and a caress comically mixed up together in every sentence.

At lunch the following day Walter Lippman gave me a much
more formal school text-book sketch of the U.S.A. I had to
remember that each State was a law unto itself, that the federal
principle meant a total lack of uniformity, that I could go out and
find whatever I set out to find, beauty, terror, fine living, unbeatable
squalor. And, above all, I had to remember that America had drawn
its population from every part of the world. That, in itself, presented terrific educational and economic problems.

And so ding-dong, one after the other, all crammed into my first
week on the other side of the Atlantic, I listened to representative
Americans describing their country.

It is, maybe, just perversity on my part, but it was those of them
who made no attempt at all at official flag-waving who left me with
the best feeling towards America. I am thinking of men like
Norman Thomas, Scott Nearing, Roger Baldwin, Professor John

Dewey, Garfield Hays, John Dos Passos. I listened to their criticisms of the society they lived in but also took note that they too were part of that society. That evened things up quite a bit.

When I was ready to return to England a telegram arrived for me from the idealistic young man, who, at that time, was secretary of the National Canadian Clubs. It was an invitation to spend a month in Canada as the guest-speaker of the clubs. I had plenty of free time just then so I wired back saying I was on my way.

Once in Ottawa I found it difficult to know whether I was standing on my head or my heels; whether to treat the whole affair seriously or as a huge joke. For there I was, dumped solemnly in the centre of an enormous stuffed-shirt type of luncheon party with the then Prime Minister, Mr. W. B. Bennett, on my right hand, and Mr. Mackenzie King on my left. Someone, just before we took our seats, whispered to me that the two men had no affection for one another. It was to be up to me to keep everything going nicely.

When everyone had reached the coffee and cigarettes stage the president announced that I would now give a lecture on 'The Younger Generation in Soviet Russia'. And so I did. Very willingly. It was evident that Russia had few friends in that very official assembly. Because of that I praised it all the more ardently. If the U.S.S.R. lives up to just one-tenth of what I promised in its name, it will be doing very well indeed.

A bit alarmed by the luncheon I decided I had better find out what sort of jamboree this was that I had let myself in for. What was it all about ? Why had I been asked ?

I got hold of the idealistic young secretary. Looking a bit reckless, worried and rather pleased all in one, he explained. The club was a non-party association. Its guest-speakers from England were usually high Tories or Liberals. He had got the idea that having heard Tory and Liberal versions of European affairs over and over again, it was only fair that club members should now hear what a British socialist had to say. So here I was.

That seemed to me reasonable enough. So I set off across Canada. And even within the carefully cotton-woolled atmosphere of the clubs I met many fine people who helped me to see a good deal of the real working life of their country.

I don't keep a diary and have forgotten the name of the small agricultural centre somewhere to the west of Lake Winnipeg, where I spent my pleasantest evening under club auspices. But I don't forget the gathering of working farmers and their wives and families who were my hosts that evening. I had wandered a long way from the formal atmosphere of Ottawa.

That was in the winter of 1932. Canada, like the rest of the world, was in the doldrums. Its poorer farmers were going through hell. But that particular evening they were bent on forgetting their cares, and one after another drove up in their antiquated Fords and still more antiquated buggies to a barn-like building that had been made into a banquet hall for the occasion. It was to be a supper-party, a dance, a sing-song and a meeting all in one. Someone had put a small piece of heather on my plate. I was the guest of honour. They intended to do me proud.

I heard good radical talk that evening. But what I remember best is the way we all stood up around the great supper-table and how much I enjoyed myself when instead of the usual pious national anthem there came thundering about my ears a chorus that went something like this: 'Hor-sie, keep your tail up, keep your tail up, keep your tail up,—Horsie, keep your tail up,—When the spring comes you'll get corn.'

You need the noise and the tune and the atmosphere before you can catch on to what it was all about. The song and the singing were just a bit of fun. Part of the jollifications. No one tried to draw tiresome morals. But I am certain the reason why I remember them so especially was that both at the time and in looking back they seemed to me a pretty good summary of the lives of the people I had wandered in among.

But it was the wild geese who came flocking to meet me wherever I went who taught me most about Canada. People from the derelict parts of Scotland, people without money, without influence, uprooted from their former homes because there was no work for them there and now finding Canada's welcome colder than its coldest winter day.

One of the sights to be seen in most Canadian cities that winter were the queues where unemployed men lined up for food rations. I was taken along to have a look at them. I am not good at that kind of sight-seeing; stepping forward squired by the official in charge; invited to taste the soup to see for yourself that it is not at all bad. You need a tough skin to do that kind of thing well. I found myself averting my eyes from the long line of shabby men standing quietly and patiently waiting for food. Why should I invade their privacy ? Stare at them as if they were so many animals on parade ?

How would I like to be stared at if I were standing in such a queue ? But it was a different matter when two of the unemployed men started signalling to me and I turned and saw who they were. They were old friends. They had worked with me in the North Lanark by-election. So we got together and first they insisted on hearing all my news, then they started telling me about themselves. They were willing enough to talk—but on terms. I had to promise that when I went back to Scotland if I met any of their relations I would not 'let on' how and where I had met them. They were down on their luck, but they would get over it 'and there is no sense, see Jennie, in worrying ma mither!'

It was the same old story, wild geese on the wing and wanted nowhere. In Canada families that had been ratepayers in a fixed place for a certain number of years and then found themselves out of work, had a chance of being provided for in a bald kind of way. But no place would accept responsibility for newcomers. Recent immigrants had the worst time of all. If they arrived in a town in search of employment they might be permitted to sleep there overnight (as likely as not housed in the local gaol) but in the morning they had to move on. If they looked like giving 'trouble' a police-escort accompanied them to the city boundaries.

It is a crazy world. At that time we were all already being deafened by the German and Japanese clamour for more territory. Poor little Japan (so it said) could not feed its teeming millions through lack of land. (But it could afford to maintain a most expensive military caste and fantastically costly arms equipment!) Germany the same. Both governments howled, give us more space and we will make our people happy and prosperous.

Well, here was Canada, 3,694,843 square miles, a population of under twelve millions, short of colonizing the moon no state could hope to have more territory at its disposal, yet wherever I went I was finding poverty and unemployment.

Canada must always remain for me an unsatisfactory jumble of irreconcilable elements. It treated me as a privileged guest. Club officials, Labour Members of Parliament, even its very Conservative Prime Minister, seemed to take a paternal interest in seeing that I missed nothing they considered worth seeing. I don't forget and I am not ungrateful. If a little flattery and a lot of spoiling could blind the eyes and still the tongue, all I need do is curtsey and nicely say thank you very much, I enjoyed the party. But the wild geese who gave me their unofficial welcome wherever I went meant more to me than all the rest. I had known some of them in Scotland. Others who came to my meetings or found other ways of getting in touch with me had never met me before but perhaps knew the district I came from, or perhaps just wanted to hear a Scotch voice or to ask about places and people that had once been their whole life. Sometimes just to shake hands and hurry away blinded by tears.

I hate the foul business of a nation pretending to be just one nice big family when it is no such thing. No class society can be a reputable 'family'. All that happens is that well-to-do patriots sing their own praises so loudly that they cannot even hear the cry of those they are trampling underfoot. And if at any moment the cries of the poor threaten to drown the Hallelujah chorus of the prosperous, then legislation is rushed through Parliament (if it is not already on the statute book), the soldiers and the police are brought out, a 'state of emergency' is declared, and at the wrong end of a machine-gun if need be, the poor are taught that it is dangerous even to complain.

I did not, of course, need to cross the Atlantic to learn anything so elementary. But a new setting, new situations, underlined the old problems that I had lived with all my life. I was eager to be home again. I have a lot of restlessness in me. I like travelling, new places, new people, new experiences. But, best of all, I like the return journey, the coming back to where you have roots that go very deep down into the earth, the coming back to familiar places and people. I have heard it said that that is a collier trait; that we have this homing instinct more strongly than most. I don't believe it. I think most people have the same need. One of the most ghastly sorrows in the world to-day is the tragedy of the millions of people who, because they are poor or because they are Jews or because of their politics or religion can find harbourage nowhere. Uprooted, unwanted, wild geese flapping their pitiful wings from country to country.

I am totally incapable of parcelling out these unfortunates into separate groups. They are all part of a common indictment against the economic and cultural values of capitalist society.

Nowadays I don't use abstract words such as capitalist, socialist, fascist, democratic any oftener than I can help. I am profoundly distrustful of them. For each of us, according to our social background and political leanings, means something different when we use such terms. I wish politicians would stop using them altogether. That would not of itself solve any of our problems. But if, instead, they would use concrete and particular language, we might at least begin to understand what our problems are. You can quarrel for ever over an abstract phrase and not even come to any common agreement as to what it is that you are quarrelling about.

The later chapters of this book would be easier for me to write if I had not such a hearty dislike of abstract generalizations that can mean anything or nothing. And that covers a great deal of current political jargon. Take the word 'socialism', for instance. At one time I was for ever using it. In my own mind I gave it exact and satisfactory content. I thought it quite all right to use it as a kind of shorthand to indicate the economic and cultural values I would like to see governing the world. But it has since been dirtied by every kind of contemptible and equivocal usage.

Hitler borrowed it for the name of his party. MacDonald clung to it to the end of his life. The Labour Party swears by it and, at the same time, by the King and the Royal Family and knighthoods for Labour leaders and full compensation even for millionaires with shares in any industry a future Labour Government might venture to nationalize.

Hitler, MacDonald, the official manifestoes of the British Labour Party, may interpret the word correctly. But if they do I have been using it falsely all my life and just haven't the faintest notion as to what it actually means.

I think, therefore, I had better continue to tell a rather personal story, hoping that in the telling, by the time I catch up with the present, it may all sum up to give at least some general notion of the compulsions that have driven me to write at all. But I cannot be sure of that. I must take the risk. And anyhow, for a bit yet, it is not so difficult for me to write on. For I am looking back seven years, which is almost the same as saying, looking back to life on another planet.

10

INTO THE WILDERNESS

IN 1932 most of us still felt we could plan for the future, be leisurely and casual, wilful and unconcerned. There was not the present grim tension in the air. But even then the atmosphere was quite tense enough for those of us who by temperament and circumstance were keenly involved in political happenings. Politics, for me, means the fight against poverty. That is what it meant to working people in the days of the Chartist agitations. That is what it has always meant and always will mean. Well-to-do liberals find it very hard to understand that. Sometimes they totally fail to do so and when and where that happens, poor people betray them to fascism. For libertarian principles, 'democracy', 'civil liberties', lose all vitality whenever an attempt is made to call a truce in the fight against poverty. Poor people look on political liberties primarily as instruments to be used in fighting their economic battles. Democratic institutions used aggressively on their behalf can count on their allegiance. But they are just not interested in a passive kind of democracy that expects them to put up quietly with a ten-shilling old-age pension, means tests, and slums.

The main source of my disillusionment with the Labour Government of 1929-31 was that it was far too half-hearted and apologetic in fighting the battles of the poor.

I expected nothing from Tory government so they had no power to wound me. But for me a Labour Government was a very different matter.

When I got back from America in the spring of 1932 I was still in a mood of violent revulsion at the memory of how shabbily poor people had been treated by the Government they had worked so hard to create. I knew all the official excuses: none of them satisfied me.

All the same, when the Independent Labour Party at its annual conference that same year decided to break off all organizational contact with the Labour Party, I had considerable misgivings as to whether or not that was a wise thing to do.

I envied some of my I.L.P. friends who were able to see the whole situation in terms of biblical simplicity. For them it was as uncomplicated as a Passion Play. It was a struggle between Right and Wrong, Good and Evil. The Labour Party had become in their eyes a kind of political anti-Christ. It besmirched, it betrayed, the True Faith.

I was intellectually impatient of that kind of mumbo-jumbo, but emotionally a good deal under its influence. I did not want to leave the Labour Party. But I did not see how I could do otherwise. I did not see how I could go on making socialist speeches for a party some of whose leaders I was as much out at elbows with as I had been with MacDonald, whose programme I could accept only with considerable reservations and whose structure was such that it was arithmetically impossible to amend either its leadership or its policy however hard one might campaign inside the local Labour Parties.

It was that last point I stuck on more than any other. It is so important and explains so much that may seem mysterious to the outsider trying to understand how to account for the behaviour of the British working-class movement that I want to return to it later in greater detail. I did not want to leave the Labour Party. I dreaded the kind of dog fight that was bound to develop in North Lanark once rival I.L.P. and Labour Party candidates took the field. I longed for a nice, easy, straightforward political situation in which there would be two great parties in the State and only two. The workers *versus* the rest. I had taken it for granted in all my growing years that my special job in life was to fight coalowners and all they stand for. I loved that particular fight. It raised no divisions inside myself. It was unanswerably, triumphantly worthwhile. It was a fight for bread. It was more than that. It was a fight for status too. My grandfather and my father were proud men. So were their workmates. The thought of them as under-dogs, mere work-beasts labouring for the greater glory and profit of a caste-ridden plutocracy was intolerable. And such a plutocracy! It gave us 1914-18. Families like mine tried to stop the butchering. It gave us the vindictive reparation clauses of the Versailles Treaty. Families like mine tried to curb their rulers' greed. About ten years too late Britain's most distinguished economists began to talk a language that Fife colliers had made me familiar with while the post-war world was still in the making; while Germany could still have been securely won as a friend, a good neighbour, an invaluable ally in lifting to unprecedented new levels the whole standard of European life. Our people were wiser than all the pretentious highly-placed 'experts' who made such a parade of their learning. Their daily experiences made them so. They knew it was nonsense to talk of squeezing Germany until the pip squeaks. And they knew, too, humane considerations apart, that it was bad economics. Reparations paid in German coal might make the distribution of wealth between nations and within nations just a little more crazily lopsided than it already was. But what good would it do to the overworked underpaid German collier? Or to the British collier idle and hungry because his former market was being glutted by supplies from the Ruhr?

I did not want to leave the Labour Party. I wanted to take part in a political contest where the alignments were as energizingly simple as the one penny fairy-tale and two comic-cuts that had delighted my childhood. I wanted to slay all the dragons and set poor people free. I wanted it to be All of Us *versus* The Others.

But in 1932 the British working-class movement was in no mood to accommodate me. It had split into warring faction. Tempers were brittle and hearts sore with the memory of how utterly, abysmally, MacDonald and his Cabinet had failed. I had to choose. It had to be either Labour Party or I.L.P. It could not be both.

One of the ironies of that 1932 situation was that those who had been closest to MacDonald and who, after he left the Labour Party, stepped into leadership positions, immediately opened fire on those of us who had warned the movement where it was drifting, who had dared to criticize the Labour Government, and who, again and again had even voted against it. I found myself presented with an ultimatum. I was ordered to put my signature to a document in which I had to promise that I would never again 'misbehave' in the future as I had done in the past. The 'misbehaviour' in question being that I had found out MacDonald before they did and had dared to oppose the policies that led us to disaster. North Lanark Divisional Labour Party wrote inviting me to continue as Parliamentary Candidate for the division. But the condition they laid down was—I had to sign on the dotted line. I tried hard to bring myself to the point of signing. But, ultimately, the reply I sent was as follows: (It was written at a time when I still assumed that the word 'socialist' was self-explanatory.)

> 12 *Paul Street,*
> *Lochgelly,*
> *Fife.*
> 5th *August,* 1932.

Dear Mr. Lashley,

I have received a letter from the Secretary of Shotts Labour Party inviting me to accept nomination as prospective Labour Candidate for North Lanark, but regret it is not possible for me to do so.

In view of the three contests we have put through together and the devoted service that workers of every shade of Labour opinion have given in order to make the work of a Labour and Socialist Movement possible throughout the Division, I am anxious through you to make clear the reasons that force me to take this difficult and unpleasant stand. I have no personal grievances whatsoever against the Labour Party. It has showered kindnesses and opportunities of every kind upon me, and if at this moment I were consulting my own comfort and convenience, I should most certainly remain with the larger and more powerful organization.

But, as a socialist, it is quite impossible for me to give the written promises that are being demanded by the Labour Party as a condition of endorsement. I am more than willing to promise to support any future Labour Government so far as it is carrying out our socialist policy. But that promise will not be accepted by Party Headquarters. They are demanding that here and now I pledge myself to give unqualified support to any future Labour Cabinet irrespective of who may compose that Cabinet or what its policy may be. That I cannot do. It would be cowardly and hypocritical on my part to pretend that I can. So far as a Labour Cabinet is carrying out socialist policy the question of my loyalty does not arise. But if ever again a Labour Cabinet asked me to vote for Tory unemployment commissions and economy committees that I felt sure would produce reports to be used against the workers and unemployed, nothing would induce me to act otherwise than I did in the last Parliament. I stated my difficulty in this respect to high officials within the Labour Party and they replied that I had always the right to abstain from voting. That right is not enough. If a Labour Cabinet or any other Cabinet produces legislation that means reduced wages or worsened conditions for any section of workers, no socialist has the right to remain merely neutral. I must be free to support the socialist alternatives in keeping with pre-election promises and propaganda. That right I am definitely and categorically denied.

Hence I must carry on my socialist work outside the Labour Party. If I remained inside, I should feel every socialist speech I made a form of fraud. Any intelligent worker would be entitled to ask me if I could be trusted to act and vote as I spoke, and in reply to such a question I should be compelled to admit that I had already promised one hundred per cent obedience to any future Labour Government so that he could have no guarantee that I might not vote contrary to anything I might say. I know of no way of evading this point. If socialists are prepared to sign pledges that they do not really believe in, in order to save themselves from embarrassments and splits, then we cannot blame the ordinary worker if he becomes sceptical and distrusting of all of us, arguing that if we are willing to act so in such issues, he can have no certainty of our stability in other things.

I deeply regret that after the failure of the late Labour Government to stick to socialist policy the party machine is not directing its energies at present towards devising rules that would compel both Cabinet ministers and rank and file members in the future to stand by socialist policy and would deal promptly and effectively with any attempt to compromise the party by feeble or anti-socialist legislation. That I believe would have brought real unity to the movement and a sense that we really were preparing to make a serious socialist challenge to capitalism. The responsibility of the Labour Party in taking an exactly opposite course and forcing socialists to leave it at this moment rather than give up their right to vote and act as socialists as well as *talk* socialism, is a grave one. I can assure you that I hate and deplore the necessity of leaving the Labour Party, but hope that every socialist will do likewise rather than carry on a semblance of false unity when no real common purpose and intention remains.

May I express my gratitude and appreciation of the work that has been done by scores of good comrades in every part of the Division to make a Labour and socialist movement possible. I am fully conscious of the trust that North Lanark was prepared to put in me at an age that made the rest of the country gasp, and hope to go on attempting to justify that trust by doing what my socialist faith compels me to do.

I know that in 1926 when I helped to get MacDonald out of the I.L.P., many older people cried out treason and folly. I know that in the late Parliament the votes that I gave against wage-cuts and Tory economy committees were criticized and deplored at the time, although supported later. In the present issue I am convinced that time will once more be on my side.

A united working class is essential for the achievement of socialism but the preliminary to such real unity is that both high and low are pledged to carry out socialist policy. Such a pledge the Labour movement is not asking and will not accept. Instead it asks me to support future governments whether they act for or against socialist policy.

That I cannot do, so I must work elsewhere for the creation of a real socialist movement and hope in doing so to have the support of all workers who are more concerned about socialist action and principles than about an autocratic enforcement of rigid rules of discipline compelling acceptance of what might well prove as ineffective legislation as that of the last Parliament.

Yours sincerely,

JENNIE LEE.

Once my letter was in the post I felt very naked. The door-bell rang. When I saw Aneurin Bevan outside I had half a mind to pretend that I was not at home. But I had better get it over. I knew what I was in for. Pedant, bigot, Salvation Army lassie—all the familiar abuse flowed over my head. I myself had quite a command of invective. The bullying was by no means all on one side.

I could survive the anger of a friend of my own generation. What hurt much more was the sadness of some of the older people inside the Labour Party to whom I was deeply attached. Why did I do such a thing? Did I know what I was letting myself in for? What hope was there of any progress at all if socialist fought socialist? The Labour Party like every other party had its undesirable elements. Some of its leaders were not much use. But its rank and file? Where could you find such people? Loyal, uncomplaining, hard-working, selfless? Were they not worth sticking by?

I listened, impressed up to a point, but at the back of my mind struggling unsuccessfully to find words that would clarify what I felt about 'the splendid rank and file' argument. I did not deny it existed. I had no wish to deny it. I knew it to be true. But the structure of the party was such that at critical moments the will of the rank and file seemed never to prevail. I felt about the majority of ordinary people inside the Labour Party, as I felt about the great majority of people inside Germany. Who in his senses would deny that the average German means well, loves children, loves homely worth-while things, has a right to be proud of the contribution that Germans have made to music, to literature, to philosophy, to the sciences. But that did not alter the fact that Germany was a police state; that its people were not free; that individual judgment had been trampled underfoot; that whenever Hitler decided to embark on war, the will of the ordinary Germans simply would not count. Only that of the Führer and the small clique with whom he had surrounded himself.

In 1932 I was sadly, reluctantly driven to the conclusion that there was no real democracy inside the Labour Party, that the personal ascendancy of Ramsay MacDonald had been replaced by the cash plus voting power ascendancy of a trade union junta headed by Sir Walter Citrine and Mr. Ernest Bevin. The latter were no more to my liking than the former.

I had no choice but to remain with the I.L.P. I was by no means happy about my decision. I had no lack of personal friends inside the Labour Party who went to great pains to point out the unpleasant personal consequences that were bound to follow. That sent me off in search of reasons that might justify my staying with the larger organization. But the more I compared the structure, policy, programme and recent record of the two parties, the more convinced I became that my place was with the I.L.P.

And, of course, I hoped and trusted the British working-class movement would one day fulfil the promise of its early pioneer years. I looked eagerly both towards the I.L.P. and to the left wing inside the Labour Party to justify my hopes. One day, I told myself, these two streams would meet again!

11

THE RISE OF FASCISM

POLITICS, in the sense I use the word, continued to take up most of my time and energies. But I managed to sprawl around in a good number of other directions as well.

For one thing my home people wanted me to do something about the law degree I had collected in my student days. Someone put the idea into their heads that I ought to read for the Bar. In their own modest, unclamorous way they rather fancied the idea of seeing me strutting around in a curly grey wig. I don't think I took the proposition seriously for a single moment. There always seemed to me a Gilbert and Sullivan element in the whole thing. I took my politics seriously. Very little else. But I was at a loose end. I was no longer a Member of the House of Commons. And I had seen so many people let their minds go to seed by abandoning themselves exclusively to the making of propaganda speeches, that I wanted some balancing interests. Anyhow, for all sorts of reasons, muddled and otherwise, I got as far as becoming a member of Middle Temple and eating my way through a number of the ceremonial dinners that are part of the ritual that all intending barristers must observe.

A note arrived from Lord Sankey, then Lord Chancellor, inviting me to have tea with him in the House of Lords. There was nothing 'official' about his invitation. It was entirely a private matter.

I do not approve of Lord Sankey—not since he followed MacDonald into the National Government—but I have a great liking for him. The name Sankey means a lot to colliers. It is associated with the most hopeful period in our history. Bob Smillie giving evidence before the Sankey Commission; Lord Sankey, then Sir

John, presiding over the Commission and making no bones about his warm sympathy and concern for miners. Because of those memories, when first I came to London and was introduced to Sankey, I beamed goodwill—and he beamed back.

The next time I met him I had a young worker from a colliery village in Lanarkshire with me who had travelled four hundred and forty miles to see London and visit the House of Commons. It takes a lot of money to travel so far. I could guess what the saving of that money had meant. I was anxious to give him as good a time as I could. When we had had the inevitable tea on the Terrace and seen all that was to be seen in and around the Houses of Parliament, we walked along the embankment in the direction of the gardens that adjoin the House of Lords. I saw the Lord Chancellor approaching and told the young fellow who he was. I could see the eager interest with which he looked in Sankey's direction for, like me, he had grown up in a mining village at a time when the name Sankey was on everybody's lips. This was history walking towards him. When Lord Sankey passed I grabbed hold of him and introduced the two. And I was grateful to the Chancellor for the gentle, unaffected courtesy with which he helped me entertain my guest. We walked on into the gardens together, talking lightly of this and that: the Thames, the fine weather, politics, colliers. My young lad's visit to London was now quite complete.

A year later MacDonald formed the National Government. Sankey stayed with MacDonald. The Parliamentary Labour Party was summoned to Transport House to consider what next. Who would now lead the Party? What policy should be pursued? MacDonald, of course, did not attend that meeting. But Sankey was more man than that. He turned up and asked to be allowed to explain what he thought of the situation and why he had felt it his duty to go with MacDonald. At the end of his statement he put his hand on the shoulder of Arthur Henderson who was sitting on the platform beside him, and pronounced an all-inclusive benediction. MacDonald had saved the country. Arthur Henderson had saved the soul of the Labour Party. Good luck to both!

What could you make of it? Only a man of very fine personal integrity could have got off with a statement like that, to such an audience, at such a time. I decided the only thing to do was to laugh. This was 'Alice in Wonderland' politics. Lord Sankey had plainly wandered in and out of the Labour Movement with only the faintest notions as to what it was all about.

I had time to recall those things on the afternoon some time later when I went to have tea with him, for when I arrived, the House was still sitting. The Lord Chancellor was still on his wool-sack. I wandered around a bit then was shown to his retiring-room. A few minutes later he came sailing along in his enormous robes. We talked for a few minutes then while, at his request, I rang for tea, he disappeared into his dressing-room to disrobe. It did not take long. Almost immediately he smilingly reappeared. I felt I was playing at charades. He looked as if he felt a bit like that too.

Well, how did I like Middle Temple? It was his own particular Inn and he was much attached to it. I enlarged on a grievance that was annoying me at the time. Why could I not be permitted when I dined in the hall of the Inn, as the law obliged me to do if I wanted to be called to the Bar, to sit at table with any students or barristers present I happened to know? Why the atmosphere of a Victorian boarding-school? Why a special table isolating women students? What sort of fraternity was this that parcelled us out into separate groups according to sex, then subdivided the men accord-ing to colour? Nice memory for Indians and Africans to take back with them of their 'mother' country! Unless they were fools or had no personal dignity, they were entitled bitterly to resent such segre-gation. It was the element of compulsion that was all wrong. Left to themselves, coloured men might prefer to dine with coloured men. Women might prefer to cluster together at the one table. But to be compelled to do it? What a silly, belittling arrangement.

Sankey listened and nodded sympathetically. Yes, but the Middle Temple was a very conservative institution. Its customs were centuries old, hallowed by time. To attempt to amend them in any way raised terrific prejudice. But he would see. He would consult his colleagues.

The rules governing dining in hall were slightly amended. But not the spirit of the place. Rather belatedly I started taking stock of what I was up against. The prejudice against women barristers in English law courts is colossal. To make even a modest beginning you must have exceptional ability, an independent income to keep you going for an indefinite number of years and a willingness to give your time and energies exclusively to furthering your professional interests. Even then it is a big gamble.

I decided I had made a mistake. I had none of the qualifications. I ought never to have begun. Above all, I was too much preoccupied with outside happenings. Other activities seemed to me much more urgent and worth-while. And so the attempt to get myself settled into a safe, respectable groove entirely failed.

For the next five years I lived the life of a glorified hobo. At least sometimes glorified, sometimes just plain hobo. Every January I crossed to America and remained there until Easter, singing for my supper from place to place.

Looking back, I can see that America influenced my way of looking at things, much more than I suspected at the time. In Britain for ten months of the year I was politically a partisan, feverishly, bigotedly partisan. In America, for about two months of the year, I found myself an onlooker, a reporter. A reporter hired by socialist, radical, or at least internationally-minded organizations and presenting European affairs from the standpoint of my own philosophy. but, nevertheless, a reporter. That makes a difference. I had somehow to fix all sorts of new experiences into my preconceived notions of things.

Every spring when I returned from America I brought back the same hope. Faint, but never entirely extinguished. I was longing to be free to spend my energies clearly and extravertly fighting the social system that keeps working people weak and poor. And even at its best, even when it gives them work and bread, brands them with inferior status and torments them with uncertainty about the future.

Instead, I had to turn to with as much relish as I could muster and take part in the never-ending warfare between rival Labour, Communist and Socialist organizations.

I regarded a great deal of that warfare as a criminal waste of energy. Disagreements, of course, there had to be. That was in the very nature of things. But I was deeply shocked and antagonized by the barbaric level at which a great deal of the controversy took place.

In Scotland, whether it is politics or theology we are quarrelling about, we are good haters. And we each and all go into battle armed with a self-righteousness that sometimes staggers people of a more easy-going disposition. Each Easter when I returned from America I felt with increasing keenness that the general political knock-about I was expected to take part in was almost as primitive in its nature as the behaviour of our eighteenth-century kirk elders who upheld their theology by burning old women suspected of witchcraft.

What worried me most was that all the time a near-fascist National Government went on ruling Great Britain, and looked like continuing to do so indefinitely unless a drastically different mood could be brought into the working-class movement. I believed it should be possible for sincere differences of opinion between Labour Party, Independent Labour Party and Communist Party to be stated without the controversialists becoming mortal enemies. I believed it honourable when these differences became acute that separate organizations should exist side by side and each of us choose the party with which we had most in common. I insisted, above all, that on agreed issues and for specific purposes, alliances ought always to be possible. There were many people in all three parties who felt as I did. There were also elements in all three parties who believed in a war of mutual extermination. It was the latter who gained the upper hand.

In November 1935 the National Government went to the country. I was once again I.L.P. candidate in North Lanark. All through the campaign came the cry, sometimes wistfully, sometimes angrily, from rank and file workers for working-class unity. Left to ourselves we might have been able to answer the cry. But the official policy of the Labour Party forbade. And quite a number of key-people inside the I.L.P. agreed with the Labour Party in this respect. The zealots in both camps wanted a war of extermination. They got it. When the votes were counted the Conservatives had won with 22,301. I followed with 17,267. The Labour Party nominee had 6,763.

And all this against a background of world events that was becoming more and more macabre. We looked on, as, with awesome momentum, calamity after calamity befell the workers of first one country and then another. First came the news that Hitler was reducing to pulp the great mass movements of the German working class. Socialist, Communist, Liberal parties, Jewish minorities, Catholic minorities, the Lutheran Church, all in turn were being flayed by the fascist whip.

Throughout Britain, we dimly took note of these things, regretting it all, but each warring faction rendered impotent by its exclusiveness. We were each the Lord's anointed, so could not unite with the other. Though the whole world should crash about our heads yet would we give no quarter to those who were our natural and only possible allies.

Then from Austria came a desperate appeal for aid. Our beautiful Vienna and its socialist administration and all the tender, careful work that had been done there was in deadly peril.

I thought of Austria as I had first known it in the summer of 1929. The hospitable and charming household of the Scheu family. The pleasant company of newspaper men I at that time regarded as merely playboys, good companions for an occasional evening out but only remotely and trivially connected with serious socialist politics. John Gunther, large, blond and looking almost idiotically good-tempered; Frances, his wife, so tiny and dainty that I wanted to lift her up and put her on the palm of my hand. 'Watch Frances, she has a jagged edge to her tongue,' some acquaintances said to me. I felt very safe. It is the sickly sweet, oh, ever so sweet women who frighten me! And Gedye was there, and Bill and Tess Shirer, and Fodor (*Manchester Guardian* correspondent and a sort of father to the whole journalistic colony), and Knickerbocker breezed in and out, the most conservative of the lot in his opinions but the best dancer.

'Gedye is the pick of the bunch,' young Friedl Scheu advised me. 'You ought to see more of him.' But I was on holiday. My standards were purely hedonistic! If I wanted to talk seriously to a newspaper man, it was Dr. Pollak I turned to, editor of the *Arbeiter-Zeitung*, Vienna's socialist daily paper.

I had a very good time in Vienna. I saw all the sights of the town —all the things that workers had built for workers. The houses and the schools and the crêches and the gay gardens and swimming pools, finer of their kind than those in any other capital in the world.

Herbert Morrison was visiting Austria at that time too, learning from Vienna how to make the parts of London where poor people live less squalid. I wished I could see more evidence that he had also learned the other lessons of Vienna. Now only a hunted illegal movement remains in our once great socialist citadel.

In Britain we were sorry when Vienna fell. Sorrier than about Germany. The Austrian workers did not run away. On every formal calculation they ought to have. They had not an earthly chance of winning. But they fought back. And for that we honoured them and felt that we ourselves had grown more wholesome. We were sorry, truly sincerely sorry when Vienna fell. But we did not see that that was any reason for pooling every scrap of strength that we could muster in a common drive against our own near-fascist Government that had helped to destroy Vienna and was preparing to destroy a good deal more. We were all so sure we were right; all so scathing about the errors of others; and all so ridiculously impotent.

12

RUSSIA IN 1936

I HAD sunk into a mood of acute depression. The 1935 general election was approaching. The Labour Party had introduced a third candidate into the North Lanark constituency, thus making a Conservative victory certain. After the election I would have to decide what next I intended to do. I had come to a complete dead end. I was no use as a politician. I clung stubbornly to the proposition that the I.L.P., the Labour Party and the Communist Party, each and all professing a socialist objective, each and [all having in their ranks loyal and trusting working people, should know how to come to terms with one another. But that apparently was heresy, mere sentimentality. I could find no echo of support in official quarters anywhere. So what was the use of going on ? What hope was there ? I hate and despise bigoted sectarianism. It is a violation of the mood and a betrayal of the hopes of rank and file members of every section of the working-class movement. I have no gift, no heart for spending myself in that sort of warfare. One would have thought that the fate of Germany would have been a lesson to the rest of us. The German Social Democratic Party had no lack of brilliant theoreticians very, very sure of the immaculacy of their doctrines. The Communist Party of Germany was equally convinced of the perfection of its policy and tactics. But Hitler won. The ordinary people lost. And nothing it seemed could prevent the British Labour Movement from dying a similar death.

I was very weary and utterly discouraged. Here is the sort of thing that there seemed no cure for. John, Jack and Jim live in the east-end of Glasgow. John belongs to the I.L.P., Jack to the C.P., Jim to the Labour Party. They are all unemployed and line up in the same queue in the same unemployment exchange to collect their weekly 'dole'. Each thinks he knows everything that has happened in Russia since the Revolution, during the Revolution and before. (After Russia they were going to have Spain to quarrel about.) On the strength of listening to a speech or two, perhaps reading a pamphlet or two laying down the official 'line' of their respective parties, they are for ever ready to slander and curse one another. And all the time they need only look down at the state of their boots, homewards to shabby firesides, disheartened wives, children lacking so much, so very much of even the barest necessities, to find ample and understandable territory about which to agree. Their party leaders could easily make allies of the three men. But instead they encourage them to quarrel about remote places and abstract theories regarding which they can have at most only the flimsiest second-hand knowledge. That, of course, does not make it more difficult for them to quarrel. It makes it just so much easier.

What can you do against that kind of grotesque misdirection of energy? From time to time the I.L.P. made heroic efforts to bring the various groups together. The Socialist League inside the Labour Party tried to respond but was exterminated for its pains. The Communist Party developed an ardent desire to join up with the Labour Party, but had not enough sense to realize that Labour leaders like Herbert Morrison were aware of every abusive epithet that at the same time the Communist Party kept throwing at the I.L.P. 'What kind of loving, trustworthy brother is this, that we are asked to open our doors to?' men like Morrison could well ask. And, indeed, he did.

In face of all that, I decided that there was nothing, absolutely nothing, that my own solitary self could do. Nature has its own way of carrying you through that kind of phase. Your mind and body react on one another. You become ill. The doctors calls it 'a nervous breakdown'. Then, somehow, as your physical self gradually repairs, your courage and hope come back too.

By the spring of 1936 I had got over my bout of depression. In particular, I was eagerly following every scrap of news that came from France. The Left forces there were learning how to unite. Perhaps this was what I had been waiting for. Perhaps this was the answer to many of my questions. Perhaps France would light the way for all of us. I wanted very much to go to France to see for myself what was happening. It was then I re-read an encouraging letter from W. Midgley, editor of the London 'Star' and wondered if I might not try my hand at being a journalist. Why not find out whether he could use an article or two on how France was looking and behaving during its 'Front Populaire' election ? I decided it would be bad tactics to go the whole hog and ask him to send me to Paris. That would probably frighten him off. Instead I would telephone and say, casual like, that I was going to France anyhow, would he like an article or two ? And so I did. And the perfect editor replied in the way that I had gambled on him replying. Yes, he could use two, perhaps three, descriptive articles.

That bucked me up sufficiently to approach 'Reynolds'. The voice at the other end of the telephone decidedly did not sound as if my offer was manna from heaven. It was a cautious Scottish voice. But all the same, I fixed up for two more articles so all I had now to do was to collect the necessary letters of introduction to key people in the various parties of the Left and set sail.

As a last preliminary I zig-zagged across a few Bloomsbury Squares from my flat to where John and Frances Gunther then lived. I went with all the humility of a novice seeking priestly benediction; but I was so excited that I said the wrong things. John, usually so easy-going, looked at me almost primly. Then he read me a lecture. Journalism was not something that any inexperienced amateur could step right into. It was a craft, an exacting craft and needed a long, often painful, apprenticeship. I agreed so sincerely that he relented. All right, when you get to Paris, make straight for Edgar Mowrer, then contact the rest of the boys—Here you are—names, addresses, telephone numbers.

There was a very different flavour to this spring-time election in France than the one we had muddled through in Britain the previous autumn. I hurried from meeting to meeting, from place to place, with evidence everywhere that the Front Populaire, the electoral alliance formed by socialists, Communists and liberals, was going to be a terrific success. It was a bit strange at first getting used to seeing the tricolour and the red flag intertwined, with socialists trying to keep the emphasis on the red flag and Communists insisting that it be placed on the national emblem. I had always contended that workers' organizations made a mistake when they handed over all the emotional drive behind patriotism and tradition to their opponents. Well, here was an example to the contrary. How did I like it ? The Communists, it seemed to me, were making their usual mistake; getting on to a good idea then applying it so rigorously, so mechanically, with such false, unconvincing emphasis that they made it sound just silly. I wished they would show a little more discrimination. But why grumble ? If the tactic succeeded, if the people of France elected a reliable antifascist, pro-workers' government, that was a good deal. It then remained to be seen if the workers could, under the wing of such a government, win solid advantages, and, having won them, keep them. What happened in France as a result of this election would have a good many lessons for the Labour movements of other countries, particularly Great Britain.

The Paris election meetings I attended, whether Communist, socialist or radical, were all alike. Large crowds, a loud-speaker booming over our heads, the platform party rather remote and unreal, the same old speech invariably keeping Hitler to the fore as the supreme reason why every Frenchman who loved liberty and France should vote for one or other of the 'Front Populaire' candidates.

After a surfeit of large city demonstrations, I was keen to attend some village meetings where the atmosphere would be more intimate and more time allowed for 'heckling'.

I found exactly what I was looking for in the enormous, sprawling constituency, not unlike North Lanark, that Gaston Bergery represented. Gaston Bergery had been described to me as a 'lone wolf' type of politician, out at elbows with capitalist society but totally unable to see eye to eye with either official socialist policy or official Communism. My chief interest in him was that he had been one of the first people in France to advocate an electoral alliance of all the progressive parties with the object of carrying through a programme of social reform, outwitting the growing fascist elements inside France itself and, above all, holding Hitler at bay.

I liked the whitewashed village hall where I was one of about two hundred people waiting impatiently for Bergery, the candidate, to arrive. It looked very spick and span. The dark blue shirts of the working men who sprawled about the back of the hall showed up vividly against the whiteness. So did their weatherbeaten faces. They looked intelligent and aggressive. I did not like so well the people who occupied the three front rows. They were obviously the small tradesmen of the town. They wore rather shoddy conventional lounge suits and had pale, ungenerous faces. Probably all just prejudice on my part! But there you are. That is how they struck me and I had plenty of time to look at them for Bergery arrived very late. I sympathized with him. He had obviously been going from hall to hall, from village to village around a French edition of North Lanark.

When at last he arrived a group of Communist workmen at the back cheered loudly and saluted him with clenched fists. I thought Bergery gave a rather irritated look in their direction. He certainly attempted no reciprocal fist clenching.

After he had finished speaking, quietly, conversationally, persuasively, the questioning began. The small tradesmen were on the warpath. One moved to the front, removed his coat, draped it cloak fashion over his shoulders, all the time gesticulating excitedly and putting his view on the situation. And always he came back to what was for him the key question. How could Bergery pretend to be on the side of property and on the side of Communism at one and the same time? Let him choose. One or the other. But not both, not both. That could not be done.

Bergery answered competently and calmly. Then another of the *petite bourgeoisie*, and still another, rose to his feet and assailed him in almost the same words. Bergery repeated his answer again and then all over again, keeping his temper but with an increasing effort. The gist of his reply was an appeal to the village butcher and baker to remember that the common enemy of France was Hitler's Germany, not Stalin's Russia, and also to remember that the Communist Party had come far to meet their views on property. No one's savings would be in the least danger. Would they not be well advised therefore to suppress antiquated prejudices, close the ranks, defeat fascism and *Vive la France*!

A few days later, when all was over except the declaration of the poll, I went to the Place de la Bastille to listen to the loud-speakers

that everywhere in the streets of Paris were booming out each constituency result as soon as it became known. The people around
me were mostly working-class and were dancing with joy. After
that I moved on to the Café de la Paix, where the crowd looked
mainly well-to-do. And there too, although less unanimously, the
biggest cheers were for 'Front Populaire' victories.

I was invited by a group of middle-class people, (you could
fairly, I think, describe them as tepidly progressive in outlook), to
join with them in toasting a Communist victory that had just been
blared through the air. Champagne cocktails were handed round. I
said, chaffingly, were they not afraid of such a toast ? Surely they
had revised their opinions very considerably 'Ah no madame, you
do not understand. It is not *we* who have changed,' was their
smiling reply.

It was all very complicated. I had certain fears, certain reservations at the back of my mind, but I hoped it would work out all
right. I hoped the ordinary people of France who were dancing in
the streets with joy would not be disappointed.

That same year I found my way back to Russia. I had been there
twice before. I wanted to compare notes; to see what kind of
changes had taken place.

Before I left I collected a commission to write five articles for
the *Daily Express.* The bargain was that I signed what I wrote and
what I wrote would not in any way be censored. But I had to keep
off the tread-mill as far as possible. No one wanted to hear that
Russia was building factories, using tractors, abolishing illiteracy.
That was not news. That had all already been said. Find new
angles. Make a different approach.

Shortly before then the newspaper had carried a paragraph
announcing that Schiaparelli had been to Moscow and had been
invited to design model gowns for Russian women. I rapped my
head against the wall and hoped I would remember that that was
the sort of thing that was news. 'Off you go in search of Schiaparelli,' I advised myself. 'Find out what she has been up to. Find
out if she actually has been designing clothes for Russian women
and if they are being worn and who wears them, commissar's wife
or ploughman's wife.'

Once in Moscow I found Schiaparelli exceedingly elusive. I

could find no trace of her anywhere. No one knew anything about her. No one had heard of her. I was given a permit to attend a mannequin parade at the Dom Modelei, central fashion house for Moscow. That in itself was surely news. Mannequin show in Moscow! I go, take my seat in an elegant room, all very modern. Find factory girls, some with shawls over their heads and a peasant look, others with manicured nails, clothes and hair styles indistinguishable from those of a London shop-girl or typist, filing into the surrounding seats. The show begins. Handsome mannequins parade before us, displaying bathing and holiday garments for that trip to Odessa when summer weather comes. Afternoon gowns suitable for a quiet party or a visit to the theatre. One evening dress actually had a train to it; surely only for the very grandest of official balls!

These Russian girls enjoyed themselves enormously. Their eyes popped with pleasure each time a new exhibit was brought forward. The leading demonstrator looked at them severely and said they must not be so undiscriminating. They must consider each garment carefully and make suggestions and criticisms. I, too, was invited to criticize and promptly found myself out of favour when I sincerely did so. Lots of Russian women have short, squat figures. These types look anything but their best in jimped skirts and bodices that are entirely uninspired imitations of the cheaper ready-made clothing you can buy in a second-rate department store in London or New York. Why not strike out on their own ? I suggested. Why not beat the *bourgeoisie* fashions ? I am afraid I got rather carried away with my subject. I would like to think that the interpreter who spoke for me to the girls did me less than justice. For I was rather crossly told that I was quite mistaken, The fashions I had been looking at were by Russian designers. Russia had nothing in common with *bourgeois* nations.

And still no sign of Schiaparelli. In despair I appealed to my friend, Philip Rabinovitch. He had a small pointed face with pock markings and looked rather like Lenin. Sometimes he came to London on trade delegations. He was a kind of cross between a junior Cabinet Minister and a big business executive. His home was a simple four-roomed affair and his wife as competent and hard-working and charming a Bolshevik as he was. I had the pleasure of going to supper with them in their home. The great thing that evening was the photograph of a new grandchild that had just arrived. They looked at it and displayed it and loved it in that way that makes war and hatred between peoples such a foul abomination. For always in foreign countries when you get through the formalities and sit down to a family supper, you find just folks.

But I did not intend even the grandchild to sidetrack me from Schiaparelli. 'Philip,' I insisted, 'you must help me. A real journalist would get to the bottom of this and here am I absolutely stumped. Get out the army, get out the Gay Pay OO, take whatever emergency measures may be necessary, but find me that Schiaparelli model!'

With an amused, tolerant gleam in the corner of his eye my friend lifted the telephone. The machinery of the State was set in motion. With mock solemnity he promised that if such a thing existed anywhere in the whole length and breadth of Russia, it would be found and I would be informed.

The following day a note arrived at my hotel along with a permit to enter the building that in Czarist times had been the Moscow Stock Exchange. I hurried along and found that one enormous room was now being used to house a sample of every kind of article that the Soviet trading authorities imported from France. It was not open to the general public. It was simply a trade show. In a humble remote corner I found Schiaparelli at last! And very nice, too! A simply-cut black dress to be worn with a matching three-quarter length reversible coat. One side of the coat was black, the other side was bright scarlet. A perky black fish-net beret completed the outfit. So this was news. Off and tell the world! Schiaparelli rejected! Schiaparelli to be re-exported to France. Not suitable for mass reproduction, say Russian fashion experts!

Having at last tracked down Schiaparelli, I then went in search of Stalin's two youngest children. I did this with a right good will. What I would discover might or might not be 'news', in a newspaper sense, but I myself was going to be supremely interested. For both of them, Svetlana, a bright little girl about ten years old, and her brother, Vassily, about five years older, were attending one of Moscow's *pukhir* high-schools. The importance of this school to me was not that it was unique—there were thousands of others exactly the same as it scattered throughout the U.S.S.R.—but that it was a sample of Russian education, 1936 model, at its most official and best.

Its competent headmaster, a distinguished Soviet pedagogue, well over sixty years of age, guided me from room to room. Each time we entered a classroom, the children rose from their desks and stood stiffly to attention. Discipline was perfect. I blinked a bit but reserved judgment.

The pride of the school was plainly its science laboratory and its workshop where model engines and aeroplanes could be made. It had a fairly good library of general literature—a group of the children told me that Dickens and Rudyard Kipling were their favourite English authors—but the school authorities were undoubtedly placing the main emphasis on technical training.

I tried to read a wall newspaper stuck up on one of the classroom walls. The main feature of the newspaper was quite a clever caricature of a very stupid-looking little boy. What was it all about ? I asked. The headmaster explained that corporal punishment was not countenanced in Russian schools but to help in maintaining discipline and, at the same time, to stimulate each child to do his or her best work, prizes were given to the most successful scholars and the children themselves dealt with particularly trying pupils, by black-listing them on the wall newspaper, sometimes, as in the one I was looking at, tacking on a caricature.

The round of the school completed, we returned to the headmaster's private study. I had duly noted that the boy Vassily had great shaggy eyebrows like his father and that his teachers regarded him as in no way exceptional. The little girl, an attractive pretty child, was praised much more warmly. She was intelligent above the average, everyone said. But Stalin's children never even entered into the conversation that began between the headmaster and myself immediately we could settle down to talk. 'What did I think of the school ?' was his opening question. 'Very German,' I replied. That, of course, was a challenge and a criticism. I made the remark deliberately. I knew I could safely do so for the man I was talking to was no robot. Some of his friends had told me something of his background to prepare me for meeting him. In the early years of the Revolution he had been under a cloud. Krupskaya, Lenin's widow, was his friend, and helped him as much as she could. In Russia, as everywhere else, it pays to find out which way the wind is blowing and blow that way too. But in the years when Russian schools were one riotous non-stop political demonstration and every type of educational experiment, hair-brained and otherwise, was being tried out without the equipment or the trained personnel to give even good ideas the ghost of a chance, he had had too much integrity to shout hurrah and pretend that all was better than well.

Now he was back in favour. I intended, by shock tactics, if necessary, to find out if the school I had just been through represented his highest educational ideals. Without a moment's hesitation he said no, most decidedly no. But what did I suggest should be done ? What would I do in his place ? I knew, did I not, that throughout the U.S.S.R. there was a dangerous scarcity of skilled technicians. A modern factory, a mechanized army, could not be built, equipped and made to function efficiently without trained personnel. And how long would Russia survive if its enemies abroad decided that they had no cause to fear it ? I had to remember that I was not visiting a Russia surrounded by friendly neighbouring powers. The Russian worker, even the Russian schoolchild, had to pay a price for the political backwardness of countries like my own. It was we who were responsible for Russia living in constant fear of invasion. And so long as this was so, a state of emergency existed inside the Soviet Union which must inevitably colour its cultural as well as its economic life.

As he talked I thought of Walter Duranty. I first met Duranty when Frank Wise took me to dine at his Moscow flat in the summer of 1930. Throughout dinner and for a good many hours afterwards, Duranty's wisecracks and stories kept everyone greatly amused. But the recurrent refrain in all he had to say was serious and sensible: 'Remember, you have come into a country that is at war. War is not pretty and not ethical. The judgments you apply to a country at war are quite different to those that fit a country that is safe and at peace.'

Frank Wise was a great expert on Russian economic affairs. I had great goodwill towards the country and had read all the usual books but beyond that was a complete ignoramus.

Throughout that first visit to Russia and again in 1932, before coming to even the most tentative conclusions about much that I saw, I kept Duranty's Moscow conversations firmly in mind.

In 1932 I found a second and considerably sharper corrective against any tendency I might have had to mere querulous complaining. And I needed a corrective, for that was a famine year in parts of Russia. Very few foreigners were permitted anywhere near the famine areas. I went right through them; first the Ukraine and then into parts of the Caucasus where there was also a good deal of hunger. At the end of it all I looked like the illustrations in Bernard Shaw's *The Adventures of The Black Girl in Her Search for God*. A hot August sun had baked me a dark brown and lack of food had made me comically angular.

The 'adventure' element in that kind of journey wears thin very quickly. And the importance that food comes to have for you, has to be experienced to be realized. You reach a stage when the whole meaning of life seems to consist in getting through to somewhere where you can have white rolls and butter.

It so happens that the place I got through to was Persia. Of course, if I had lingered in Russia, once I was back on the ordinary Kutais-Tiflis-Baku route there was food to be had. It was only in certain areas that it was unobtainable.

But by going straight on to Enzeli and then to Teheran, I had the important corrective of seeing hordes of emaciated, disease-ridden beggars, weird caricatures of human beings, for whom famine was apparently a permanent condition. That was invaluable in helping me to keep my balance. The hunger, disease and illiteracy I saw tolerated in parts of Persia where British interests had dominated for centuries was an unforgettable lesson in much that South-eastern Europe takes for granted.

I could look back to Russia with new respect. There was a war on there. And in that war, peasants who killed their live-stock and refused to cultivate the land rather than conform to Soviet methods of farming and land-holding trapped themselves into famine. It was famine from such causes that I had seen in the Ukraine. But the plus factor added by Russia was not poverty, or disease or illiteracy. It was exactly the reverse. It was the fight *against* these barbarities. And finally in Persia, I saw for the first time in my life, women walking about in what looked to me to be shapeless, black cloth coffins. Only their eyes could be seen. I was told these monstrous drapings were called *paranjas*. This was the ancient eastern way of life for women. And against all that, too, Russia was fighting a terrific, lonely and many-sided battle.

In 1930 and 1932 Walter Duranty and Persia helped me when looking at Russia to keep in mind what many people seem to forget. Not just where it was trying to go but where it had come from and the stupendous obstacles that slowed down its advance at every stage of its journey. In 1936 a Moscow schoolmaster helped me in a similar way. He said nothing I had not already heard. There was nothing dazzling or original about his arguments.

But I knew no answer to them. Russia expected any day to be drawn into war. Everything it did was necessarily conditioned by that prospect. And in spite of the burdens imposed by war preparations, the ordinary Russian worker plainly enjoyed better food, clothing, medical services, opportunities for education and entertainment than ever before in his history.

I travelled back through Europe in a much more optimistic mood than I had been in the previous autumn. The general balance of power in the world had by no means toppled over on the side of fascism. I was quite sure that even inside Hitler's Germany there were millions of people secretly opposed to the policies of their government. Franklin Delano Roosevelt, a liberal, was America's President, Léon Blum, socialist, was at that moment Prime Minister of France. That did not mean as much as it looks, of course. I knew perfectly well that in France and America there were powerful influences at work irreconcilably pro-fascist whatever the passing character of their government might be.

And, adding enormously to the general feeling of confusion and uncertainty, there was the problem of Great Britain's behaviour. I was anxious to be home again. Wherever I went I had been asked if British people realized the extent to which the British 'National' Government was helping the fascist powers. I could honestly say 'no'. Was there any chance of getting rid of it ? Was there any hope of a Labour Government ? Or a 'Front Populaire' Government ? What sort of socialist movement had we in Great Britain ?

All these were more difficult questions to answer. But I did so as fairly as I could. When in doubt I perhaps tipped the balance over on the side of optimism. But then I felt optimistic. That was in the early summer of 1936. We had not yet betrayed Spain.

13

THE SPANISH CIVIL WAR

IN the autumn of 1936 I looked forward with a good deal of pleasure to revisiting Edinburgh. There were several good reasons for that. The most important of these was Aneurin. We had been married for more than a year. I had been trailed all around Wales, north, south, highlands and lowlands. I am not complaining about that. Indeed, I am very grateful. And the pride and careful generalship with which he presented his country to me made me chuckle under my breath for his behaviour was far from squaring with the irreverent things his tongue was for ever saying.

Now I was anxious to show him Scotland. And I had made a firm resolution not to be unchivalrous. Not to point out that the mountains of Wales are lovely, but the best of our Scottish scenery is much lovelier, that the cities of Wales have their points but not one of them can compare with Edinburgh.

Our marriage had put my mother in an awkward political dilemma. Aneurin was Labour M.P. for Ebbw Vale. I was, of course, still a member of the I.L.P. Mother was nothing if not loyal. Until that time she had been a staunch member of the Independent Labour Party. After our marriage she continued to be a staunch member of the I.L.P. but became a supporter of the Labour Party as well. Mother had a special genius for that kind of thing, and no amount of arguing or chaffing on our part could make her budge from her position. I had to resign myself to this very disconcerting fact. For more than four years, the I.L.P. and Labour Party had been separate, often hostile, organizations. She had attended scores of I.L.P. meetings, lived in an atmosphere of continual political discussion, heard the case put for the I.L.P. from every conceivable angle. And in spite of all that she still had not the faintest notion as to what the quarrel between the two parties was really about. For her spirit refused to listen to any of the formal arguments. It simply cried out for unity and insisted on having it.

It was quite clear that the I.L.P. could make no great headway so long as it had people like mother to grapple with. For her way of looking at things was typical of ninety-nine per cent of the men and women who, either actively or passively, take part in Labour politics.

I had her very much in mind as I travelled up to Scotland in the autumn of 1936. The annual conference of the Labour Party was being held in Edinburgh that year. I went along to it with great goodwill. I was very anxious to see the old alliance between Labour Party and I.L.P. re-established. Aneurin was in Edinburgh attending the conference as a delegate. I was there to report for the *New Leader*. Immediately it was over we planned to begin our holiday.

But we had no holiday. We had no heart for holidaying. Not after what was done in our name at that Edinburgh conference. Perhaps you already know all about it, but in case not let me tell you, for it is a very important part of this whole history.

The main issue before conference delegates was the civil war in Spain. Right on the dot from the firing of the first shot, there seemed to me one stand and only one that any socialist could take. Uphold the right of the Spanish Government to buy arms. Spanish generals and *grandees* had barricaded themselves in behind German guns and opened fire on the working people of Spain. The Spanish Government needed arms to quell the rebellion. It tried to purchase the material it required in the usual way, as governments have always done and as every principle and precedent of international law entitles them to do. But the Spanish Government found that its way had been barred. It was not to be allowed to buy arms. The governments of France and Britain had evolved an extraordinary scheme called non-intervention. Neither Spanish insurgents nor the elected Government of Spain were to be allowed to buy arms from abroad. They were to carry on their fight strictly within the frontiers of Spain, having at their disposal only such arms as they possessed or could manufacture for themselves.

The British Government called into conference the leaders of the British Labour Party. At the annual conference of their Party those same leaders turned up with a more than usually 'weighty' air. Their manner conveyed that they knew a great deal more than it was expedient to say. The conference had better take their word for it that non-intervention was in the best interests of the Spanish people, of the British people, of the cause of peace.

Isabel de Palencia, a member of the Spanish Cortes, who had been sent from Spain to explain to this working-class assembly her people's desperate need of arms, was, after a good deal of backstair diplomacy, granted permission to speak. When she ended her appeal almost everyone in the hall was in tears. But the speech and the weeping were carefully timed. Those responsible for conference arrangements saw to it that the Spaniard was not allowed to present her case until *after* the vote had been taken that told the world British Labour had come down on the side of 'non-intervention'. The Spanish Government had informed us quite definitely and categorically that 'non-intervention' was a farce. That the fascist powers were sending arms and men to aid the Spanish fascists.

Nevertheless, British Labour voted in support of 'non-intervention'. While the votes were being counted I was facing the delegates from the press table at the front of the hall and could see the cards held up. The Little Fellows, that is, the local Labour parties, were doing their best. By an overwhelming majority they asked that Spanish working-men should not be denied arms. But the Big Fellows, the holders of the block trade-union votes, controlling almost five-sixths of the total votes cast at annual Labour Party conferences, decided otherwise. Up went the cards with hundreds instead of ones and twos on them, in support of 'non-intervention'.

When the result of the voting was announced, and again after the Spanish visitor had made her appeal, a howl of protest went up from the body of the hall. The party leaders rode the storm by promising that they would make the British Government make the German and Italian Governments carry out 'non-intervention' with rigid impartiality. If the Spanish Government was denied arms they would see to it that so were the Spanish fascists. Mr. Ernest

Bevin, leader of the Transport and General Workers' Union, went so far as to say that he would sit on the doorstep of 10 Downing Street and not budge until the Prime Minister had given him satisfactory assurances.

It was very silly of Mr. Bevin to talk in that way. He ought to have known better. But British Labour leaders have a monotonous willingness to trust to promises made to them by Conservative politicians; and the equally monotonous aftermath is the air of hurt surprise with which they later return to tell us that we have all once again been let down.

Not many delegates in that Edinburgh conference hall got any real comfort from Mr. Bevin's speech. Very few indeed were ingenuous enough to believe that it was safe to place any reliance on promises made by Mr. Chamberlain, still less, promises made by Herr Hitler.

The dreadful reality behind all our talk was that Spanish workers were waiting on Spanish battlefields for arms with which to hold back steel-clad fascist troops. Almost all the world had taken side against the working-people of Spain. They had hardly anyone they could look to except us. They were appealing to us to uphold their right to buy arms. And we, their natural allies, friends and supporters, were dithering and equivocating, lost in a mist of words.

At the end of the proceedings delegates were called on to rise to their feet and sing the 'Internationale'.

'Then comrades, come rally'—that was too much. I was not supposed to have any part in conference business. Neither had I officially. I was at the press table. But I was not made of wood. I crept miserably out of the hall and stumbled into Aneurin. He looked haggard and careworn. He was ill anyhow at the time and in no condition to stand punishment. He looked as if he had just dragged himself out of a torture chamber. And he was not the only delegate who looked like that. Out they came, singly and in groups, the most unhappy, guilty-looking collection of people I have ever seen. Their very misery made me hope again. If they felt like that something perhaps could still be done.

That evening there was no need for me to ask Aneurin where his thoughts were, for mine were there too. We had been to Sinap

together a year before the civil war began. We went there to
recover from the fuss of getting married. There was nothing at all
political about that first visit to Spain. It was planned entirely as a
holiday. While there we were both as nearly carefree as the circumstances of our lives had ever allowed either of us to be.

If you live most of your years in a Scottish or Welsh colliery
district, then one day you find yourself breakfasting out of doors
in January (in January, mark you!) with orange-groves around you,
the Sierra Nevada on the sky-line and a brilliant blue-green sea at
your feet, you rediscover all your childhood's faith in miracles.

Aneurin, who when he was among Englishmen always seemed
to me an alien figure—he was much too unequivocally alive to suit
staid English ways—looked utterly at home in Andalusia. He loved
it all. The vivid colouring, the smell and flavour of the place, the
warmth, the dark, proud-spirited people.

The fishermen and field-workers of Torre Molinos were almost
all socialists or Communists. Once they knew we were on their side
they smiled and were friendly. It was a great lark the day Aneurin
got himself a magnificent Spanish cloak, a sombrero, a scarlet
facha to wind round his waist, and because we had dared him to do
it, went swaggering dressed like this along the winding village
street that leads down to the sea. As he passed along, the older
people grinned to him more broadly than usual. The young
señoritas shrieked with delight. I can see them all as they were that
day. I am sure those Andalusian peasants thought we were quite
mad. But I am also sure they trusted us. That is why he and I had
such bitter reason for shame. We made promises to those Spanish
people that we failed to keep. I don't mean promises made in so
many words. There was no need for that. The pledge we made was
implicit in our relationship.

After what came to be called the Spanish 'civil' war began,
Madame Vandervelde was the first to give us news of Torre Molinos.
She left shortly before it fell to the fascists. Sick with foreknow-
ledge, I listened to what she had to say. On the day she left, a group
of women gathered around her in the main street of the village crying brokenly, 'Los Moros, los Moros'. I could see those Spanish
women; hear the dread in their voices. I had known some of them.
'Los Moros'. The Moors. The Moors were coming. Black troops

were being rushed along the coast road. Black troops with German guns and Italian conscripts to aid them.

The men of Torre Molinos, its fishermen and field-workers were mobilizing to defend their homes armed with little more than spades and fishing tackle.

Spades and fishing-tackle and antiquated rifles and home-made explosives against the devilish perfection of the most up-to-date armaments that the most up-to-date factories in the world could produce. That was how we left our friends to fight. The fascists of Germany and Italy kept faith with the fascists of Spain. They promised them arms and men and gave both in full measure. It was only we who failed to keep faith. It was we whose stock-in-trade for generations had been phrases such as 'Workers of the world unite', who, when it came to a show-down, ratted.

It was not even as if we had been asked to do anything very heroic. The Spanish people did not ask us to send our men to fight for them. They did not even ask us to make them a present of guns. All they asked was that the voice and vote of every member of the British working-class movement should be united in demanding that the Spanish Government should not have to hold back fully-armed fascist troops with the bodies of unarmed Spanish workers.

Nine months after the Edinburgh conference, two miles from Huesca on the Aragon front, I saw for myself how non-intervention worked out in practice. Fascist troops were in possession of Huesca. Suddenly I heard what sounded like the recurrent noise of thunder in the air. I was stupidly slow to grasp what was happening. There were soldiers in Huesca, fascist soldiers who had pointed their guns in the direction of the mill-house where I was sheltering. They were concentrating on hitting the building. They knew Government troops were quartered there. I had only the vaguest notion as to what the effect of cannon-fire discharged at a range of just over two miles would be if the fascists should make a direct hit. But I had sense enough to know that that was not the moment to start trying to make any inquiries. If I could not be useful, I had better at least stand by quietly and not make a nuisance of myself. We had all been ordered to go down into the large basement kitchen of the mill-house. In a small side-room I could hear two telephone operators at work. Sometimes they tried a dozen times before their rapid tapping brought any response from other parts of the line. I wondered what that might mean. But my chief attention was given to young Galahad. He looked about seventeen but had told me at least half a dozen times, when I had been chaffing him, that he was twenty-two. Small, dark, vivacious, very completely a young Catalan worker. He had been told when we left Barcelona to keep beside me because of his knowledge of French. His command of the French language was about as sketchy as my own, but we managed to talk together reasonably coherently. His chief concern as we drew nearer the fighting line was that the support holding his rifle on his shoulder had snapped. It looked to me a feeble piece of string, not worth mending. I produced a leather belt that I had wound around my attaché-case and offered it to him. That made us indissoluble friends. The old support for his rifle was thrown away and my bright new British belt took its place.

I watched him standing in the mill-house kitchen while the fascist guns barked around us, alert for whatever might happen. He stood at an opening that had once been a window, looking in the Huesca direction. Several times he turned his head to look back to see how I was taking it all, each time tapping the belt on his shoulder and grinning as if to say, 'Leave it to us. My belt and I will hold them back!'

I know nothing about military matters. I barely know the difference betwen one end of a rifle and the other end. But a child could have told that these youngsters with their antiquated guns, their improvised quarters and their eager air, had not yet seen any real fighting and would go down like chaff before efficiently-trained and armed soldiery.

That, in fact, was what happened later in the war when the fighting began in earnest on the Aragon front. There is a great deal more to that Aragon story beside lack of arms. A tortuous and terrible tale of sectarian fighting behind the lines that may some day be fully and fairly told. But I am not qualified to tell it. Nor was it the decisive factor that enabled General Franco to march through Barcelona. He got there primarily because the Spanish people were starved of arms. I saw that side of things with my own eyes. I listened to groups of soldiers in place after place along the Aragon front demanding arms with which to consolidate the ground they held and prepare a great offensive. I listened to a Spanish officer addressing group after group of Catalan soldiers in these terms: They must be patient. They must trust. There were not enough arms to meet the needs on all the fronts. The main brunt of the fighting was in the Madrid sector. Arms had had to be concentrated where the enemy offensive was heaviest——

Back in Barcelona I called at the head offices of the C.N.T., the mass trade union of the workers of Catalonia, to ask advice regarding what should be said to young men in Britain who were beginning to offer themselves as volunteers for Spain.

The union official I talked with took me to the window of his office and pointed to the street below. A steady stream of young men in civilian clothes were promenading up and down. 'We are not short of men,' he muttered, with an undercurrent of anger and hostility in his tone. 'Particularly we don't want foreigners coming here to tell us how to conduct Spanish affairs. What we need is guns. Look here,' going to his desk and taking out a handful of cartridges, 'we don't even have enough of these to feed the rifles already in use. Send guns. Break down the embargo on arms. That is how those of you in other countries who feel well disposed towards us can best help us to win. If you send the guns, we will do the fighting. Spaniards don't want to look on while foreigners do their fighting for them.'

Access to arms. That was the essential thing.

The evening before I returned from Barcelona I bought a huge slab of marzipan. I bought it for young Bob Smillie. That was in the first year of the war before the food situation had become acute. The marzipan, I was told, was Catalan Christmas cake. I knew Bob was very fond of it and I had noticed that the food he was having in the very spartan hotel where he was quartered, although at that time adequate, was exceedingly stodgy and monotonous.

I had arranged to have a farewell cup of coffee with him in one of the cafés about nine in the evening. I had business to attend to that kept me occupied until nearly midnight. So, by the time I reached the café, Bob had decided I had forgotten about him and had gone off to bed. John McNair, who had been with me all evening, took me to the room that he and young Smillie shared. A tousled mop of straw-coloured hair appeared above the bedclothes.

Bob was at once eager to get up and begin the evening all over again. There was a photograph of a very young woman on the small table beside his bed. I asked him who his 'girl' was. He grinned and refused to tell. 'Was she Spanish ?' At that he nodded in a way that plainly meant 'No'. 'Was she Scotch ?' This time he smiled happily in a way that very evidently meant that my second guess was a success.

I offered to look out of the window and whistle while he jumped into his clothes. He was up like a shot. We all three went out together.

About one o'clock in the morning, John McNair shook a middle-aged head and advised young Smillie to leave the marzipan until the next day. But Bob was at the sweet-tooth age. And I had by no means passed it. So we dined handsomely on coffee and cake.

I was very attached to this grandson of another great Bob Smillie. I had not known him at all intimately for long. But that was not necessary. There were no layers of guile or deception to be got through in order to know him. I was thankful he had not a penny-in-a-slot machine kind of mind with a ready-made answer waiting to pop out in reply to every question under the sun. He did not pretend that he knew the answer to everything. He had much too good a mind for that. He was fumbling his way with utter integrity towards his own verities.

He was obviously a great favourite with everyone around him. He was speaking French competently and making good progress with his Spanish. And he was following with an acute and un-prejudiced mind not just the broad issues of the fight between the fascists and the government forces, but the infinitely wearing and complex polemics going on among the various socialist, communist and anarchist groups. I liked above all the generosity of his temperament and judgments.

Scotland is well supplied with socialists puritanical and parochial in outlook to a degree that stultifies a good deal of their usefulness. Bob's mind and experiences were outgrowing the swaddling clothes of his early environment. But that did not mean that he was losing any of his passionate sincerity, his incorruptible devotion to the service of the poor.

When the military situation in Spain became more critical, he was one of the army of young men who (we having failed to send arms) tried to make amends by offering their bodies. He had been in the firing-line but was recalled to Great Britain to help the Independent Labour Party to explain to the British public what the real situation and needs of the Spanish people were. He got no further than the frontier. He was detained there and died of appendicitis. An illness of that kind would have been a trifling matter if he had been in Scotland. It would have kept him in bed for a few weeks. It would not have killed him. He died for the Spanish people just as surely as if a bullet had been put through his heart in a front-line trench.

And he was just one of many. I do not add a catalogue of names. That would be too paltry, too mechanical a tribute.

In time the British Labour Party came to see that 'non-intervention' did not mean what Mr. Chamberlain had assured them it would mean. In a perfunctory kind of way it declared in favour of the right of the Spanish Government to buy arms.

We all redoubled our efforts to send food and medical aids to Spain. But on the larger and decisive issue of arms, nothing was done; very little was even attempted.

The Spanish Government, no doubt biting back the bitter words that could easily have come to its tongue, said thank you to us very nicely for the food and bandages we sent. The fascists of Spain had more substantial cause for thanking their friends in other countries. Even the very best type of British bandage is not much use against a German gun. The fascists won the war.

14

HOME TO FIFE

AFTER Edinburgh I went home to Fife. Over the Forth as I had done so often before, back to home-people and home-places, back to a colliery district where very few people give themselves fake fancy airs and graces and where you have more chance of hearing people say what they really have in their minds, in simple forthright language, too, than anywhere else I know.

First I wanted a long sleep. Our mother was very good about sleep. It is the best kind of medicine, she maintained. You could be quite sure she would leave you undisturbed for what she called a good round of the clock and when at last you woke all your clothes would be washed and pressed, you would know the beatitude of finding a pair of stockings waiting for you miraculously free from ladders, but you would be lucky if you could find a pair of shoes to put on. A little patience, though, and your shoes would be back from the cobbler's and you would promise for the hundredth time in your life that you would never again let yourself get so far down at the heel.

This time I had come back to make Lochgelly the starting-point in a long pilgrimage. Not so long, measured in geographical lines, as many of the journeys I had made already, across Europe, down through Russia, zig-zagging in a kind of stagger dance from one lecture engagement to another up and down, out and about, and around the whole of the U.S.A. But much more important than any of these others. At least much more important for me. I was set on exploring right into the heart of my own discontents. I felt I could hardly bear to go on living unless I could get to the bottom of a mystery that was poisoning the whole of life for me. Why was Aneurin so often sad now ? Why did my father sit by the fire, gently

cynical about the whole socialist movement that had once been for
him ground so sacred that he taught us to tread reverently whenever we approached it ? Why were all the finest people I knew in
the grip of a kind of spiritual paralysis ? Where was all the vigour,
the belligerency, the robust certainties that had characterized the
Labour movement as I remembered it in my teens and early
twenties ? Or was I merely the victim of a very ordinary piece of
self-delusion ? Was it merely my own age and circumstances that
were changing, making me raise a querulous voice, the sort of
voice that has been heard from the beginning of time, to complain,
'Ah, it was not like that in *my* young days.' I did not feel as old as
all that. But I had better be careful! I was in my early thirties. Not
old, but certainly not a child any longer.

I decided I would begin my quest by strolling through the town,
talking less and listening more than I was in the habit of doing. I
wanted to know what people were thinking about some of the
decisions the Labour Party conference had just reached. I wanted
to know what was in their minds regarding the whole gamut of
current affairs. I knew that if I had lost my way, got badly out of
step, I would very soon be told about it.

At the corner of the street I met John ——, collier. His brother-
in-law, the dust-cart man, joined us a few minutes later, and,
before I got home again, I had run into Jack ——, joiner, Joe ——,
butcher, and half a dozen others as well. None of them seemed to
have any enthusiasm about any of the sort of things I wanted them
to talk about. Minds flicked off as quickly as possible to the football team, the weekly pool, the weather. To all sorts of inconsequential things. Politics was very much a back number.

All those men voted Labour in the Parliamentary elections. But
voted with an indifferent shrug of the shoulders. What else was
there to vote for ? Tories and Liberals were no use to a working-
man. All those men had lived through phases of intense social and
political concern. More than once they had thought that Jersualem
was just around the corner. They had grown jaded with so many
emotional ups and downs. Now they seemed to be settling down
to a grey twilight of indifference. They could no longer be searingly
disappointed. For they no longer hoped for much. Politics ? It was
all a game—everyone out for himself. You are a fool, Jennie. A

fool for yourself. You ought to get back inside the Labour Party. And, anyhow, splits are no good. No good to anybody. You can't expect to get anywhere with the I.L.P., the Labour Party, and the Communist Party all at one another's throats. People don't know which of you to believe. It is about time you all learned to agree among yourselves. You might have a chance them.

I got the talk round to Spain. You know what's the matter, don't you, says John ——, collier, with a grin once removed from a sneer. The Labour Party is afraid of the Catholic vote. Honest to God, some of them would sooner see the whole of Spain go up in smoke than damage their election chances. That's what is at the bottom of it. So-an'-So is lying low. He is trying to wangle so as to please everybody. I tell you it's a scream watching some of their antics.

I trailed home, not feeling very encouraged and wondering just what it would take to bring back the old clean fire. I knew it could be done, but what would it take to do it? Would anything short of dynamite be able to pierce through so many years of dwindling hopes ?

In our house, supper is anybody's meal who likes to drop in. Sandy Brown called to see about some I.L.P. business. Sandy is one of my heroes. You could boil him in vinegar for a hundred years and still not make him sour. I have a small brown jug he sent me as a wedding present standing on a ledge above my desk. I had admired it once—it has real beauty—when I looked in to see him in his tiny single-roomed cottage where he keeps house for himself, managing somehow on his ten shillings old-age pension, a shilling or two extra from the P.A.C., another shilling or two from his garden, total from all sources, well under £1 a week.

I remember his present arriving at my bright new London flat. Beneath the brown paper on the outside of the parcel there were layers of newspapers, then the jug itself carefully wrapped in some of Sandy's old pit socks that had been darned and darned and crept in with the wash until it was a problem figuring out what in the world it was he had got hold of as packing. The plump little warm brown jug looked rather like Sandy himself. It was not in the least put out by its rather uppish modern surroundings, but settled down with such a friendly look, such good-tempered self-possession, that I decided whatever else might have to be displaced, Sandy had arrived to stay.

But what I started to tell you about was that other evening when Sandy dropped in in time for supper. He had on a new pair of trousers. At least somebody's old trousers made down to fit him. Sandy is short in the leg. 'What do you think of them,' he demanded, and it was plain from the twinkle in his eye that he had something more to say. 'You look a toff,' we replied. 'What do you think yourself ?' 'Ah, weel,' says Sandy, 'they are a' recht, only ye ken, when I want to put my hands in ma pockets, I declare to God I hae to gang doon on ma bended knees.' Sandy enjoyed his joke. So did we all. And it would have been quite out-of-place for me to have broken into the chaffing with a dull harangue explaining what another part of my mind was thinking.

But I did not really enjoy seeing my old friend going around in these made-down trousers. It was not just the trousers, it was the whole pack of values they symbolized. Sandy had had to work, as all colliers have, very hard for his living. He had gone on working until he was too old to be needed any longer by the pits. And now here he was thrown on the scrap-heap; left to make do with a ten-shilling old-age pension and 'pickings' such as the cast-off clothing of some other man who had probably not worked half as hard as himself, if he had worked at all. Probably some other man who thought he was behaving with the utmost Christian charity in thus helping his poorer brethren.

Ugh! I hate the stench that rises from the word charity. The well-oiled conscience of the well-to-do, or the relatively well-to-do, satisfied to see working-people harassed and humbled by poverty, hostile to every honest-to-God effort to root out the causes of poverty, but at hand to plaster over the worst of the wounds that they themselves have helped to inflict, with a nice warm blanket for the children's bed, Mrs. Jones; a packet of tea for grandma, Mrs. Brown; would you like me to send down my last winter's coat, Mrs. Murphy ? You can turn it and make quite a grand school dress for Mary Jane.

One of the snags when you tried to settle down for a quiet evening under my mother's roof was the number of times people came knocking at the back door. Particularly on Thursday night. Out she went to the kitchen, you heard a slight scuffling and whispering then back she came trying to look as if there had been no one there. If you asked her she might tell you who it was, or, more likely, she would say, 'Never mind. Poor folks don't like to be affronted with everybody knowing their way of doing.'

By Thursday evening last week's pay has dwindled to nothing, if it has survived till then, and it is not everybody whose credit is good enough to tide them over until pay-day comes again. And if you have no money, no credit, young mouths to feed, what can you do ? Smother your pride and try to think which of your neighbours is kindly enough, and at the same time able, to lend you a loaf, a store 'check', a shilling or half a crown on the strict promise that it will be repaid in two days' time.

Almost any neighbour could knock at any other neighbour's door in our mining villages and ask help and be given it, if it was only a matter of finding someone kindly disposed. But when you put on your old coat and the grey felt hat you bought at a clearance sale the year before the flood and go out to borrow a shilling it is not such an easy matter as all that. For you have to find someone who besides being well disposed, is not in quite as desperate a plight as yourself. Mother had all the qualifications—feeling-hearted, discreet, just a little above the hunger line.

She did a thriving business. Thursday night, 'Please could I have a little obligement, Mrs. Lee ?' Saturday night, 'Here you are, Mrs. Lee, and thank you very much. I'm very much obliged!' Sometimes, when I questioned her about these very private trans-actions, she would look at me distrustfully and shy away. What did I want to know for ? But if I persisted she would first threaten me with what she would do to me if I should as much as breathe a word to a single soul of anything she said. Then she would talk. Talk soberly and tenderly, first of this one, then of the next. How could Martha be expected to manage with only one man's pay among so many of them ? And they were the unlucky ones, too. Always some little accident. Nothing serious, but enough to keep putting them back just whenever they thought they were getting their heads above water. Bessie used to think it would be easier on her once her family was up a bit and started to work. But now she is learning her mistake. It would take a fortune, she said to me, to keep them going. Puir young things! The things they want are innocent enough. It would be unnatural at their age if they were not for ever wanting. But it is hard on Bessie. She tries to do too much and just lands herself in a hole.

Did I know that Jean's laddie had got a start? That would give them a lift. And not before time. She has hungered herself for those bairns. I was thankful to see her out at the whist drive the other night. Take her mind off her troubles for a little bit. That's right, Jean, I said to her. You start looking after yourself for a change. You'll be all the more thought of.

Once started on this kind of monologue, mother could go on for ever. Not sitting down to talk—it never occurred to her that talking in itself could be an occupation—but keeping on at the same time with whatever household task she happened to be doing, sometimes disappearing into the kitchen for quite a time then re-emerging to ask if I remembered So-and-So, and did I know——

I did not often go visiting in Lochgelly. I didn't have to. I could sit by our own fireside and know all that was going on. Friends and neighbours kept coming out and in, bringing their news and their views with them.

But when I heard that Mrs. Foote had been ill, that was a different matter. I must go and see her. And ex-Provost Foote, too. I was feeling restless. I was looking for something. These two were part of the legend, of the story that had started me off on all my escapades. They were old socialists. I would find a bookcase in their parlour containing the same mixture of standard classics and socialist literature as in my father's bookcase. Our two families had been friends for three generations; since the time when my grandfather, an orphan of twelve, brought over from the Lothians by his uncle, first saw a coal-pit. Both families were colliers, scholars, socialists of long standing. There had never been a time when they had not rebelled against the raw, racking poverty and labour of a miner's life.

The struggle to build a union, a Co-operative movement, a socialist party; the eager reading of books and pamphlets and the weekly socialist Press. The punishment and distresses that are thrown on people whose views are in advance of the majority; the feeling of growth, of future greatness, of the society that is to be that keeps you going through all the darkness. Old Mrs. Foote could tell you more of the inwardness of such things than ever you will find in books.

When I walked down through the town and knocked at her trim cottage door, it was past teatime. But we started tea all over again. If you know Scotland at all, you know that the freshly-made pot of tea has very little to do with the needs of the stomach. It is a symbol, a ritual, a sacrament. You are a friend. You are being made to feel welcome. And there is nothing in the world more pleasant than such homely, sincere hospitality.

We talked until the darkness closed round the fireside and the curtains had to be drawn and the lamps lit. New-fangled electric-lamps, bright and clean, much less work for the housewife than the old-fashioned paraffin oil.

But there was no electric light in the Lochgelly our minds had travelled to. We had wandered back through the years. Back much further than my memories, back to when they themselves were children. 'Yes,' said Mrs. Foote, 'I can remember my father coming in and saying to my mother, "How many bowls of porridge Tib can you make from a peck of meal? Don't lose heart lass. Don't lose heart. If you can spin it out, we will beat them yet." '

She is telling us about 1870 and '71. The Fife miners are fighting for the eight hours' working-day. I forget the present. I have gone back more than sixty years. I am a collier hewing coal in a narrow underground seam and every little while peering out anxiously to see if the hutches[1] are arriving. None come. I curse and understand quite well what is happening. The coal company is out for murder again. Out to break me or starve me. No hutches. The swine. No hutches, so no wages and hunger enough at home already. Just before finishing time the hutches come hurtling through. I load them like a man gone mad. It is bread I am shovelling not coal. Bread to take home, bread for the wife and for the bairns. For John and Jean and Tam and all the rest of them. It will soon be two o'clock. I must stop then, dead to the minute. Not a shovelful, not so much as a single pebble of coal after two o'clock. I promised that. I pledged myself to my workmates. None of us to work a minute longer than eight hours. I must keep my word. I must not have eyes looking at me accusingly and folks spit at the mention

[1] Hutches or 'trams' are small trucks for carrying the coal to the surface of the pit and the miner's wage is reckoned only after the coal is taken to the surface, weighed and checked.

of my name. I must stand true. What other hope is there? Last winter I scarcely saw the light of day. Up in the dark morning, the bairns still all in bed. Home in the dark evening, the bairns already sleeping. Soon they'll hardly know their daddy. What a life for a man! No life at all. Just slavery.

But patience, thole a bit longer, and we will win yet! Alexander Macdonald said we could. He had a grand turnout to his meeting on the Birnae Braes. Hold together, men, he said, hold together and you will win. You will establish an eight hours' working-day for the miners of Fife and be the first in all the land to do so. Aye, but who would have thought the Company would hold back the hutches so that a man could get no coal carried away and that then, like the devil himself, they would tempt tired, penniless men by sending in the hutches as fast as they could follow one another, in the last hour of the shift. It's plain what they are after. Tempting us; tempting us to betray one another. To go on working long past the eight hours. And if we do, what then? Nothing to look forward to but the life of a pit rat, starvation wages, never seeing the light of day, not so much as a single hour when we can look up at the sun and call our souls our own. We must stick it no matter what it costs. But at two o'clock I must not think of the wife or I may weaken. Poor girl, it is a hard life for her. Harder, maybe, than for me. She can't work miracles. She can't feed us if there is no money to feed us with. I must get her to come out to the meetings. She would understand better then what it is all about. She is shy about coming out, prideful, woman-like, not wanting to be affronted showing everybody her old patched clothes. As if others were not as badly off as herself. And what can a man do? The Company has the pull. It has the money and the power. There is only one thing we have; just one weapon in our hands. We can hold together, keep our plighted word, not give in, stick whatever suffering may be entailed until the Company learns we are men, not beasts, and that our union is something they will have to reckon with, have to learn to respect.

And so, racked with anger, sorrow and labour, the miners of Fife in 1870 and '71 and '72 held out for the eight hours' day. They won. The Franco-Prussian war helped them to win. Coal prices soared. The coal companies saw their chance of quick, easy profits. But for that they needed the co-operation of the men. The men said they could have it—on terms. The eight-hour working day.

The years pass. It is 1894. I am my grandfather sitting by the roadside wondering where next I can turn. I have been a ring-leader in a recent strike. The men are back at work, but no colliery will employ me. My friend, Jock Simpson, passes by. 'Where are you off to, Jock ? To the Mary Pit ? No use. There are no openings there. I have just been inquiring!' Jock tells me to sit where I am till he comes back. He goes to the Mary, fixes up a job for himself and a neighbour and comes back gleefully to tell me. I am to start work with him the following day. I hurry home with my news. We are uplifted and much relieved. One of the bairns goes round to Tam Dicks for a pennyworth of pease meal. There is some churn-milk in the press. We can make brose and survive somehow until payday.

The next morning I rise at dawn and get into my working clothes, thankful, very thankful that the weeks of trudging from pit to pit in search of work are over.

But when I reach the 'Mary' the oversman meets me and asks where I am going. 'No, Michael, you are not wanted here. I did not know it was you Jock was bringing as a neighbour. Sorry, Mick, I'm very sorry, but these are my orders. It is not in my power to let you start!' And so sadly home again. The men have been at work three weeks. I have tried everywhere. The bar is up. Managers have their orders. I am not to be employed. The whole world looks black. No hope, no help anywhere. And then comes the news that causes that great lifting of the heart. The men have heard what is happening. They are angry and loyal. Strike notices are being sent round the lodges. Michael Lee must be given a start or every miner in Fife will lift his graith.

1897—the coal company thinks it can dictate even who my doc-tor is to be. I won't submit to that. I don't want their hand-picked nominee. I want Dr. Dandial, who lives among us, is liked and is a fine doctor. The men stand by one another once more. Every fort-night you will see them lining up outside Hendersons' hall waiting to pay their union dues and their pennies for Dr. Dandial. I am a committee man sitting at the table inside the hall, collecting and

counting the money, planning all the things our union will one day
do as the men learn more and more the power that union gives
them.

1898—I have been elected to Lochgelly Town Council. During
the campaign I say exactly what I think about slum property
owners and their sinful rack-renting ways. My opponent is also my
landlord. I win the election but lose my home. I, the wife and all
the children are thrown out on the street. I have been evicted.

Such was my grandfather's early life. It is in no way exceptional.
It is the typical history of a socialist agitator, a working-class
leader, in these stark pioneer years.

You will find many present-day Labour town councillors, county
councillors, Members of Parliament, trade union officials, who can
tell a very similar story.

One of my last memories of my grandfather is also my saddest.

The Fife Miners' Union was situated at the bottom of Rose
Street, Dunfermline. My grandfather's home was within five
minutes' walking distance of his office. Even after he retired he was
in the habit of making a daily journey back to the office just to hear
and to see how things were going and occasionally lend a hand.
This particular day I dropped in to have tea with him. I wondered
what could be the matter. He hardly looked up as I came in. Just
sat looking into the fire. That was very unlike his usual warm
welcome. An aunt was washing-up at the kitchen sink. There was
a vehemence and a clatter in the way she lifted and laid each dish
that conveyed she too was in no sunny temper. I sat down by the
fire conscious of atmospherics, but not asking any direct question
for that is not the way in our family. Grandfather got up and said
he thought he would go out for an evening stroll. Immediately he
left, my aunt, taut with indignation, told me what had happened.
It was too sore a thing for him to have been able to talk about it
himself.

He had gone down to the office as usual. He had been standing
on the front step looking about him, ready to walk home again. A
Communist delegate from one of the districts arrived for a miners'
meeting. The young man going in met the old man coming out
and bawled at him: 'What are *you* doing here? I thought we had
got rid of all you old buggers!'

One miner can say that to another and by his tone make the words positively an endearment. But there was no kindness, no wisdom, no understanding in the young man's spirit. He might just as well have lifted his fist and stuck the old man physically. He could not have hurt more. My grandfather did not go again to the office. His union, his life, all the pride and the labour and hopes he had put into it! Then to end up sitting looking into the fire, sad, perplexed, afraid to go near his old workplace lest he should be spat on. I walked down Rose Street, Dunfermline, the evening I heard of that encounter, with murder in my heart. I think if I had met a known Communist I would have been gaoled for manslaughter. That sort of incident told in bald outline may sound silly and trivial. Multiplied a thousand times and repeated all over Great Britain in a thousand different variations, it goes far to explain the dislike and distrust of the Communist Party that baulks all their efforts to achieve friendly relations with the rest of the working-class movement.

In visiting my old friends in Lochgelly and going through the years with them, I was not engaged in pointless reminiscing. It is all too easy to escape into the past. That was not my purpose. It was the present that concerned me.

For several years I had been living with a great fear; the fear that my grandfather's movement was a doomed thing. The fear that it was destined to travel the same road as the pre-Hitler socialist movement of Germany. And for the same discreditable reasons. Not because it had championed the cause of the poor too strenuously, but because, again and again, since 1926, when it ought to have stood its ground, it had found plausible reasons for running away.

And added to all that, making the situation just so much more impossible, because of the failure of a vast hinterland of comfortably situated people who hated fascism as much as I did, to realize that they could only preserve their liberties by making common cause with working-people who perforce must primarily fight for bread.

Those are precisely the mistakes that the organized working-class movement of Germany and liberal-minded, middle-class Germans made in the years before Hitler came to power.

The German social-democrats thought they could conquer by everlastingly retreating. Well-to-do German liberals thought they could enjoy their privileges without paying for them. Civil liberty, intellectual and spiritual liberty were very precious to them. But so was their property. They left too many German workers to face the threat of fascism on empty stomachs. A democracy that had reduced them to bare bone poverty and kept giving them reasons why they should agree to become still poorer, did not seem to vast numbers of German workers such a dazzling thing to fight for.

It was asking a great deal of an unemployed or underpaid working-man that he should not be inclined to believe that a change of any kind must be for the better. It is on that sort of mood that fascism, not at all necessarily under that name, knows how to batten.

In the summer of 1933 I revisited Berlin. Wondering if it was entirely a discreet thing to do, I sent a note to a German lady of great wealth and vivacity whom I first met in 1929 at an international peace conference in London. I promised that next time I came to Germany I would call on her. 'Next' time was September 1930, on a homeward journey from Russia. I telephoned from a Berlin hotel and inside an hour an exotic outsize bouquet of roses was spilling all over my minute back bedroom and an elegant car was waiting outside to take me along to a party that was going on at my friend's house.

It was then I met her husband. We wrangled good-temperedly about some current political affairs. He was a liberal. I was a socialist. With a friendly, mischievous smile, he made a point of showing me a signed photograph of Hindenburg that occupied the place of honour on his desk. He was every inch a patriot, very proud of being German. No one could have seemed more on top of the world than my charming host as I remember him then, with distinguished artists and scholars, as well as merely fashionable people, surrounding him in his very grand home. That was the only time I met him. Before I returned to Berlin Hitler had come to power. My friend's husband had been driven to commit suicide. In 1933 she was alone when I called. The vast drawing-room (I think I should say *salon*) that formerly I had seen crowded with gay chattering people, was now a ghostly room to walk through.

There were exquisite paintings by Cézanne and Gauguin on the walls. But the master of the house was dead. He had been too unhappy to want to go on living. Great possessions may be important, but they look very paltry in the home of a man who has committed suicide.

Millions of Germans learned too late that wealth cannot buy laughter, nor lighthearted fooling, nor peace of mind, nor even any real comfort once the spiritual values of a household are slain.

15

THE SECOND WORLD WAR

IN the summer of 1939, it looked as if Britain had no power left in the world unless the power to betray.

I returned again and again between '36 and '39 to my home district in the Fife coalfields hoping to find in this place I knew so well some evidence of fresh life, new beginnings. I could find only frustration and decay.

I turned from there to my comfortably off liberal friends. They were very much alive to the dangers threatening them from Germany, but there seemed no way of rousing in them the same sense of urgency about this other battle in which I was so eager to engage them; the fight against suffering right here at home.

In those dismal prewar years, with the betrayal of Spain still heavy on our souls, there followed the surrender of Austria, and the dismemberment of Czechoslovakia. Looking back, I can see now much more clearly than I did at the time, just how greatly discouraged I had become about the general drift of public affairs. There seemed nothing that people like myself could do. Fascist values were seeping in all around us. It was like a slow paralysis.

But luckily public affairs are not the whole of life. That summer of 1939 had for me another and very different side to it. When I could forget about outside happenings and think only of personal matters, it was a rather wonderful time.

Aneurin, who had had an appendix operation, was at home convalescing and beginning to recover all his old arrogance and verve. And our way of life had completely changed. We were no longer living in a suitcase with a diminutive London flat as sketchy headquarters when we were not flying from one part of the country to another. We had begun to take root. We had a home now; an absurdly unpractical but attractive one. I had been told that I must take him to the country when he left hospital and see that at least for some months he had lots of quiet and was not allowed to over-work. That meant looking for somewhere to live in the country. We fell in love with an old thatched cottage three miles from the nearest railroad station and fifty miles west of London. It had the one thing those old cottages so often lack. It had a feeling of space and lightness inside it. Then Aneurin discovered that the fireplace which had been built over in recent times could be opened up and restored to its original Elizabethan proportions. That settled it. This cottage he would have and no other.

Gaily we tackled the thousand and one settling in problems. We worked as the traditional navvy is supposed to work. Besides fixing the cottage there was a three-acre garden to be taken care of, most of which had been allowed to go derelict. We two numbskulls had not the least notion of all the work that would be needed to make this anything like the garden of our dreams. I was deter-mined to have an extravagantly large flower garden. Aneurin developed an ardour for planting cabbages and fruit trees that astounded me and was the joke of the season among all his friends.

But it became clear as the months passed that we would have to dedicate our entire lives and energies to the cottage and the garden, helped out even at that by a young country labourer and his sister, if we were really to cope with this business of living in the country. We who had always been footloose and fancy free, scorning com-pulsory ties of any kind, now found ourselves in hopeless bondage to this deceptively simple-looking old place.

Then we found the solution. We sent an S.O.S. to Scotland. Would mother come and take charge? Would father come with her? He had been ill, and we feared his life would be shortened if he went back to his work in the mines. But could they be persuaded to leave the land and the people they had lived among until their sixtieth birthdays? I knew that for them it must be a balance of good and evil. Their one son was in Australia. Their one daughter was tied by her work and her marriage more and more to the south. That meant that Scotland was less attractive to them than when the family was complete. But even at that, I realized it would be a big wrench. I was dubious as to how the experiment would work out. So we put it on a temporary basis. They were to come for a long holiday. If they did not like it they could always go back. They came and I think were happy from the first day because of our helplessness. They enjoyed our dependence on them.

Soon they were completely in command. Sometimes I had wondered if my childhood memories of home were the usual illusion of distance. Now I had proof that it was not so. Here again was the bright fireside, the easy, happy hospitality, the general air of comfort and well-being. Aneurin, who had already gone a long way towards seducing my parents, made them completely his own. We sketched a tiny three-room cottage that would be built in the far corner of the garden and be entirely theirs. They liked the idea and so did we. It is never a good thing for different generations to live too completely together. Each must have their own private quarters to retire to and each must be given free play to gather round them the sort of household goods that taste and association have conditioned them to need before they really feel at home. My parents, I could see, though very polite about our rather spartan and clean-lined taste in furnishings, thought their own cosy clutter definitely better. With two cottages, we could make the best of both worlds. We could join the old with the new, the familiar Scottish background with our more modern needs and tastes.

It all ought to have been as nearly perfect as a design for living can ever hope to be. So it was in a material and family sense. Also, now that Aneurin and I were emancipated from the routine work of the place, my parents doing what we had formerly tried to do in a third of the time and with three times as good results, we began to discover the countryside. And we had time to read, time to write, time to entertain our friends. This convalescent period was a heavenly interlude between the public work that we knew lay ahead of us and the restless busyness of the past.

But there was something lacking. When you read what do you read about? When you write what do you write about? When you talk with your friends where does your conversation take you? There are ghosts looking over our garden hedges, sitting beside us at our country fireside. Not the story book ghosts that belong to an ancient cottage. Those we could have lived with and joked about very happily. But it was not so easy to make light of the memory of the many friends we ourselves had known and loved who had been murdered, exiled, betrayed in the long seemingly endless night into which Europe had been plunged.

Aneurin was an adept at escaping to his cabbages. He could talk about them for hours and on the strength of his three-acre garden rather fancied himself as an expert on agriculture. Then often in the evening we would ban any talk about politics and he would read to me or he would scold me for being so unmusical and do his best to share with me his own fierce Welsh love of good music.

But why pretend there was any real escape ? Aneurin picks up a volume of A.E. Housman and begins to read. Soon he comes to the passage 'Be still, be still, my soul; it is but for a season: Let us endure an hour and see injustice done.'

A poisoned barb strikes into our nerves. We are back on the same old treadmill. There is no escaping.

The summer days shortened. We moved into early autumn. A thick pall of rumour deepened around us. In stunned wonderment we heard of the Stalin-Hitler pact. What did it mean ?

We were still trying to piece together all the available evidence when Hitler marched into Poland. That settled it. Whatever anything might mean there was at least no doubt as to what must be done. The British Government was bound to declare war. Mr. Neville Chamberlain had no choice in the matter. Nothing else would have been tolerated in that September mood. It had taken millions of our people a long time to make up their minds. It had taken them a long time to reach breaking point. Because they had wanted peace so badly they had backed wrong judgments. They had trusted. They had been misled. But this was once too often. A howl of wrath spread through the press. It was the echo of what was being said in the homes, in the streets, in every place where people met for work or fellowship.

And thus it came about that we fooled Hitler. For he could not have expected that declaration of war. In terms of the immediate military situation it was madness. After his pact with Stalin he must have considered the Polish invasion plain sailing. For without Russia, what could Britain do ? Protest once more, complain, save face as best it could ? But Hitler had reckoned without the stolid, slow-witted, gentle, peace-worshipping, and essentially

moral ordinary people of Britain. At this moment it was they who
stepped forward and took charge. It was they who dictated policy.
It was they who demanded action. Now that the final showdown
had come they were ready to go to war without so much as counting
their guns. They were going to war because they had to. If, in
that fateful September, we had failed Poland after the long sordid
story of other such failures, Britain would have gone to pieces
morally and in every other way. It was now or never. That was
how we felt. That was the motivation behind the tidal wave of
public opinion that swept the Chamberlain Government into war.
Maybe this was not a very intelligent way of behaving. Certainly
many who clamoured for action did so without full knowledge of
the military and diplomatic factors involved. But that is how it was.
I simply record the facts. There were clever people like Mr. Lloyd
George who counselled caution because we were so ill-prepared
both militarily and diplomatically. There was a handful of people
who urged peace at any price. Tory, Liberal, Labour, I.L.P., C.P.
and non-party elements, all contributed their quota to this small
minority made up of persons whose motives varied from genuine
pacificism to well meaning humanitarianism to coldly calculating
pronazism. But the main flow of public opinion would have none
of those. Quite quietly, almost sadly, with none of the old-
fashioned jingoism, flag-waving, shouting, parading, mass hysteria
of the 1914 mood, but with an utter steadiness and unbreakable
conviction, this strange island had decided it must fight. There was
nothing bellicose in its mood. Rather it was rooted in an exceedingly great love of peace. Almost everyone was now ready to face
even the hell of war since it was clear that only through and beyond war could we hope to find peace again.

Aneurin and I were at the cottage that Sunday in September
when war was declared. We tuned into the one o'clock news for
official confirmation that the fight had really begun. We had discussed all this so often and so much. Now at last it had come. Our
enemy Hitler had become the national enemy. All those who hated
fascism would have their chance now. They would have their
chance to fight back. No more one-sided massing of all the wealth,
influence and arms of international reaction against the workers of
first one country then another. I thought of Spain. I had a guilty

feeling about Spain. I said something to Aneurin that must have indicated the drift of my thoughts. He had been pacing up and down our long low whitewashed cottage room, for once too excited for words. He stopped walking up and down to rummage in a corner among a disorderly pile of gramophone records. He found what he was looking for. He found records we had not dared to play for more than a year: the marching songs of the Spanish Republican armies. Now we may listen to them again. We need not be ashamed. They ring triumphantly through the cottage. We are on our way back to Spain. We are bringing arms this time. We are coming fully armed. There are some memories too painful to live with unless you can do something about them. We cannot bring back our dead. But at least we can undo some of the wrong that official British policy has done there. I see young Bob Smillie's straw-coloured tousled head as he scrambles out of bed to spend that last evening with me in Barcelona. Young Bob, whose grandfather and mine began so much for us. Those two who were rebels, pioneers, colliers, great gentlemen. Those two who believed in their fellow men. And for a time it all seemed to be coming about as they had worked and planned and suffered that it should. Bob, do you remember how they talked? How they thought the hardest times were over? How they dreamed of wonderful cities in a world at peace and of their grandchildren dedicated to the fulfilment of their dreams? They could not know, Bob, that you would be buried under Spanish soil within two years of leaving College. They could not know that the Tories of England would still be in control. They could not know that the Labour Party they did so much to build would leave us stranded, would become the prey of piddling little career politicians, would measure up so inadequately to events, would be so dangerously timid, so depressingly orthodox, so unsure of its distinctive purposes. But the fight is not over yet. A new phase is just beginning. Opportunities recur in strange oblique fashion. Even those in England whose diplomacy helped Hitler to power must now unite with us in destroying him. To destroy Hitler and the power of the German war machine is not necessarily to destroy Hitlerism. But at least we are off in the right direction. There is no need to be hopeless any more; nor inactive. There will be plenty for everyone to do. We shall all have to help maintain the military front against nazism and many of us, more of us than ever before, will keep pounding away at the nazi creed as well. It is quiet now in the cottage. The music has stopped. My thoughts stop too. I pull myself back to the present. What has a declaration of war between Britain and Germany to do with much that I have been thinking about ? With Spain for instance. Formally, Britain is not at war with Spain. Franco is supposed to be neutral. So is Mussolini! But those are absurd suppositions. It is only a matter of time and secret planning among themselves until all the Axis powers are lined up against us. Otherwise there is no meaning to anything. It is all senseless killing. The blind and the deaf in high places who helped bring us to our present pass may take some time to grasp those things but in the final outcome even they will be forced to see that it is win all or lose all. There can be no half-measures.

Later in the day Aneurin became too restless to remain in the country. He set off for London. There was a rumour that an air raid alarm had already been sounded there. He went charging along in his Rover fourteen as if he were a whole crack regiment going into battle. I imagine he felt like that. He had no doubts. He was all out for fighting Hitler and not particular who his allies were or what weapons he used provided he gained his end.

Once Ni had left, I was alone in the cottage. It was very quiet now. After the first excitement of hearing the official declaration of war cold doubts began creeping in. Had I been carried away by the fervour of a Welsh husband ? Were his truths my truths ? What was the war about ? Who would lead us ? And for what ends ? Had Spain anything to do with it ? Or liberty ? Or democracy ? If so what about India ? Would India go free ? Why did Britain declare war when Colonel Beck's near-fascist Poland was invaded after acquiescing in the betrayal of democratic Czechoslovakia, the occupation of Austria ? Were not Britain and France the two controlling powers at the League of Nations Council that turned away unhearingly when China cried out against the theft of Manchukuo and Italy grabbed Abyssinia ?

Was it all a black-hearted game of power politics with ordinary men's lives and aspirations counting for nothing ? What was I to do ? Support the war, standing in with Chamberlain and his

Cabinet, knowing all the time that whatever I might want to be fighting for, my war aims were not their war aims and it was they, not I, who were in control ? What was I to do, I whose group loyalties were not a matter of geography but a thing of the spirit ? My tribe for whom I was prepared to fight were those who shared my values, who loved their fellow men and wanted to see them, whatever their nation or race, dignified, happy and free. Could we rally an army of such as they and fight Hitlerism wherever we found it ? Or was that romantic twaddle ? Was the only choice open to me to decide whether or not to fight against Hitler in the con- crete ranks, not of Utopia, but of a British Imperialism that had, in all truth, sins enough of its own that needed redressing ?

Ni home again, full of news and views and gossip. Funny driving today, says he. Everyone went a little faster, more erratically, more recklessly. C'est La Guerre! We may not be a danger to the Ger- mans yet but we are sure trying our 'prentice hand on one another.

In those first months of war Great Britain behaved in a fantastic fashion. Life went on very much as before. Some young men were conscripted. Others voluntarily enlisted. Still others who were brave enough to stand up to public ridicule and criticism joined A.R.P. services or campaigned for a Home Guard. We wrangled over the three pounds per week paid to full time A.R.P. wardens and behaved generally as if it were all a comic opera war against a cardboard enemy that need not be taken too seriously. Hitler care- fully encouraged this fearful levity. He left us pretty much alone, concentrating on mopping up, country after country, the whole continent of Europe.

The course of events brought one shock after another but we continued to have a good deal of the spectator attitude. The Government made few demands on us. We were lulled into a false sense of security.

When Russia invaded Finland a ferocious anti-Russian campaign broke out in sections of the press. There was much more fervour and drive behind speeches and writings condemning Russian aggression than behind any expressions of hostility that had as yet been voiced towards Germany. It was only after Hitler out- manoeuvred us in Norway that the British Government began slowly to wake up to the realities of this war it had undertaken to fight. But so slowly, so very slowly! The Maginot mentality of the Chamberlain cabinet, even after Chamberlain himself had been deposed, continued to poison the air with a deadly complacency. In May 1940, when Mr. Winston Churchill became Prime Minister and Labour and Liberal leaders were brought into the Cabinet, everyone counted on a vastly more energetic conduct of the war. We knew that the reverses in Europe were serious. We knew that a drastic speed-up of our war effort was essential, but even at this late hour we had nothing like a realistic appraisement of what was happening. We were still half asleep.

Apart from my ordinary peacetime activities, in those early months of the war, there was nothing much for me to do. There were many of us, millions of us, in that position. It was not that we were not willing enough to do whatever might be asked of us but that little or nothing was asked. Trade and industry continued hobbling along almost on a peacetime basis. There were two million registered unemployed. A vast unused reservoir of machine power and labour power was as yet barely tapped.

Then almost overnight the whole situation changed. France had fallen. The war for us began in earnest. The news that France had fallen came as a shock to most people. The public was not prepared for it. Every hour of the day the correctly modulated unemotional voices of our radio announcers had given out news reports that made each new retreat sound like a victory.

Then came the deluge! Then came Dunkirk! Then came the rummest turn of the war; the snatching of strength out of weakness, of victory from defeat. In the first tense moments of expected invasion you think of yourself as a soldier, quite literally a soldier. Your instinct is to reach for your gun. But millions of us had no guns to reach for. We were civilians. We were of little use as fighting units. We had neither training nor equipment.

But of course, this gun-reaching mood passes very quickly. Your common sense comes to the rescue. You realize that your imagination has been over-dramatizing, over simplifying. Modern warfare means more than the firing of guns. Guns have got to be made as well as fired. Transport has got to be maintained to carry people and goods from place to place. The whole industrial life of the country has to be kept going.

Therefore, even although the Germans might any moment appear on our doorsteps, what was asked of most of us was simply that we carry on with our normal occupations, not permitting ourselves to be thrown out of gear whatever might befall.

In this phase of the war workers in the defence industries became of paramount importance. Our pilots had to have planes. The factory workers had to produce the planes. Failure in the aircraft factories meant failure in the air. Failure in the air meant invasion and defeat. In the defence plants working hours were lengthened, labour was diluted, effort was intensified.

The standpoint of the trade union movement was that it was better to make a temporary sacrifice of some of its rights than for Hitler to win, which would mean the permanent loss of all its rights. Also the union leaders received solemn guarantees from the Government that at the end of the war every trade union practice temporarily abrogated would be fully restored.

But all this extra spurt in the factories was more than cancelled out by the time lost during air raids. Air raids had now become a daily, nightly occurrence. There was only one thing to be done. All essential industries would have to be kept going even when there were German planes in the vicinity. Millions of men and women who were civilians, not soldiers, would have to learn to stand up to direct enemy fire, taking their chance like soldiers of the line.

Lord Beaverbrook, then Minister of Aircraft Production, was impatient to have this new policy adopted. But he alone had no power to enforce it. This was something that no one Minister could accomplish; nor any one political party. It was the ultimate test of national unity, of national will to survive, of national morale. In the final analysis the initiative had passed to the working people of Britain. Everything depended on how much they were prepared to do, how great the risks they were prepared to face. That there was nothing they were not prepared to do is now recorded history. Never once has the Government of Great Britain run into difficulties by asking too much of the people of Britain. It is only when it has asked too little, or applied measures that people, rightly or wrongly, believed to be less than adequate, that it has had to face serious criticism.

In those strange, terrifying yet exhilarating days following the retreat from Dunkirk I, like millions of others, was for the first time called into active service. And I, like all those others, was thankful. The worst possible hell at such a time would have been to have nothing to do. For the only alternative to work was to hang around fretting and worrying. Home life, in any peacetime sense, had for the time being come to an end. Aneurin's time was spent between Parliament and his constituency. The tiny cottage that we had planned and built for my parents was almost completed but they were not to be its first occupants. It was handed over to Nicola, an adorable ten months' old red-headed baby. Kay, Nicola's mother, came too. Their home was in Chelsea, one of the worst blitzed London areas. They were old friends and we were happy we could offer them the relative safety of a country district fifty miles west of London. Nicola's father was at that time 'somewhere in France' serving with the Royal Air Force.

16

LONDON BRIDGE IS BURNING DOWN

I HURRIED down into the East End of London with a slip of paper in my hand. It made me feel safer. It was my talisman. London town is burning down, burning down, burning down, London town is burning down, my fair lady. No, that is all wrong. It should be London bridge is falling down, falling down, falling down . . .

The silly old jingle kept churning around inside my head. My taxicab had to make a dozen unexpected detours where roads were barricaded off because of unexploded bombs and there was the smell and the smoke from massive piles of debris where the effects of the blitz the night before had not yet been completely brought under control.

I was on my way to a factory that made army overcoats and was right in the heart of the district that had been hardest hit by one of London's worst air raids in the middle of the previous night. The factory was unharmed but the homes of the factory workers living in the surrounding streets had been terribly mauled. There had been many deaths. More than half of the employees had had their homes or their nearest neighbours' homes destroyed. Some of the families had been trapped in the burning buildings. Others were assembling their relatives and what little might be left of their household possessions in the rest centres that had been established close at hand.

I was on my way to the factory in answer to an S.O.S. that had been sent to the head office of the Ministry of Aircraft Production that morning, although this type of factory was not normally under its charge. I had been working in the Aircraft Ministry for several weeks now, helping with the emergency problems created in the factories as a result of incessant air raids. This morning's task was not unusual.

Only a third of the coatmakers had come in to begin their day's work. And even those who had reported for duty were in a dazed condition. The factory supervisor wanted help in pulling them together, in getting the work of the factory going again.

What inhuman monsters some newspaper reporters would make of the London cockneys! Always smiling! Homes blasted, families wiped out and never a tear. Hell let loose all round them, yet no one showing any sign of fear. That is all nonsense. Human beings don't react like that. The glory of the working people of London was something much greater. It was not that they did not taste the full bitterness of grief and fear. It was that blinded by tears, half sick with fear, they somehow kept going. After the shock of each new raid they gathered themselves together in an amazingly short space of time and went on with the work they knew had to be done and that they were determined to do. In this factory that morning, for instance, I noticed a woman of my mother's age working at her sewing machine with desperate speed and concentration. Her home had been struck the night before. This was her way of carrying herself through the shock. And there was another thing sustaining her. Her youngest son was in the army. 'And who,' she said to me when I went to her to pay my respects, 'is going to make a coat to wrap around him with the cold days drawing in if his own mother is not willing to help him ?' That was the first time I heard an industrial worker so simply, so directly, link her work with the needs of her family serving in the army. Later I heard this sentiment again and again. Workers were working for wages and employers were employing for profit but cutting through and above this peacetime relationship was the plus factor of helping to serve and protect those others of themselves who were in the fighting services.

I said I went to the East End of London with a slip of paper in my hand. This paper went everywhere with me. I felt incomplete without it. It was marching orders of a strange new kind never before known in our country. The first sentence read, 'All key men must stand by their posts throughout air raids or until relieved.' There was nothing unusual in the wording. Those words at such a time were very ordinary.

But this particular order was unique because of the manner and source of its origin. It was the marching orders that the Welsh miners, after meeting together in the lodges throughout the valleys and after full and democratic discussion, had issued to themselves.

Aneurin brought a copy home with him in the first days of the blitz. I pocketed it, saying it might be useful to me in some of the defence factories. So it was. I handed it around to groups of shop stewards in the process of making up their minds whether or not to carry on with production during blitz periods. What the shop stewards decided, you could depend on the rest of the employees endorsing. The bold black headline on this paper I had with me, 'South Wales Miners' Federation', and the instructions that followed, interested them enormously. Here was a document above suspicion. There was no private profit motive behind it, no petty politics. This was their own kind calling to them. This was one worker calling to another.

In times of emotional crisis most of us are apt to fix on some one thing and give it an importance that rationally considered may be quite disproportionate. With some people it is a lucky charm. With others a rosary or some other tangible symbol of their religion. A friend of mine who was a senior officer in the air force told me once about a young fighter pilot, already decorated for bravery, who asked for and was given exemption from duty one evening because he had forgotten the mascot he always carried with him. I am not superstitious in any of the more obvious ways. Nor am I religious if religion means attending any particular church or chapel. But I admit that this document issued by the people I knew best and who had the first claim on my loyalties, this document was a tangible something I could hold on to, linking me with the colliery districts and the men and women there, and meant more to me than any rational use I could make of it. What the miners had decided to do, the transport workers did, the defence workers did. Each group of workers in turn fell into line. It was for me a deeply moving spectacle. Those people I had always believed in, whose cause I had tried to champion through the lost years between two wars, those people who had been despised and forgotten and so shabbily used, were bigger than any clique of men who had ever governed them. And they were coming through! Modestly, competently, kindly, no bragging, no posturing! I was excited and happy and proud, for at the heart of all the terror and suffering something was struggling to be born, the Britain of the future, the Britain I had always hoped for and believed in. I knew there would be setbacks. I knew that though the common people were the toast of the town in this time of crisis, when safer times returned there would be those who in cultivated accents would try to push them out of the picture again. But my hunch was that this present generation would be less easily pushed than their fathers were, those fathers who marched back in 1918 expecting to inherit the new world they had been promised, only to find themselves back again in the heartbreak army of the unemployed.

A group of mechanics working at their benches in a famous Lancashire aircraft factory were among the first to impress on me the essential difference between the 1940 mood and that of the men of 1914. I thought they were singing 'There will always be an England.' But when I listened more carefully I found that to the same tune they had invented words of their own. Instead of 'There will always be an England' they sang 'Will there always be an England—with a job in it for me ?'

Those men were good-tempered, patriotic and ardently anti-fascist. Even when we talked of the pre-war years when many of them had been unemployed, there was remarkably little bitterness in what they had to say. But there was one thing on which they were resolved. They came back to this theme again and again and again. Grimly, resolutely, unanimously they insisted that they were not going through war for a second time to end up in the bread-line once more at the end of it all. That sentiment cut right into the heart of the contemporary mood.

It did not mean that the present generation was cynical or disillusioned. It was neither. It was simply that there was more astringency in its thinking, a greater sense of awareness. Memories of the 1914-18 war and of what happened afterwards had warned it of how possible it is to win on the battlefield, and then at the end of all the fighting, return to peacetime conditions, only to discover that you have lost most of what you had hoped you were fighting for.

In 1914-18 men were more trusting. They did not wonder quite so much if there would be a job for them after the war. They took all that for granted. They took everything for granted. When they thought of the future it was in Messianic terms. There was to be a new Jerusalem in England's green and pleasant land. Never for a moment did they doubt it.

Vague abstractions about a new heaven on earth, a land fit for heroes to live in, were definitely out of date. Occasionally an old-timer in politics attempted that kind of oratory. His audience were quite unmoved. It had all been said before. It was only words, unhappy words, that carried the mind back to memories of 1914-18, then to the years of disenchantment that followed.

Yet, paradoxical though it may sound, it was this very lack of response to grandiose oratory that encouraged many of us to feel optimistic about the future. In seeming to ask less than was promised to their fathers, a younger generation was actually asking more. It wanted the deed, not the word. It wanted the immediate and the particular, not the remote and the abstract. It was less easy to cheat. It had been warned by past failures. It was thinking ahead. Its basic demands were modest enough. But to ask that your country's resources shall be organized in such a way that no one need beg for his daily bread, is not as modest as it sounds. Its fulfilment has revolutionary implications; and that too, the present generation was beginning to understand. But even when it used words like 'revolutionary', which it did not often do, it did so in a balanced, businesslike way. It was not thinking of streets running with blood, of guillotines, of violence and destruction. It was thinking constructively of the economic and social changes essential before a nation can provide work for all its citizens at fair wage rates and under reasonable conditions.

And one thing more it was thinking about, even as it fought and worked; how man can enjoy all that—and freedom too.

This was the big issue; the biggest in the world. No country had yet won through to so much. Germany had hacked its way through to a scientifically planned and controlled economy but in the doing had murdered all liberty. It had given to the twentieth century a gruesome caricature of what a modern society might be. Soviet Russia was another contemporary example of a new attitude towards property within a state, who shall own it, control it, and for

what ends. In Soviet Russia there was not the race and sex discrimination, nor glorification of force as good in itself, that black-
ened the face of nazi Germany. The two countries were very
different. But the Russian model was at best a primitive unsatisfactory foreshadowing of what an enlightened modern state could
do with its resources, economic, social and cultural. There too this
issue of individual freedom had not been solved. Could Britain do
what the dictatorship countries had failed to do ? Could it plan its
material resources yet leave men's spirits free? Or was that a dream?
Was that Utopian ? Did that belong maybe to some future century
but not to ours ? But why not to ours ? The war had broken down
all the old boundary lines. We could not go back. Our only
safety lay in being daring enough in the demands we made on ourselves, our neighbours, our institutions. If we were not to be
trapped by the past, to be made too weak, too timid, too divided
by it to be equal to the challenge of the nazi creed, we would have
to learn to move forward very fast. After all the nazi had no
modesty. Why should it always be those who uphold the rights of
ordinary men and women who lack the arrogance of their mission ?

All those things we talked about in that atmosphere of heightened apperceptiveness that war conditions had brought to us.
Even that we should talk so was in itself a great new gain. But it was
still early days. We were only at the beginning. There was no
clarity, no finality, only a new confidence in ourselves, in one
another, in all that we had been too diffident to do in the years
before the war, but now so firmly realized would have to be done.

17

MANNING THE FACTORY FRONT

WE had settled down by the autumn of 1940 to what was to be wartime routine for many months to come. When the raids were severe the shops closed early. There were no cinemas nor restaurants open in the evening. Everyone not engaged on essential work took cover where best he could. When the blitz lifted, out we all came again. The shops, restaurants and cinemas reopened. As much as possible of normal living promptly reappeared.

The invasion scare began to recede. The exaltation of the Dunkirk days was not forgotten. But we had ceased to be quite so tense.

One of the tragi-comedies of wartime was the commuting of thousands of children between town and country. Once in the country where they had been sent for safety, they ought to have remained there. But children grew homesick, parents grew lonely. Only strict compulsory disciplining could have kept them apart. Should that kind of discipline have been applied? That would have been the mechanically efficient thing to do. Instead, the Government muddled along in a tentative, traditionally English way. Eloquent appeals were addressed to the parents. Cheap travel rates for periodic visits to their children in the country were arranged. That reduced but by no means stopped the ebb and flow. There was only one thing to be said for the Government's behaviour. It was very human. The emotional needs of parent and child were calling the tune. In the long run it was perhaps not such a bad way of doing things. There is more than one way of sustaining a nation's morale. Compulsory separation of parent and child is not necessarily the best.

Some city parents chose to keep their children beside them, even through the worst of the blitz. You could see those youngsters asleep in the shelters at night. It was a strange, macabre atmosphere for them in the early months of the war. But there are human beings who can make a home even out of a corner of a public air raid shelter. It was fascinating to watch this home-making instinct at work. Family groups became used to one particular spot. In terms of comfort or safety it might be no better, perhaps not as good, as a hundred other locations. But this was their own particular corner, and each night it was this and no other they insisted on having. In time all this became systematized, the hygiene and general amenities were improved, the shelterers themselves formed committees responsible for the cleanliness and good order of their sleeping quarters.

A mighty controversy broke out in the press about the provision of deep shelters. It would have been very fine to have had them. And it was remiss of the Government not to have done much more in this direction in the earlier months of the war. But all that having been said, it was obvious that there were some political groups who were willing to ride this particular horse to the death. They cared more about using men, time, machinery and building materials for this purpose than for any other aspect of the war. Russia had not then become a belligerent.

In this second winter of war we were still far from complete mobilization. 'Go To It' placards adorned every billboard. They were looked at ironically by at least a million unemployed who were still looking in vain for work.

Everything was in a transition stage. All the time new defence plants were coming into production and absorbing new labour. But there was an awkward hiatus in many districts while luxury and less essential industries were being closed down and war industries were not quite ready to take over the men and women thrown out of their peacetime occupations. Some of the delays were inevitable. Others were part of the price a nation at war is forced to pay if its industries are a highly complicated maze of conflicting private interests. It takes time to sort out all the various claims, eliminating some, consolidating others, attempting to construct a workable scheme equal to wartime needs.

While waiting for the new defence plants to come into production, those already functioning had to carry intolerable burdens. We were short of guns, tanks, planes, every single military necessity. The established plants were urged to work seven days a week, ten to twelve hours a day. I had sometimes to go into a factory with an S.O.S. from headquarters asking that an emergency order be rushed through. When I saw the tired faces around me of men and women who had already completed a full working day, I marvelled at their response. Instead of serious grumbling there was a little good-humoured 'grousing' but, basically, their mood was one of great pride and heightened self-respect. They were needed. They were essential. The rest of us were depending upon them.

Each factory had its own personality. In some it was all grim endurance. Management and men had not yet learned how to adjust themselves to a wartime atmosphere. As a patriotic duty they worked all the hours they were asked to work and that was all. There was no warmth, no easy cooperation between employer and employee. The employer was probably of the old-fashioned kind with a feudal attitude towards his employees. The employees in turn were defensive and resistive to any demands until they were sure they were not the whim of their employer dictated by profit motives, but official requests made directly by the Government and endorsed by their union leaders.

Other factories were entirely different in atmosphere. You could sense the difference within five minutes of entering the building. The old feudal relationship had vanished. Everyone in the works was trying to humanize life as much as possible for everyone else. There was a fellow feeling, a family sense stronger than any difference in opinions and status. And this change in atmosphere was not just an intangible something floating in the air. It made life pleasanter in all kinds of concrete ways. The factory canteen for instance was a happy place to go into. It was a club, a concert hall, a debating society as well as a place to eat. Concert parties came into the canteen during the dinner hour break, the best known artists in the land proud to help in this way. But some of the best fun were the improvised concerts made up from local talent among the workers themselves. Also the wiser works committees knew the value of the short ten-minute breaks several times a day. They did not wait until the Government ordered these rest periods. They had worked out rest periods for themselves and the inevitable cup of tea was the high spot of the break. Especially where women were employed, those breaks for tea were a great feature of the working day. Life was strenuous, life was earnest, but there was also drama, excitement, a heightened sense of living in those war-time factories. The men and women in them were earning their living. But they were doing a great deal more than that and were very conscious that they were. This was their way of fighting Hitler. They were answering back in the one way they knew.

This mad race could not go on forever. There is a limit to the length of time men can work seven days a week, ten and twelve hours a day. But for those emergency months following the fall of France this tempo was maintained in thousands of key defence industries. This was no long-term policy. Everyone knows that when hours are lengthened beyond a certain point output is retarded, not increased. But an emotional exaltation giving the body powers endurance far beyond the normal, falsified for a time the ordinary laws of industrial psychology and carried us through the crisis. Also long before the end of 1940 it was quite taken for granted that our industrial workers would face up to maximum risks as well as maximum physical strain. The real miracle of the factories was not so much individual acts of excep-tional bravery, although these were plentiful enough, as the general level of steady nerves and good manners. I was in a room with three or four hundred other women in one of our factories that make barrage balloons when the warning was given that German planes would be passing over our heads in less than five minutes. This was the moment when work stopped and we had all to hurry to the basement.

I had expected to be among the last to go below, which is the routine procedure in the case of the local supervisors in charge of each room, but the women decided otherwise. A plump matronly woman stood still in the queue and insisted that I go ahead of her. That was the general wish and there was no time for arguing. I felt humble in those women's presence. No panic, no hysteria. I was a visitor among them. They could be gracious even at such a moment. When we were all below I had a gentle argu-ment with my friend, Mrs. Johnston, who had stopped the queue and insisted that I go on to safety ahead of her. She was the wife of one of our merchant seamen, had worked in the cotton mills twenty years ago and was now back in the factories 'doing her bit.' She would have been surprised and embarrassed at the thought that anyone should regard her as a heroine. All she did was to volunteer for night shift work so that she could be home by eight in the morning, make breakfast for three children before they went off to school, attend to housework, washing and shopping, cook an evening meal for the family, then report for night duty at eight in the evening. 'But when do you sleep ?' I asked her. 'I manage,' she said, 'I manage fine if there is no air raid to wake me up. I go to bed about eleven and sleep until five. The oldest boy will soon be fourteen and he is the man of the house while his daddy is away. He keeps the younger two quiet and makes up the fire and prepares the tea when he comes in from school.'

The sheer modesty of the requests made by some of our defence workers who had to carry on under specially dangerous circumstances was breath-taking. I was puzzled when the report came into the London office that there was some sort of trouble among the shop stewards at one of our great southern aerodromes where planes were made as well as tested. I knew there was a very good group of workers there and went to meet them, wondering what could have happened. Once at the aerodrome I called a meeting of the shop stewards. I always enjoyed those encounters and was invariably predisposed to believe that if they had a grievance it was a genuine one.

On this occasion the soreness that had arisen had nothing to do with anything inside the aerodrome. But dotted around the aerodrome, only a field or two away, were the small houses where the workers' wives and children lived. The aerodrome itself had magnificent underground air raid shelters but those small homes had no air raid shelters of any kind. When the siren sounded, the workers were nervous and wanted to quit work and run off home. They were not thinking of themselves. They knew they were safer in the works. It was anxiety for their families that broke their nerve. That, remember, was in the autumn of 1940 when there was an acute shortage of cement and we had not yet got round to building all the shelters needed by the civilian population.

The following day the works personnel manager, the leading shop steward and myself were in conference with the county authorities responsible for the provision of shelters to private households. The county authorities were themselves in a jam. They were willing enough to build shelters but the army had priority rights in building materials, so they could promise us nothing. What we did then is not for publication. It was an enjoyable act of piracy. All that mattered to us was getting hold of enough cement. That we did, and before a single shelter had been actually built, with only the knowledge that they were going to be built to comfort and sustain them, every worker in the aerodrome agreed to carry on even when the nazi bombers were over their homes.

The steadiness and reliability of the entire population gave the Government its chance. It gave it a breathing space in which to work out long-term defence plans both in industry and in the services. That was what we were now waiting for. That was the next logical stage in the war. By a series of improvisations we had held together during an exceptionally dangerous time. A great deal was taken on trust. No one was overcritical. No one expected Britain's industries to be remodelled overnight. But it was time to move on now. We were becoming impatient. Once again the people of Britain were ahead of the Government. They were ready for the third phase in the war and the Government was still lingering in the second phase. First there had been the phoney months, then, following Dunkirk, the heroic months. Now it was time to move on to a solidly constructive all-out effort. The chief ground for complaint against the Government was the dilatory piecemeal way in which production problems were being handled. Nothing like maximum use was yet being made of Britain's man power and machine power. It was not enough for national leaders to make constant reference to the bravery of the common man. The common man had learned to take his own and his neighbour's good nerves for granted. He was now becoming increasingly anxious that those qualities should help the Government forward to new achievements, not become its alibi for muddling along doing less than enough.

In a defence factory near Manchester I was given a sharp reminder of just how much room for improvement there was if this Battle for Production that we were now all talking about was to be won. I had been warned that the managing director in charge of this particular plant was a surly, disgruntled fellow. In the first five minutes after my arrival he did his best to live up to the descriptions I had had of him. He wasted no time in coming to the point. Almost his first words were: 'There is no need for you or anyone else to come here asking us to do more than we are doing. It is damned impertinence. Your head office would be much better employed if it applied itself to correcting its own shortcomings. If you want increased output go about it in a businesslike way. I am sick of Government people *asking* me how much I can step up production. If this thing was being handled properly they ought to be *telling* me, not asking me.'

I skipped the first part of his remarks. Lord Beaverbrook had urged all essential industries to work Sundays as well as weekdays. So far this plant had not done so. It was working fewer hours per week than other factories similarly situated. I had already talked to the employees' representatives and they assured me that so long as the national emergency lasted, they were willing to work as long as was required of them but that so far, the boss had not asked more than a handful of them to come in on Sundays. That cleared the ground so far as they were concerned. It was now up to me to find out what was in the mind of their employer. He was a rather crusty old Tory, opinionated and set in his ways, but quite certainly not consciously sabotaging. After his initial explosion, he mellowed charmingly, sent for his production experts, charts, graphs, all complete, and explained his point of view.

He had an excellent case. There was a bottleneck in one of his departments. He had done everything possible to maximize production at this point, then adjusted the work of the other departments accordingly. By keeping the entire staff working on Sundays, as Lord Beaverbrook had urged, all that would have happened would have been a useless accumulation in the number of some of the component parts without any increase in the one thing that mattered, the number of completed machines dispatched from the factory.

From there he went on to expound what he called the elementary principles of wartime economic planning. First find out where the bottlenecks occur. Find out not in terms of individual factories or even groups of factories, but by a nation-wide survey of the materials, machine power and man power available. Leave nothing undone to maximize production at these points, including, if the men and the machines can stand it (which few can and none can for long), working a seven-day week. Then regulate the production of all other processes so that by the final assembly line there is a scientific balance of parts, not a madly lop-sided over-production in some departments, and under-production in others.

As gently as possible, I edged into the discussion the consideration that his was a counsel of perfection. The Government would ultimately arrive there but in the meantime piecemeal improvisation had been inevitable. He thawed enough to concede the time factor but sent me away with his main theme ringing in my ears. Modern warfare depended on industrial output. Haphazard production was treachery to the fighting services. Maximum production could be achieved only after centralized planning. Centralized control was not enough. In some instances it merely obstructed the more enterprising business executives. It told them what they could not do and what they could not have without organizing the skill of their employees and the precious machine tools to maximum national advantage.

Many other men in charge of defence plants talked to me along similar lines. They were not only ready for more centralized planning. They were panting for it. Those men were seldom the main shareholders of the companies they were working for. Some of them were not shareholders at all. They were simply salaried officials. In the peace years they had worked for private companies and had been quite satisfied to do so. In war circumstances they were anxious that their best services should be given to the State. But what they objected to most bitterly was the untenable halfway position in which many of them found themselves, their salaries and hopes of promotion dependent on the skill with which they safeguarded the present and future interests of the particular firm they were working for, their general instructions coming from Government departments and the two loyalties not always by any means squaring.

Among rank-and-file factory workers there was also a growing number of critics of production methods. Shop stewards and trade union officials were giving an increasing amount of their time and thought to queries addressed to them on this issue by the men they represented. After Soviet Russia entered the war a new impetus was given to this kind of questioning. Until then a small but active minority of shop stewards under Communist Party direction had used production deficiencies as a stick with which to beat the Government and as material for 'stop the war' political agitation. From the moment Hitler attacked Russia they changed their tactics, henceforth regarding any hold-up in production as a challenge to constructive criticism.

But whatever the reasons for men's actions, and the dominant reason was simple uncomplicated determination to win the war, what was well worth noting was that rank-and-file workers, for the first time in Britain's history, had become production-conscious and were discussing industrial output with an avidity that in the peace years had been reserved for football and racing results. Wherever, with or without good reason, men considered that less than the best use was being made of man power or machine power in the factory where they were employed, they demanded explanations. Employers in tune with the times knew how to meet this mood and turn it to mutual advantage. They readily accepted, and sometimes themselves were the first to suggest, that a wartime Production Council be set up composed of representatives of management and men. A competent patriotic employer had nothing to lose and much to gain by this arrangement.

On one occasion, inside a defence plant I was visiting, a blue dungareed mechanic approached me, glared at the personnel manager who happened to be with me and said to me, 'I want to talk to you—alone.' We stepped aside. First he talked about the fall of France and all the highly placed Quislings there who had not been found out until it was too late. Then he went on to hint of sabotage inside this very plant. Queer things were happening. It was not all as it appeared to be on the surface.

I looked at his strained, anxious face. Whether there was any truth or not in what he was saying, he undoubtedly believed it. We walked together to the room where he worked. I wished to find out if his workmates took him seriously, or if he was regarded as a crack-pot. A number of the mechanics who worked beside him, although less melodramatic about it all, were plainly uneasy and unable to make up their minds.

This was a most unwholesome atmosphere. The manager was entirely to blame. It could never have occurred in a factory where a trustworthy Production Council was functioning. The root of the trouble was that the manager was a die-hard of the 'theirs not to reason why, theirs but to do or die' mentality. There was a perfectly simple explanation of the hold-up in production which had become the starting point of the sabotage rumours. But the manager thought it was sufficient that he himself should know the reason without sharing it with anyone else. Trade unionism was anathema to him. Any kind of working-class representation was anathema to him. He had not thought fit to establish any kind of communication between himself and his workpeople. The world had moved on and left him on his dreary pinnacle of obsolete isolationism. But he was on the losing side. Eventually he had to compromise. Democratic co-operation and consultation on the basis of common citizenship, not the old-fashioned master and man relationship, was the new order of the day.

Or at least it is true to say that it was in that direction the tides were flowing. Working men and women, in their anxiety to win the war, had given up cherished trade union privileges; they had accepted what was virtually industrial conscription; they were not free to move from job to job but had to remain wherever the Minister of Labour, Mr. Ernest Bevin, decided they could be of greatest national service. Men working for three pounds per week in the coalpits for instance, who had left and found work in factories where they earned twice as much, were asked to return to their former work and wages when the pits became seriously denuded of able-bodied miners. Those who did so felt they had earned the right to be something more than dumb cogs in their country's industrial machine.

It was too early yet to say where all this was leading us. There were those who bade us be careful lest all this economic centralization should undermine our general citizen liberties. Other countries, they pointed out, had travelled this self-same road, only at a later stage to lose their way and end up in a concentration camp. Only one thing was certain. The Britain of the future was being hammered into shape, bit by bit, here and now, under the inescapable compulsions of military necessity. It was not a question of war-time, then peacetime. Much that was happening was a continuous flow.

18

WHAT ARE WE FIGHTING FOR?

I WAS glad to be back at the cottage for a quiet week-end. Aneurin was there too. After the scarred cities, this was delightful. The war seemed suddenly far away. But ten minutes later it caught up with us again. On the way home we called at the Pineapple, our local pub. Our kind neighbour, the landlord, had just received news that his soldier son had lost a leg. We sat for a while trying to find the right words. But what was there to say? The boy's mother joined us. She had been crying. It was the boy's future that worried her. There was an undercurrent of angry resentment to her grief. Why had this to happen to *her* boy? He had never done anyone any harm. What was it all about? What would be the end to all the maiming and the killing and the sadness? Would the world be any better for it all? Would it? That was what I was hoping to think out a little more clearly in the relative peace and quiet of the countryside.

But baby Nicola, our wartime baby, had extended her rule over both cottages. She could now do an enchantingly uncertain stagger walk from the one to the other. On Sunday afternoon I made a bid for favour by offering to take her to the lily wood. Nicola loved a jaunt. Kay and Aneurin and Dad decided to come too. I was surprised to hear voices in the woods. Usually we had them entirely to ourselves. But of course. Evacuees. I had forgotten that almost every cottage was now sheltering families from London or from Portsmouth. A group of children passed us. They were intently talking to one another and looked happy and absorbed. They hurried on into a part of the woods I scarcely knew; the part that before the war had been sacred to the breeding of pheasants. Mere humans had not been permitted to walk there.

There was a certain primitive symbolism in this picture. As between pheasants and children, the children, for the time being at least, were being given priority rights. How would it be after the war? Would the children once more be crowded into the back yards of mean little streets, confronted, whenever on rare occasions they ventured into the country, with those barbaric 'Trespassers Will Be Prosecuted' notices? Or would this densely populated little island learn to space out its population with more all-round justice? In a sanely planned world there was no reason of course why there should not be ample room for man, bird, and beasts. I thought of Mumford's *Culture of Cities*. It had given Ni great joy. Its main thesis, that there was an optimum size for a city and its industries and that expansion beyond that point was wholly bad, had long been one of his favourite themes. He became clamorously eloquent whenever this subject was raised.

There was a great deal to be thought out if we were to rebuild Britain after the war. I was getting along nicely with my daydreams. Then suddenly I was brought sharply to earth. A surly old game-keeper was shouting at the children. Maybe they were doing something they ought not to do but there was no need for so much venom in his voice. How he loathed seeing those city youngsters playing in the woods! How he loathed for that matter seeing us or anyone else in the woods. For the woods were Private Property. They belonged to his titled master. He too belonged to his master. Body and soul this old fellow was a product of England's feudal past. His presence was a reminder of just how much of England still belongs to that past. We were at war and there was much vague talk about building a new Britain after the war. Yes, but how and where would we build it? Would it be possible to plan for the general weal or would the many have to be suppliants paying high ransom to the few for the privilege of building so much as a hen-house? One of the things that was worrying me at this time was the gap between our generalized statement about the fine new world that was to be, and the practical steps we were, as a nation, prepared to take to implement them. It was fashionable to talk about liberty and fraternity. It was not nearly so fashionable to come down to earth and ask, for instance, who after the war, would own Britain's land. The Government in trust for the People?

Or would there still be the great landed estates fenced off as private pleasure grounds for an exclusive few with, as their corollary, the rest of the population crowded into over-built, rack-rented, ill-planned urban areas?

Back at the cottage and all of us sniffing a wonderful odour that reminded me of my school days: scones and pancakes freshly baked for tea. Some friends had come in. Mother had set tea for a dozen. There was no butter on the table. The little there was had been used up in baking. But we were not complaining. There was a wonderful assortment of home made jams. Altogether, a most lavish looking wartime tea table. I knew perfectly well what was happening. Mother was doing a food blitz over the week-end while Ni and I were at home. The entire week's rations of meat, butter and the rest were being used up. But there was no use remonstrating with her. She was built that way. This was her happiness. Nor was there any need to be tragic about it. She would find substitutes. Also, as she continually reminded us, we had lots to be thankful for. We were not nearly so badly off as the average family in town. Our vegetable garden had become an important asset. Eggs at that time were not yet rationed. Nor fish and poultry. They were expensive, but available for those who could afford the price. All this meant that there was a cushion under the rich that the poor could not share. We were not rich but not so poor that we need go hungry. To know what wartime rationing meant you had to be too poor to be able to afford meals in restaurants or to buy the expensive extras such as fowl and fish not included in the rationing schemes. The unfairness in all this was another of the problems that were worrying me.

Nine o'clock, Nicola long since in bed, our friends departed, no sound except the crackling of the logs in our great open fireplace and the occasional zoom of planes overhead, German bombers on their way to our cities or our own leaving for enemy territory. We switch on the radio to hear the nine o'clock news bulletin. Immediately it is over we switch off again. At one time we had waited eagerly at the end of the Sunday night news service for the J. B. Priestley broadcasts. Now there was no speaker we cared to listen to. Priestley had been put off the air. That was another of the problems that were worrying me. In itself it was a small thing, but as Priestley had made himself the spokesman of the 'little man' did this in effect mean that it was such as they who were being pushed aside ? Had the few high Tories who deplored his broadcasts more influence in the land than the great majority of the listening public who heartily approved of them ?

Strange the successive moods that sweep over a country at war. Or were they so strange ? Was there not a quite understandable pattern running through it all ? In the Dunkirk days when we had thought we were all about to die, the Tories of England had undergone a kind of death-bed repentance. They had written a will in favour of the common man. It was all very spiritual. All very moving. In this rarefied atmosphere people had become more important than property. The old internal frictions had disappeared. Happy, elated, at peace with ourselves and one another, we prepared for battle. The days of battle came. We fought our way through. It was no picnic but not as bad as we had expected. There was no invasion by German troops. It was merely their planes we had to contend with. Only the few were called on to die. The many were still alive, very much alive, and looking forward to their inheritance. So an effort was now being made to bury that unfortunate will. It had promised too much.

And the great Tory families of England, like blind Samsons, were unable to see that if they buried that will they buried our hopes of victory along with it. We could not win an old-fashioned territorial war. We could only win a great social crusade. If we attempted anything less than that we would be no match for Hitler. We would be no proper antithesis. It was tantalizing. We had been so near to something great and good and now we were moving backwards again. The heart of our dilemma was summed up in the personality of the Prime Minister himself. He was brave. He was eloquent. He had made it clear to all the world that he would fight on whatever the odds against him, that he would die rather than surrender. In all that he was the very embodiment of the people of Britain. But this brave man was in love with the past, was inspired by the past, was fighting with the hope of returning to the past. He had no twentieth-century vision of a world federation of free peoples. He was, and ever would be, a flamboyantly romantic imperialist. His hopes lay in a great Anglo-American alliance, powerful enough to defeat Hitler yet conservative enough to hold at bay those liberating forces throughout the world that threatened the prestige and the property rights of the British Raj. I had a proper appreciation of all that we owed to him. At a critical time he rallied the Tories of Britain as only one of their own could have rallied them. He falsified the calculations of both Stalin and Hitler, for both believed that Britain had muddled into war and at the first opportunity would find a way of muddling out again. Their specialists in British affairs no doubt provided them with impressive lists of all the high and mighty ones who remained appeasers at heart. But the two dictators underestimated the power of democratic public opinion in Britain combined with the hot-headed gallantry of a Winston Churchill. That combination had committed us so absolutely that there was no going back.

So far so good. But where did we go from there?

We had come to a new crisis in the war. It was a moral crisis as much as a military one. Typical of our dilemma was our attitude towards India's demand for independence. There were many of us in Britain who wanted to call out to Jawaharlal Nehru, 'Fight, man, fight. This is your battle as much as ours, your future as much as ours, your freedom as much as ours. We need you as much as you need us. The past is dead. We are friends, equals, allies. We are fighting to end all tyranny, not to perpetuate our own particular form of it.'

But Churchill was holding us back. He was too blinded by class and property interests to realize what such a step would mean in rallying and inspiring a world-wide army too numerous, too fanatically devoted for any combination of Axis powers to be able to withstand it. I blushed at the presumption of any of us in Britain imagining that the whole world could be summoned to fight for the British Empire. British domination, or rather, as it would have to be, Anglo-American domination with Britain as the junior partner, was preferable to nazi domination. I had no doubts at all about that. But the difference was not impressive enough for the conquered peoples of Europe to feel that they would gladly fight and die for it; or for the subject races of India, Africa, Malaya to fight shoulder to shoulder with us in comradeship and trust; or for men and women in the very heart of Axis territory to risk death and torture to befriend us; or even for the great majority of the people of Britain and America to be roused to their highest pitch of devotion.

It was late, time to go to bed. I had to catch the early Monday morning train for London. Aneurin had already left for a miners' conference in Wales. Mother had gone to bed. Dad was out paying his nightly visit to the local lads on Home Guard duty at a bridge half a mile away. He would be back soon saying there were red lights in the sky in the direction of London, or maybe, that London looked quiet tonight but the south coast was having trouble.

In this quiet dreaming room it was hard to believe that the world was at war. Maybe I had been having nightmares. Maybe this was reality and all the rest a frightening dream.

I was disappointed with myself. My week-end was over and I had not made any brilliant discoveries nor come to any world-shaking conclusions. We were at war and we had to win it. But we could not win until as a nation we emancipated ourselves from many of the property entanglements that were impeding our efforts. How could we hope to rally the whole world to fight for freedom when within the Empire there were vast populations seeking for freedom and being denied it ? There were many complex and sophisticated answers to that question but the guts of the whole painful problem was—property considerations. Within Britain there were men, materials and machines that ought to be switched immediately to war production. Why were we so hesitant, why were we doing less than we could, giving less than our all ?

The ordinary people of Britain were game. They were clamouring for an intensification of the war effort. The Government believed that it too was game. So it was according to its lights; but those lights had been dimmed by generations of good fat easy living.

That was not a comfortable thought on which to end the evening. But there was no use telling lies to myself. That was the picture as I saw it. Our Prime Minister, had at a time when a less brave leader might have lost his nerve, made himself our bridgehead to the future. For that we would be forever in his debt. But we were now bound to hurry ahead much further and faster than had apparently been part of his reckoning.

19

HITLER'S PEACE CAMPAIGN

ONE of his wartime friends once described Lord Beaver-brook as a mixture of Mr. Puck and Mr. God. The description is apt. 'I am going to make you my balloon-atic-in-chief,' he informed me, on the Monday when I got back to town after my week-end in the country.

What this meant was that I was being asked to undertake an executive job in the department responsible for the making of barrage balloons. I had to make up my mind quickly whether or not to accept. The work I had originally been called in to help with was coming to an end. Every factory had by this time perfected its plans for carrying on during blitz periods and had experts on the spot ready to deal with every kind of emergency that might arise.

I wished I could stop thinking about the broader implications of the war and settle down to this new job. I had been in every barrage balloon factory in Britain. I knew their problems. I was keen to help and believed I could. But the worry at the back of my mind was that I would be working and asking others to work with-in a general production set-up that I did not believe was adequate for winning the war and that, as a very junior executive, I would be powerless to alter.

Our Defence Industries were producing a great deal but not enough and not as much as they were capable of producing. In the summer and autumn of 1940 Lord Beaverbrook had done wonders. Under his direction we had met the emergency require-ments of an emergency situation. But now he was lagging behind. His methods were no longer adequate. His entire approach was wrong. He was relying far too much on the pep qualities of 'special' individuals, too little on a general plan showing clearly our resources, the relative importance of the jobs to be done, the factories, materials, men and machines to be allocated to each particular task.

A man fights best with the weapons he believes in. Lord Beaverbrook believed in private enterprise. He believed in high-power individuals cranking up everyone around them. Whatever job he tackled, in spirit and in method he remained a capitalist buccaneer.

In a furious blaze of energy, superbly supported by rank-and-file workers putting up with all the aches and pains of a seven-day working week, he had helped us through the blitz months following Dunkirk. He did everything that any man could do within the framework of an unplanned capitalist economy.

But by the end of 1940 it had become evident that something more than Lord Beaverbrook's spectacular tip and run raids into one industry after another was now necessary if Britain was to make the most of its industrial resources.

And as had happened again and again, the general public grasped the essentials of the situation long before the Government could be persuaded to do so.

Plain disinterested citizens, who knew what was happening in the factories, became increasingly insistent that it was time the right hand knew what the left hand was doing; that stop-gap methods were no longer seasonable; that we had now to equip ourselves for the long steady upward pull. Something in the nature of a modern industrial Domesday book was asked for. The placing of all the cards on the table. An end to the economics and the ethics that functioned in terms of this is my factory and that is yours. This is my secret patent, I cannot share it. These are my machine tools and I mean to keep them here although they could be more usefully employed elsewhere.

There were a thousand and one such deeply incrusted habits to be overcome. A Production Chief was demanded whose authority would be final in the allocation of materials, machine tools, skilled labour, priority rights. When pressed, the Prime Minister sulked and said he had no superman available as a Production Chief. The Opposition retorted that it was not so much a superman they asked for as an industrial traffic 'cop' with powers to regulate the general direction and flow of production. And what was just as essential as a

Production Chief was a scientifically coordinated plan for Industry. Our enemies had mobilized for total war. We on our side dared do no less. I was caught up in those discussions on every side. Earnest, well-informed union men talked to me in the factories. So too did many of the managers in charge of the plants. Few of those discussions followed along pre-war political lines. No one was interested in abstract talk about socialism, capitalism, liberalism or any other 'ism. That was my mood too. We agreed as the basis of all our discussions that what mattered, the test that every proposition must meet was, would it or would it not add to the strength of the material and moral resources at our disposal in the fight against fascism.

Of one thing I was certain. Opinion in the factories was far ahead of Government policy. That was not true of all employees nor of all employers. But it was true of the overwhelming majority of both. It was an extraordinary situation. A people ready for daring new innovations, conscious that no half measures would carry them to victory, and a Government hesitating, always hesitating, waiting to be prodded by acute danger or by indignant public clamour into taking steps that would have been twice as effective if taken sooner.

This critical mood carried me out of the Aircraft Ministry and into Fleet Street. The *Daily Mirror* invited me to become its political correspondent. It was a crazy world we were living in and this was a crazy little tabloid. But it was widely read. It was popular in the services and popular in the factories. A million and a half copies were sold every day. And I was promised all the freedom I could wish for. Mr. Bartholomew, then director of the *Daily Mirror*, assured me that his was the one independent daily in Fleet Street. It was not tied to any party or politician. His great theme was that we were fighting a People's war and he intended to slant the news from the People's point of view. And no one was going to frighten him out of his resolve. Not, he quickly added, that he had any intention of making the *Daily Mirror* a frowsy political news sheet that no one would want to read. But along with the comic strips, the racing tips, and the legs of the luscious ladies featured on its middle page spread, was to go a simple, factual warm-hearted championship of the rights of the ordinary man and woman.

I listened, much impressed. I am sure Mr. B. meant every word he said. But three months later he had changed his mind. Or rather, the Government had changed it for him. A threatening letter from the Prime Minister complaining of the critical tone of the paper threw Mr. Bartholomew completely off his balance. The *Daily Worker* had been suppressed. The *Daily Mirror* was sure it was next on the list. Every member of the staff was gagged. Cassandra, its leading columnist, who had the most pungent pen in Fleet Street, fumed and fretted. But for a time he had to do so under his breath. 'I shall write about milk bars. Revolutions never take place in a dairy,' he informed his mystified readers.

And what was it all about? An attempt on the part of British journalists to sabotage the war effort? The communist *Daily Worker*, following an appeasement policy at the time, might have had difficulty in answering that charge. Whether it ought to have been suppressed and the manner of its suppression was another matter. But the Government had certainly a case against it. Against the other papers it had no case at all. It was simply that the Prime Minister disliked criticism of any kind against any member of his Cabinet or any Government department.

We had made a bad beginning to 1941. The personal ascendancy of Mr. Churchill had become too absolute for either his own good or his country's good. His eloquence was becoming almost as dangerous a soporific as had been Mr. Chamberlain's complacency. Fine words are not to be despised when a nation is battling for its life and is short of everything else. They have a practical as well as a spiritual value. But there is a limit to their efficacy. It takes more than words, even magic words, to win a war. There is also a great deal of homely, undramatic, detailed precision work to be got through. It is here that the great prima donnas in politics are apt to fall down. They are seldom good executives. If they are wise they know how to gather round them colleagues with qualities complementary to their own. But the lavish exuberant temperament that makes the great prima donna is often a jealous temperament. It dislikes sharing authority. It resents criticism. It is susceptible to sycophancy.

A few bold spirits in Parliament, in the press and throughout the country valiantly attempted to knock the Prime Minister's wilful romantic head against certain unpleasant facts that simply had to be faced, for example, the muddles and the delays on the Production Front. It was about as popular a task as if they had gone around shouting 'Heil Hitler.' Later on the country was sobered by further disasters. It was only then that responsible criticism had any chance of being listened to.

Another important element in that early 1941 atmosphere was the signing of a new German-Russian pact. Was this the prelude to Russia entering the war on Germany's side? Some argued yes, others argued no. In Fleet Street only one thing was certain. The press had reached a low-water mark in its news service. All the morning papers read alike. No critical material appeared anywhere. For a brief period even the men of Munich who still held important posts inside the Cabinet could open their newspapers without fear of finding themselves under attack. They had been given a new lease of life by a poisonous smokescreen of insinuation that any criticism of public policy was almost certain to have originated either in Moscow or Berlin.

This phase passed. Fleet Street reasserted itself. I mention it only because it is important to remember that freedom of the press in wartime is not automatic. It has got to be fought for. The greatly increased powers of the Government, the legitimate need to prevent the printing of news that would be of military value to the enemy, the very human dislike of criticism on the part of those who hold high office, all tend towards a regimentation of both news and views.

The *Daily Mirror*, then, and in later skirmishes between Fleet Street and Downing Street, showed poor political judgment. It did a great deal of vigorous sniping but it failed to develop any constructive side to its policy. Its methods remained those of an ill-mannered street urchin, sometimes saucy and amusing, sometimes just vulgar. In those periods when the other newspapers were critical of the Government, its criticisms were always the loudest and most shrill. But when the Government threatened suppression, it would flee from the field, too terror-stricken to maintain any kind of balance.

It was left to Frank Owen, then editing Lord Beaverbrook's *Evening Standard*, to lead the fight from the Fleet Street end against undue Government interference with the newspapers. In Parliament a group of M.P.'s of all parties with Ni acting as shock absorber for most of the P.M.'s spleen co-operated with him. At first the Prime Minister in reply to their questions gave surly indefinite answers. But the general temper of the House indicated that hero-worshippers though most of its members were, on this issue Mr. Churchill had gone as far as he would be permitted to go. Even in wartime the British Government had to produce a convincing, indeed unanswerable cause, before it could win popular support for measures seriously curtailing civil liberties.

During the war, Fleet Street had its ups and downs. It had its timid phases and its more independent phases. But its general story was a creditable one. In every great crisis it insisted on speaking out. True, few papers campaigned ahead of events for measures anything like adequate enough to have prevented catastrophe. But whenever disaster was about to overtake us, the press raised the alarm and insisted on vigorous action. Apparently that is the way things get done in our kind of society. A few lonely voices give warning well ahead of events but their remedies usually entail drastic revisions of property relationships. For that reason they are left unheeded. Then at the last hour there is a general rallying and a willingness to do absolutely anything that will stave off defeat.

By raising the alarm as it so repeatedly did, the press of Britain helped to establish two important principles. First, that a nation at war is not bound to be a gagged and servile nation. Secondly, that it is not in the national interest that it should be so.

The nature of Britain's wartime House of Commons made this issue of a free press doubly important. There had been no general election since 1935. That meant that the House was of pre-Munich vintage. A fresher Parliament might have been sprightlier in coping with wartime issues. But too much can be made of this point. If there had been a more recent general election the Labour Party would probably have increased slightly in strength but the general quality and character of the Commons would not have been radically altered.

One of the unsolved problems of parliamentary Government is the high percentage of members of Parliament who are little more than party hacks. Hack is not necessarily a term of abuse. It depends on one's point of view. Personally I have never been able to accept the argument 'my party, right or wrong'. In the British electoral system a candidate for Parliament enters into a direct contract with the electors of a given constituency. The surest way I know of breeding cynical contempt for democratic government is for men and women, once elected, to be willing to vote contrary to their convictions, or even to become neutral, in obedience to the instructions of a party whip.

In recent years the party system at Westminster has become increasingly rigid. It would be hard to say whether the Tory machine or the Labour machine exacts the most slavish obedience. All this is supposed to make for greater efficiency. That is open to question. But one painfully obvious consequence is a dearth of members of outstanding intellect and character. The most distinguished addition to the Parliamentary Labour Party since 1930 had been Sir Stafford Cripps. The only thing his party could find to do with him was expel him. The most colourful personality in the Tory Party in those same pre-war years was Mr. Winston Churchill. He was almost always in disgrace.

Looking down from the press gallery on our wartime Parliament I was bound to remember those things. There had been many changes but we were still a long way from victory. The most crucial decisions had yet to be made. Could this island, at the heart of an old Empire, governed by a House of Commons with a two-thirds Tory majority, wake up in time to the real nature of the war it so sincerely wished to win? Could it be made to realize that this was more than a war? That it was a world revolution?

Hitler had vowed he would make the German people the 'herren-volk', raised above all others. If Germans were to be 'herrenvolk' what did that make the rest of us? What childish crazy nonsense was all this? Was the rest of mankind to be branded like so many inferior grades of cattle?

There was enough dynamite in that racial doctrine, if we knew how to handle it properly, to blow Hitler and the whole nazi creed off the surface of the earth. But was this House of Commons capable of lighting the fuse? Did it realise its supreme advantage? Or was it too blinded by the past and by many of its present practices?

For a quarter of a century we had been moving away from racial supremacy doctrines, pushed partly by revolts among the colonial peoples of the Empire, partly by our own conscience. Officially, as expressed in Government policies, we had now reached a half way house. But millions of us were far ahead of the Government. We had completed the journey.

I recalled Jawaharlal Nehru's visit to England in the summer of 1938. Isabel and Stafford Cripps had invited some of their friends to spend the day with him at their home in the Cotswolds. We talked about India. We talked about Britain. We talked about the kind of relationship we wanted the two countries to have with one another and with the rest of the world. There was complete identity of purpose among us.

Nehru reminded me of much that was pleasant to remember. He reminded me of all that was best in my own early environment. This great Indian leader was fighting for better material conditions for the Indian masses. But that was not the root of the matter. The hunger in this proud man could not be appeased by bread alone. He was also fighting for status. That combined purpose I always find deeply moving. It is the tradition in which I myself was brought up. It was my grandfather's tradition. Grandfather Lee fought coalowners for better wages and working conditions. But with him too, that was only one part of the problem. There could be no peace in his spirit in a world that branded working people as an inferior class. There could be no peace in the spirit of a Nehru in a world that branded the Indian people as an inferior race.

Here you have dynamite all right. Here are the great tidal waves of twentieth-century aspiration. Unleash the forces symbolized for me by Nehru and my grandfather and this war is won. We could carry the fight right to Berlin and find our own waiting for us there. Even among the German masses there would be those who dared remember the dream of a world federation of free and equal peoples. But we must give them a sign. We must prove that it is indeed those things we are fighting for. Hitler tells them that the purpose of the war is to determine whether the Germans or the British are to be top dogs. If that is all, why should any German try to aid us ?

I listened to Mr. Churchill again and again addressing the House of Commons. I tried to understand what was in his mind. How did he see the future ? Could he be brought to realize that the British Empire in the form he had known it, loved it, approved of it, had come to an end ? That the great imperial dream his ancestors had begun for him would now have to give ground to the still greater dream my forbears had begun for me ? The Prime Minister was as primitive in his loyalties as I was in mine. He was an ancestor worshipper. So was I. He believed in the future of his countrymen. So did I. But it was different ancestors we worshipped and different futures we believed in.

How would it all work out ? In May 1940 when Churchill became Prime Minister, he understood the terrific odds against him. He was game. Crusaders are always game. They go into battle for the cause they believe in, leaving it to lesser men to calculate which army is likely to win. I had heard influential British Tories with colder brains than Churchill's tear his optimism to shreds and damn him for his foolhardiness in throwing away every opportunity to come to terms with Hitler. These 'gentlemen' saw clearly what their Prime Minister was reluctant to believe. They saw that in order to win this war more would be needed than the massing of the orthodox industrial and military strength of the British Empire and the United States of America. They saw that they would be compelled to endure more enlightened attitudes to the social, racial and economic problems of the modern world than they could find it in their spirit voluntarily to agree to. They saw that whatever happened, their day was ending.

The views of the British press, Parliament and public opinion were well known to Hitler. Before the war he had won his greatest victories, not as a soldier, but as a politician. He was still engaged in intensive political warfare. His technique, whenever he saw divisions of opinion becoming acute inside an enemy territory, was to launch an appeasement blitz. In that way he calculated further to exacerbate the divisions and so prepare the way for the successful entry of his troops. The climax of a terrific 'peace' campaign was the arrival of Rudolph Hess, Hitler's closest friend and confidant, who came to Britain in person as an assurance to the British Government that German plans for an attack on Russia were no mere feint. At that time Soviet Russia was almost as unpopular in Britain as Germany was. The war against Finland, the appeasement campaign the British Communists were then engaged on, the knowledge that Stalin had signed a pact with Hitler and uncertainty as to how far he was prepared to go in his aid to the Axis powers, had created bitter anti-Soviet feeling.

The nazis were aware of all this. Also they remembered that before the war the bolshevik bogey had been their most successful device for making the British Government do whatever Germany wanted it to do.

But on June 22nd, when the Germans marched against Russia, it was not Hess the Prime Minister sent for. He sent for Sir Stafford Cripps. Together these two went off to the country. They spent the day at Chequers. Together they prepared the radio address that Churchill delivered to the world that same evening. That address was one of the resounding victories of the war. It gave two black eyes to Hitler and at the same time stamped firmly on the face of British appeasement.

20

RUSSIA, OUR ALLY

WITH the entry of Russia into the war a new wave of optimism swept over Britain. For the first time we could see the forces beginning to assemble that could carry us through to victory. Until then we had been certain of victory but it had been a mystical certainty. We had had very little solid ground under our feet.

But Hitler knew, and many of us knew, that our severest political test had still to come. In every crisis we had remained united. But hitherto it had been unity behind a policy and a Prime Minister that were essentially Conservative. What would now happen, as events demonstrated the need for a war strategy that involved a complete break with Conservative tradition ? Would we be able to make drastic readjustments in our attitude towards property and towards Empire . . . and still remain united ?

It was the Tories of England who had now to be tested. This was no small thing history was asking of them. Although living at the heart of an Empire and believing in Empire, they would have to accept entirely new values. That was not difficult for me to do. Nor for many others. Millions of us were eager to see the world rid of all empires, including our own. We had long urged that we had no moral case against nazis who sought to establish German supremacy over other peoples until first we looked homewards and cleansed our own country of the same selfish ambitions.

But the great ruling families of England, few in number, powerful in influence, would find it hard to see the world and the war in those terms. An independent India, for Churchill, for instance, would mean the end of the great imperial dream his family had lived by since the days of Queen Anne. It would be almost as bitter for him as defeat at the hands of Hitler. He would accept it only as a last ditch measure forced on him by military necessity. And there were many others, although not the majority, who looked at the world from the same angle.

It is a simple matter to write about factories and the making of planes and the training of soldiers. Those aspects of modern warfare are easily understood. It is the turmoil that goes on in the minds of men everywhere that is more difficult to define. For a time most people in Britain thought they had found what they were looking for in the leadership of Mr. Churchill. We would win a military victory. Beyond that we would gradually improve the world for ourselves and everyone else. Bit by bit, we would remedy every racial and economic grievance.

But angry insistent voices all over the Empire were shouting to us to drop this exasperatingly patronizing attitude. The subject races were not interested in vague future promises. They were insisting on immediate recognition of their status as free men. As free men they were willing to fight. On any other terms they warned us we could not depend on them.

At the same time, inside Britain itself, there were other angry voices raised in protest at our failure to achieve total industrial mobilization. Private property interests were still an impediment. Men argued heatedly that this did not happen in the dictatorship countries.

As the war moved into its third spring, the people of Britain were again pressing on ahead of official Government policy. They were insisting on new measures to meet new needs.

In the factories and the forces the ferment of ideas often blazed into heated discussions about every aspect of war strategy and of what was to happen after the war.

Everyone was bent on smashing Hitler and the military machine he controlled. But that was not enough. There was also a great longing for the kind of peace that would enable men everywhere, in allied and axis territories alike, to have work to do, something to serve, something to be proud of, homes, families, friends.

Where would everyone find work when the defence plants were dismantled ? What would take their place ? What kind of opportunities would there be for the demobilized millions ?

The great fear was lest there should be a recurrence of mass unemployment. I knew men who for years had had nothing to do but
hang around street corners or heckle from the back row of political
meetings, or space out the long empty days in clubhouses where
others as poor and unwanted as themselves were used to congregate.
Before the war they were becoming corrodingly cynical. They were
losing even self-respect. In the third year of war, when I met them
again, much of the lost pride had come back to them. They were
needed now! They were citizens. They were part of the life of the
times.

Almost always when we began speculating about what would
happen after the war, the talk would turn to the years following the
1914-18 war. We reminded one another of what was done wrongly
then. We tried to figure out how we could avoid the worst of the
old mistakes. We vowed it would be different this time. For the
purpose of winning the war, Britain's industries had to be increasingly centrally planned and controlled. When peace came we would
have to insist on the controls remaining. And not from theoretical
notions of socialism or any other 'ism'. It was simply that we saw
our best chance of having work after the war was if peace work
was planned as war work was now having to be planned.

But planning in Britain would still leave many odd unregulated
corners and a multitude of private businesses. That is how we
wanted it to be. We did not want to build an iron cage round
ourselves with the Government regulating even the way we
breathed.

I had no wish to see Britain become an imitation Russia, still
less an imitation Germany. I believed we could do a great deal
better than both. The bone structure of our economic life, our
banks, land, power supplies, and basic industries were ready for
public ownership. But around that framework there was ample
room for pleasant, casual, inconsequential, small private concerns.

Much thought was already being given as to how best all this
could be done. None of it would be easy. There were problems in
the relationship of the State to the individual and to industry that
would take careful handling. We had no wish to see established an
all-powerful, self-perpetuating bureaucracy controlling every word
we read, wrote or uttered. Nor did we wish to abdicate our demo-

cratic rights in favour of Government by managerial groups with expert knowledge of trade and industry. There were a few but not many who talked that dangerous kind of stuff. I found it hard to believe they had ever met the experts. For if so, they must surely have discovered how very foolish the experts can be about all issues other than those on which they have acquired special knowledge and skill. Skill is something to be used, respected, rewarded. But democratic countries must keep a sense of proportion. The technical expert, like the civil servant, must remain subordinate to the State and the State must continue to be primarily a freely-elected Parliament sensitive to the wishes of the private citizen.

But all this talk of the future was little more than idle gossip until we could begin to see the type of men and parties that would govern in Britain after the war.

In 1939 we had begun the war with Chamberlain as Prime Minister. By sheer mass pressure we got rid of Chamberlain and substituted Churchill. Several times we had insisted on reconstructions within the Churchill Cabinet. We were not yet satisfied. Further changes were on the way.

Before the war our various political groups had been frozen and immobile like figures on an Egyptian frieze. Now there was an acceptance of change, a feeling of new life everywhere. Occasionally I met someone who was despondent about the future, who talked about how we failed after the first world war and assumed we were bound to fail again. There was as yet no certainty about anything, but I held that those past failures could be made a source of great future strength. We knew this time some of the worst mistakes we must avoid.

21

IN RETROSPECT

THESE fragments of autobiography were first published more than twenty years ago. They reflect the growing alarm many of us felt as we met with one reverse after another during the Chamberlain era.

The second world war had its roots in class conflicts even more than in national rivalries. It need never have happened. The time to stop the rot was when General Franco betrayed his oath of loyalty to the Spanish Republican Government. My generation has an abiding sense of guilt for all that followed.

It was the measure of our despair that by 1939 even war was preferable to the creeping paralysis of the preceding years. We had visions of marching back to Spain. But after more than two decades Franco is still in power. So the second world war led only to partial victory. The fight goes on.

In 1945 the return of a Labour Government confounded most of the prophets. Aneurin Bevan insisted this would happen. I was not so sure. Mine was the more conventional attitude. Only Ni had the gift of vaulting ahead, leaving more pedestrian colleagues panting resentfully in the rear. His certainty sprang from his total involvement in the two different wars that were waged between 1939 and 1945.

I had hoped that one day it would be he who would tell the full story.

In these concluding chapters I give only a faint glimpse of the turmoil that led to the rejection of Winston Churchill in the 1945 election. Many, in retrospect, see how important it was that the British House of Commons should not degenerate into a Reichstag and that responsible criticism in the press should not be stifled, even in wartime. But not so many saw this at the time.

Our wartime prime minister was also leader of the Tory Party. Ni, more than any other Labour leader, made it his responsibility to ensure that in the first capacity he was upheld but in the latter, relentlessly opposed. Both men were conscious, dedicated class warriors. They were fighting for very different post-war worlds.

But I am anticipating what must be told another day.

Progress is a zigzag affair. By 1950 the Labour Government that had begun so brilliantly well, had exhausted its élan. It was divided, exhausted, uncertain of its purposes.

Now, once more, there is every sign of a great new forward surge.

When cynics try to cut the ground from under my feet by claiming that all our efforts to build a friendlier, gayer world are worthless, that people everywhere are too narrowly self regarding, too much the prisoners of prejudice and greed ever to respond, I am not impressed.

I have the final argument. And it does not depend on the changing whims of abstract political dogmas. It is rooted in the concrete reality of everyday experience. More than all else it draws its strength from the family and friends who have been my life.

I refuse to believe that my parents were uniquely different from their neighbours or that the man I married represented no one but himself. They were the best of their kind. Of that I am proudly and gratefully conscious. But there are others. The urge to serve is as strong as the will to dominate. The impulse to share is as much a part of our make-up as the temptation to exploit.

The torrential forward drive of those in every continent in the world who have vowed to fight racial and economic oppression wherever they find it gathers momentum, it has a raw urgency that will not be denied.

I had no need to look for a purpose in life, a cause to fight for. Growing up in the Scottish coalfields it was there, all around me. Some of our hard-fought battles eased life for many whose lot was once intolerable. That is something to build on. But it is only a beginning.

A younger generation has no need to protest as I once did, 'There will be nothing left to fight for'.

Measured against the great issues of our time, the fight has hardly begun.